Studies in Economic Reform and Social Justice

Social, Methods, and Microeconomics: Contributions to Doing Economics Better

Edited by
Frederic S. Lee

Studies in Economic Reform and Social Justice

Social, Methods, and Microeconomics Contributions to Doing Economics Better

WILEY-BLACKWELL

Studies in Economic Reform and Social Justice

Social, Methods, and Microeconomics: Contributions to Doing Economics Better

Edited by
Frederic S. Lee

WILEY-BLACKWELL

This edition first published 2011
© 2011 American Journal of Economics and Sociology, Inc.

Blackwell Publishing was acquired by John Wiley & Sons in February 2007. Blackwell's publishing program has been merged with Wiley's global scientific, technical, and medical business to form Wiley-Blackwell.

Registered Office
John Wiley & Sons Ltd, The Atrium, Southern Gate, Chichester, West Sussex, PO19 8SQ, United Kingdom

Editorial Offices
350 Main Street, Malden, MA 02148-5020, USA
9600 Garsington Road, Oxford, OX4 2DQ, UK
The Atrium, Southern Gate, Chichester, West Sussex, PO19 8SQ, UK

For details of our global editorial offices, for customer services, and for information about how to apply for permission to reuse the copyright material in this book, please see our website at www.wiley.com/wiley-blackwell.

The rights of Frederic S. Lee and Wolfram Elsner to be identified as the author of the editorial material in this work has been asserted in accordance with the Copyright, Designs and Patents Act 1988.

Library of Congress Cataloging-in-Publication Data

Social, methods, and microeconomics : contributions to doing economics better / edited by Frederic S. Lee.
    p. cm.—(Studies in economic reform and social justice)
  Includes index.
  ISBN 978-1-4443-5032-6 (casebound)—ISBN 978-1-4443-5033-3 (pbk.)
  1. Economics—Sociological aspects. 2. Microeconomics. 3. Ecology—Economic aspects.
I. Lee, Frederic S., 1949–
  HM548.S614 2011
  306.301—dc22
                                                                        2011008918

A catalogue record for this book is available from the Library of Congress.

Set in 10 on 13pt Garamond Light by Toppan Best-set Premedia Limited
Printed in Singapore by Markono Print Media Pte Ltd.

01—2011

Contents

Contents

Editor's Introduction

It is not often that an editor receives submissions from unrelated academics that actually fit together quite nicely in addressing, in a linked fashion, a particular set of themes. During my first year as the editor of the *American Journal of Economics and Sociology* this unlikely event happened to me. The starting point of the articles in this issue is Karl Polangi's mundane concept of social embedded economy, but then the "social" gets taken to identify an approach in ecological economics and even to explain the creation of money— which puts us on a slippery slope towards a more critical but better way to do economics. Once on this slippery slope, issues of methodology naturally arise, followed quickly by the query of who are these economists on it, and ending with a partial glimpse as to what the better economics looks like. If one's goal in life is to be a stalwart of the conventional, mainstream economics, and so not to be found standing on a slippery slope, then you need to exclude anything that has to do with the "social." However, from its beginning, the *AJES* has taken the road less traveled and firmly placed its foot in this slippery slope and this volume is a continuation of this endeavor.

Gareth Dale begins the issue with an investigation of Polanyi's concept of the social embedded economy, showing what contributed to the concept and how it has been subsequently interpreted. Dale's discussion of the antecedents to the concept is interesting because he shows that it just does not include Marx, Tonnies, Weber, and the anthropology, but also the American Institutionalists. It is a curious thing that much of the voluminous literature written by sociologists on Polanyi's concept virtually ignores the American Institutionalists (except perhaps Veblen) contributions, but it is in today's American Institutionalism where the concept is most alive in economics. Dale then goes on to discuss Polanyi's own work on the concept and its subsequent developments (of which more details can be found in his new book, *Karl Polanyi: The Limits of the Market*, 2010, Polity Press).

In his article, Clive Spash jumps on the social and introduces the reader to social ecological economics. In particular, he is not thrilled with the way ecological economics is moving forward, with its combination of the natural with the mechanistic and asocial mainstream

American Journal of Economics and Sociology, Vol. 70, No. 2 (April, 2011).

economics. Rather Spash sees the way forward as integrating the social with nature in a interdisciplinary manner, with the result being social ecological economics. To make his case, he first provides an overview of the historical roots of ecological economics and how it got fused with mainstream economics and thus rendered it much less useful for dealing with the ecological problems facing society today. To overcome this, Spash argues that ecological economics should turn its back on mainstream economics and become engaged with hetero-dox economics for many reasons, the most notable being its concern with the social and its non-mechanistic methodology. The outcome of the engagement, he concludes, will be a social ecological economics that has a social and theoretical vision of approaching ecological problems through social change undertaken in a democratic manner.

The slippery slope of the social continues with the articles by Alla Semenova, by Germana Bottone and Vania Sena, and by Matthew Interis. Semenova draws upon Polanyi's substantive approach and locates the creation of money not in the bargaining activities in markets but in the holy debts to Greek gods. That is, money is a representation of a social debt/credit relationship between the popu-lation and the central public authority, and one, in the case of the Greek gods, that is freely entered into. Moreover, since money emerges from and represents a non-market social debt credit relation-ship, its fundamental importance is not in facilitating market exchanges but in promoting the social engagement of society as a whole. Bottone and Sena carry the social agenda further by putting the social back into "human capital." While "human capital" is a very problematic term, it is made worse through its identification of edu-cational characteristics and training and work experiences with the individual worker. In this way, their very social nature is lost. Rejecting this, Bottone and Sena extend human capital to include labor quality, that is, an array of social capabilities and characteristics, such as health, psychological conditions, and active citizenship, that affect workers' productivity. They argue that individuals are willing to acquire additional capabilities that improve their productivity perfor-mances if the same such capabilities also help them to contribute to the society they live in. Finally, in any discussion of the social, the question of social norms is bound to arise—what are they and how to define them. The imprecision of the responses to the question has generated a large and often confusing literature. Where fools should not rush in to clarify the literature, Interis does with surprisingly interesting results. In a succinct article, he lays out a simple typology of norms that renders communication among economists that utilize them in their work more fruitful.

The issue of the social emerged in the *Methodenstreit* between Carl Menger and Gustav Schmoller. In particular, economists that favor the asocial, isolated individual as the methodological starting part for economic analysis were also inclined to deductivist methods and universal economic laws. Therefore, economists that favor the social and hence were inclined to empirical-inductive research approaches and historically contingent explanations of economic activities were viewed as near-non-economists by the former; the latter felt the same way about the former. These are some of the core issues that were part of the methods debate between Menger and Schmoller and that Marek Louzek deals with in his article. Louzek seems to conclude that this battle of methods was a mistake, since it is possible for both methods to be used in mainstream economics. But those economists imbued with the social will probably not agree.

Robert Dimand's article on Emily Balch is interesting in this regard. Balch is the only economist to receive a Nobel Prize—the 1946 Nobel Peace Prize (all the other economists have received the Sveriges Riksbank Prize in Economic Sciences in Memory of Alfred Nobel)— but she is not known by most economists due perhaps to being a woman, or maybe because she was a socialist or favored peace during World War I, or that her areas of research interests happened to be in social issues and social reform, many of which affected women. Dimand's splendid article recounting the career of this remarkable economist makes it clear that she thought of economics as "social economics" and its purpose was to deal with important social issues.

Andrew Mearman's article on the identity of heterodox economists is interesting for many reasons, including perhaps the most controversial one being that the heterodox economists are not strictly distinct from mainstream economists. However, what is noticeable in the article's empirical evidence is that those economists surveyed, those that most strongly identified themselves as heterodox also considered class, power, and gender very important variables in economic theorizing; that is, it is the social that clearly helps differentiate heterodox from mainstream economists. This point is clearly made by Steven Pressman in his article on Post Keynesian microeconomics and public policy. In particular, he identifies the social issues of crime, health care, education, and poverty as central to Post Keynesians concerns; and their resolution requires non-market government social actions, such as greater employment and less income inequality. Of course resolving those social issues requires a great deal of research. So the question is: What kind of research methods should be used— econometric or qualitative methods? Most economists, whether mainstream or not, would exclusively utilize the former method, while more social-oriented would use both. In his article, Philipp Bagus draws upon Oskar Morgenstern's critique of quantitative data used in econometric analysis to argue that its usefulness by itself is quite questionable. However, it has been shown that using a mixed method, triangular method approach that combines both quantitative-econometric methods and qualitative methods produces by far the best empirical results.

Economics is a social science and its subject matter is the social activities involved in the process of social provisioning. So doing better economics means doing more "social" when doing economics. Talking about individuals making "social choices" does not do the trick; for the social includes class, gender, power and social provisioning activities that are irreducible to individual choices. Rather, doing better economics means doing a different kind of economics than that pursued by the mainstream—an economics in which the social is not a peripheral add-on, but infused at every level from its ontological-methodological foundations, its theoretical core, to its applied research and policy recommendations. Doing a different and better economics is the trademark of the *AJES*.

FSL

Lineages of Embeddedness: On the Antecedents and Successors of a Polanyian Concept

By Gareth Dale*

ABSTRACT. Since the 1980s, much debate has revolved around Karl Polanyi's concept of the "dis/embedded economy," generating some light and not a little heat. This paper looks at three reasons that account for part of the "heat." It begins by tracing the sources upon which Polanyi drew. They include Karl Marx, Ferdinand Tönnies, and Max Weber, along with anthropology of the inter-war period, and German and American Institutionalist economics. After exploring the differing ways in which these varying currents conceptualize the relationship between economy and society, I explore the different interpretations of what Polanyi means by embeddedness, and the different purposes to which contemporary economic sociologists have put the term. For some, he is held up as the originator of a line of sociological analysis that treats "the economy" as a subsystem "embedded in" a social system. In this reading the emphasis is upon the moral underpinnings of market behavior, in contrast to the naturalism of Ricardo, Malthus and their heirs. For others, his "disembedding" thesis contains a more radical tale: of the market economy coming to dominate "society," bringing forth a sorcerer's apprentice world of untrammeled market forces that, although human creations, lie beyond conscious human control.

Since the 1980s, a great deal of debate has revolved around Karl Polanyi's concept of "dis/embedded economy," a term that refers to the relationship between "economy" and "society," generating some light

*Gareth Dale is senior lecturer in politics and international relations at Brunel University (Kingston Lane, Uxbridge UB8 3PH). His publications include *The European Union and Migrant Labour* (co-edited with Mike Cole); and a trilogy on East German history. Currently, he is researching an intellectual biography of Karl Polanyi, for publication with University of Michigan Press. Email: gareth.dale@brunel.ac.uk

American Journal of Economics and Sociology, Vol. 70, No. 2 (April, 2011).

and not a little heat. This paper looks at three reasons that account for some of that "heat." It begins by tracing the sources upon which Polanyi, who first used the metaphor of "embeddedness" to refer to the relationship of "economy" vis-à-vis society, drew. These include Karl Marx, who, when discussing the economy-society relationship, emphasizes the differences between modes of production, arguing that the separate institutionalization of "the economy" only fully occurs contemporaneously with, and as a consequence of, the rise of capitalism. They include Ferdinand Tönnies, whose couplet *Gemeinschaft* and *Gesellschaft* closely resembles Polanyi's embedded/disembedded economy, as well as the sociology of Max Weber, anthropology of the inter-war period, and German and American Institutionalist economics.

Evidently, Polanyi's concept draws upon a number of sources, some of which were quite distinct, not to say antithetical, and his own relationship to that intellectual terrain changed over time. In this article I explore the different interpretations of what he means by embeddedness, and the different purposes to which contemporary economic sociologists have put the term. For some, he is held up as the originator of a line of sociological analysis (developed further by Parsons, Smelser and Granovetter) that treats "the economy" as a subsystem "embedded in" a social system.[1] In this reading the emphasis is upon the moral underpinnings of market behavior, in contrast to the naturalism of Ricardo, Malthus and their heirs. The embeddedness of economic relations is seen as a constitutive element of all economies, with the rider that at its least-regulated extreme, the market economy represents a pathological form of economic organization, generative of institutional inefficiencies, social anomie and ethical debility. For others, his "disembedding" thesis contains a more radical, even Marxian, tale: of the market economy coming to dominate "society," bringing forth a sorcerer's apprentice world of untrammeled market forces that, although human creations, lie beyond conscious human control.

Antecedents of Embeddedness: Marx and Tönnies

"Embeddedness," a metaphor denoting a state of dependence upon or subordination to, refers to the relationship between "economy" and "society," that defining question of a discipline the founders of which approached it in diverse and inevitably clashing ways. For Marx, whose works are often cited as stimuli to Polanyi's use of the term (Halperin 1988: 34; Cangiani et al. 2005: 62–63), economic behavior cannot be studied as if it is isolated from society. In the *Grundrisse* (1973: 101) he cautions that,

> the simplest economic category, say, e.g. exchange value, presupposes population, moreover a population producing in specific relations; as well as a certain kind of family, or commune, or state, etc. It can never exist other than as an abstract, one-sided relation within an already given, concrete, living whole.

That "the economy," as a separate analytical category, came into existence, Marx explains in the *Critique of Hegel's Philosophy of Right* and elsewhere, was consequent upon the emergence of a new matrix of class relations centered on the relationship between the owners of money and the means of production, on the one hand, and free workers, the sellers of their own labor-power, on the other. Separated from the necessary instruments and materials of production, workers must contract with other parties in order to produce; they must sell their labor-power to secure the means of survival. It was upon this foundation that Marx developed the theories of alienation and of the separation institutionalization of politics and economics. The worker is alienated from the object he produces because it is owned and disposed of by another, the capitalist. The class relationship, although centered in the sphere of production, extends in its effects to other social institutions, in particular to the distinction between private and public domains. That the exploitation relation in the new society was enforced primarily through the effect of propertylessness on the workers' "voluntary" decision to hire out their labor-power, rather than by direct coercion within structures of personal obligation or ownership, had implications for the form taken by state power. Because the "political" nature of the relationship between capitalists and their representatives on the one side and their employees within the farm, factory or office on the other came to appear as the strictly "private" realm of civil society, a space distinct from civil society could emerge in the shape of the modern "political state." The production and distribution of goods and services appears to be situated within the "economic" realm, giving the appearance of "society" dominated by "economy," with social purposes and humankind's metabolism with nature subordinated to narrow economic ends dictated by market imperatives. Given the separate institutionalization of politics and economics, the central dynamic of capitalist society—the drive to infinite accumulation, with social purposes subordinated to market imperatives—appears to emanate from a particular "sphere," the economic.

Marx's theories of alienation and the separation of politics and economics were important reference points for Polanyi, but in an earlier age they had provided similar inspiration to Tönnies—and with its adoption by him, the notion that the economy in capitalist society is instituted in a historically singular manner became a staple of the nascent discipline of sociology. But on several points the founder of German sociology parted company with Marx. He was infuriated by the thesis that capitalist states are structural supports for capitalist society such that the first step towards overcoming the latter must be the deconstruction of the former and their replacement by workers' democracy, and singles out the work in which Marx develops this argument most fully, *The Civil War in France,* as by far his worst, as "pathological," no less, and motivated by "dark anger and bitterness" (Tönnies 1974: 75, 129–130). Working within the "German Historical" tradition of *Sozialpolitik,* Tönnies theorized states as class-neutral instruments that should be bent towards the reform of capitalism along collectivist social-democratic lines through the incorporation of the working classes via welfare measures and the vote.

Tönnies' well-known couplet, community (*Gemeinschaft*) and society (*Gesellschaft*), is a close analogue of Polanyi's embedded/disembedded society. His book of the same name advanced a resounding challenge to liberal certainties of the naturalness of possessive individualism, confronting it with the altogether different perspective of man's innate inclination to communal life (see Liebersohn 1988). *Gemeinschaft,* with its small-scale, face-to-face relationships, is a form of social existence in which individuals, oriented to the purposes of their group, make its ends their own. It denotes an "organic" and "natural" condition of society in which actions are rooted in an *a priori* unity and manifest the will and spirit of that unity even when performed by an individual—"a condition where the lives of men were embedded in a tissue of common experience," in Polanyi's paraphrase (1957: 69). By contrast, *Gesellschaft* is a realm of inauthentic experience—which Tönnies (1988: 76) emphasizes with the terms "abstract," "artificial" and "fictitious"—in which individuals exist in a permanent condition of separation from, and latent or overt tension with, others. In *Gesellschaft*, characterized as it is by the sharp separation of social spheres, the common values that enable group behavior to function are not rooted in custom and governed by face-to-face relations but have to be deliberately fashioned with the aid of abstract systems. Its hallmark is a novel kind of actional disposition characterized by the liberation of individual behavior from customary norms, a shift that has facilitated the autonomous conception of ends and the calculation of alternative means but at the cost of the marginalization of "community." Tönnies (1988: 82) perceived that what he termed the "great transformation" from *Gemeinschaft* to *Gesellschaft* was irreversible and tragic, and yet believed that, thanks to the waxing influence of the working classes, a new communal era could yet dawn. For him, the road thereto was signposted moral enlightenment and political reform.

If his notes from the inter-war period collected in the Polanyi Institute Archive can be taken as a guide, Polanyi studied Tönnies more closely than any other author, with the possible exceptions of Marx, Eugen Dühring and Joseph Schumpeter. His daughter, Kari Polanyi-Levitt, confirms that he "engaged intensively with Tönnies" and that the German sociologist was "certainly of importance in the formation of my father's confection of ideas."[2] But in the post-war period he was influenced to a much greater extent by another German sociologist, Max Weber.

Antecedents of Embeddedness: German Institutionalism and Weber

In the late 19th century, theoretical inquiry into the interrelationship between economy and society in the late 19th century was not restricted to sociologists, but was conducted by Institutionalist economists too. In German-speaking Central Europe—which included Polanyi's milieu in Budapest—the German Historical School (GHS) was the prevailing school of political economy for several decades following the publication of Friedrich List's *National System of Political Economy* and Wilhelm Roscher's *Grundriss* in the early 1840s. They, together with a younger generation around Gustav Schmoller and Carl Bücher, developed a distinctive approach to economics characterized by the inductive method, historicism, institutionalism, and étatiste reformism. Against the English economists' postulation of the market economy as a natural phenomenon they stressed its historical specificity and constructedness (in Tönnies' terms, "artificiality"), drawing attention to the historical novelty of the profit-motive and to the pivotal role of states in engineering conditions conducive to market formation. Anticipating Polanyi, they brought the eye of the historian and social theorist to anthropology, refusing the distinction between economic anthropology and economic history and engaging in a systematic theorization of the shifting role of economic institutions in different societies.

The research program of the GHS scholars focused upon the tasks of drawing up a comparative history of economic institutions and identifying a typology of the social conditions relating to these in different economic orders. They presented the historical sequence of these orders as stages of economic development. Bücher was the key figure in this regard. In his evolutionary schema of economic development the defining taxonomical criterion was the role played by exchange. In low-surplus economies actors are averse to exchange. In the *oikos*-economies of antiquity, goods moved from producer to consumer without intervening exchange. The medieval towns of Europe knew a limited degree of exchange, and they eventually yielded to the exchange-dominated *Volkswirtschaft* of modernity.

As regards the development of a comparative history of economic institutions, Schmoller set the tone. For him (in Nau 1998: 213), institutions should be comprehended as expressions of historically specific mentalities [*psychische Erscheinungen*]. Economic life

> takes place in political and social organs which have their unity [not only] in borders and an integrated territory . . . but in the first instance by their spiritual unity by the socialization of the actors, with law, morals, and religion . . . as their prime expressions. (Schmoller, in Peukert 2001: 104)

The common element that unites the particular economies of a nation or a state is not simply the state itself, but something more fundamental: the community of language, of history, of memories, of customs and ideas. This deeper community, Schmoller (in Therborn 1976: 202) concludes,

> is an order of life which has grown out of these harmonious psychological foundations and become an objective fact, it is the common ethos, as the Greeks called the moral and spiritual community crystallized in custom and law, which influences all human behaviour, hence including the economic.

The economic, in short, cannot be understood as a separate entity; its study must be integrated with that of the wider culture.

As regards political convictions, the GHS scholars appropriated elements of conservative-romantic and social-democratic critiques of free-market capitalism, in particular with regard to the self-interested orientation of economic activity that it promotes, but inserted them into a broadly liberal framework. They defined the role of the state "in liberal terms, as an essential condition for the well-being of the individual," and theorized capitalism as in principle a harmonious order, based on the cooperative division of labor (Clarke 1982: 123). However, they were critical of *laissez-faire* economic policy, which, in List's view, provided an unsuitable institutional framework for the enhancement of national power and prosperity. His younger followers were likewise concerned with national power and prosperity, but for them the "social question" loomed larger: they were troubled above all by the pace of social change, the threat of free markets to social harmony, and the potential of working-class revolt. Free market economic policy, they warned, aggravated tensions between the business class and workers. Reconciliation between the classes was required, and they offered social policy, along Bismarckian lines, as remedy.

In the 1870s the GHS faced a sustained challenge from a new current of thought: Austrian marginalist economics. One influential product of this encounter was the sociology of Max Weber. Weber studied economics with Roscher and was an active member of the *Verein für Sozialpolitik*. From the GHS, Simon Clarke has observed (1982: 201), he imbibed a concern to emphasise the extent to which capitalist rationality was itself a particular ethical ideal contrasting sharply with the ethical ideals of a feudal paternalism. Capitalist rationality had particular ethical implications; for example, in opening up economic conflicts that had previously been subordinated to the sense of community through the subordination of self-interest to duty.

In his studies of the development of capitalism in rural Prussia, Weber made a case that was characteristically historicist in its counterposition of culture to economics. Viewed in purely economic terms, he argued, the transformation of rural Prussia was progressive, but this had come at the expense of an erosion of the ethical and political foundations of the nation (Clarke 1982: 194–195). While accepting marginalist economic theory, he was critical of the notion that free markets provided the basis for a stable social order; rather, the economic sphere had to be shaped by ethical and political concerns, and the study of their workings requires a theory of institutional structure.

With the GHS, and its younger representatives Georg Simmel and Werner Sombart, Weber shared the postulates that economic behavior is grounded in the cultural realm of customs, language and the collective ethos, and that the dominant ethic in capitalism contrasted sharply with that of previous systems. He set the tone of discussion of capitalism in terms of its *spirit*—its "motivational basis," "motive complexes" and "historical psychology." The economy is understood not in structural terms but in terms of orientation; it is analyzed as the outcome of actional dispositions directed according to particular mentalities. By way of illustration, consider the distinction he makes between market-based and administered economies. They are differentiated in terms of the relative presence of two ideal types of meaningful orientation: towards profitability, or towards "the security and increase of resources and income" (Savage 1977: 7–8; cf. Weber 1964: 199).

If Weber's core intellectual interest was in the social structure and dynamics of modern Western society, his political commitment was, as Jan Rehmann has shown in impressive detail, to the redirection of German capitalism along Fordist-American lines. On this basis he advocated the development of autonomous power centers alongside Bismarck's patrimonial state and the subordination of the working class through integration into the bourgeois political order. In contradistinction to Tönnies, he advocated the further differentiation of economic and political realms, not least because this would strengthen the hand of conservative layers within the labor movement who wished trade unionism to be restricted to "purely industrial" issues (Rehmann 1998). But with Tönnies and the GHS he shared a sense of disquiet over the unstable character of capitalist society. For him, "the market alone was not an adequate basis for the realisation of a rational and harmonious social order"; its operation had to be confined within limits set by morality and by states, with the latter conceived as benign impersonal entities that guarantee civil order and progress (Clarke 1982: 216, 230). Given that the social preconditions for a cohesive capitalist society could not be discovered in the self-interest of market actors alone, the study of economics evidently required supplementing with a theory of its cultural integument (or "spirit") and of its institutional structure.

Although Polanyi resists classification as a follower of the GHS, or as a Weberian, that these were strong influences is evident. He cites Schmoller and Bücher as his precursors in approaching economic history from the "institutional and historical" perspective (Nafissi 2005: 127). He singles out Bücher for particular praise, on the grounds that he, more than anyone else, deserves credit for debunking the myth that exchange was a natural feature of every economy and for originating the thesis that the growth of markets cannot be understood without reference to the role of state power. What appealed to Polanyi in Bücher's approach was that it "makes exchange only a phenomenon of a particular stage of economic development, while the essence of the economy has to do with actual production, or, as one might say today, with the substantive element" (Polanyi 1968b: 163–164). Weber, too, was a major influence upon Polanyi. In particular, he found inspiration in Weber's attempt to formulate a "general economic history," focused on the problem of the changing place of the economy in human society (Polanyi 42-9). Polanyi describes his own approach to economic history, as well as some of his specific concepts that deal with the "place of the economic system in society," as having "a broadly similar focus" to Weber's (Polanyi 31-15, 37-2).

Antecedents of Embeddedness: American Institutionalism

It would not be inaccurate to describe the GHS as older sibling to the American Institutionalist tradition of which Thorstein Veblen, John Commons and Wesley Mitchell were the preeminent exponents. The similarities between the two are explicable in part through the common circumstances they experienced, but also through the direct influence of German Institutionalism upon its American kin. The shared environment included industrialization and the rise of the "social question," as well as the waning of British liberal hegemony and its associated doctrines of utilitarianism, free trade and *laissez-faire.* Institutionalists, of German and American schools alike, were acutely aware of socioeconomic change, fiercely critical of classical economics (in particular its individualistic conception of human beings as governed by natural laws), and closely attuned to contemporary research in biology and anthropology and to the new thinking on cultural variation and the evolution of societies to which it gave rise. The direct influence of the GHS on American Institutionalism is well documented, even if its strength is open to debate. In the final third of the 19th century a significant number of US social scientists engaged in postgraduate study in Germany, where they encountered the GHS. As Anne Mayhew has described (1987: 981), its ideas—including the notion that the state and the church should be in the forefront of providing solutions to economic problems—were absorbed by the founders of American Institutionalism in the early stages of their intellectual careers.

Recent decades have witnessed a growing body of literature that identifies areas of convergence between Polanyi's economic analysis and that of American Institutionalists. Jérôme Maucourant (2002), for example, has remarked upon the similarities between his theory of the institutional nature of money and that which is found in Mitchell, Commons and Veblen. Polanyi's ideas have been discussed and developed by numerous contemporary American Institutionalists,[3] one of whom has observed that "Polanyi's work has been gradually incorporated into the body of institutional economics" (Özveren 2007: 783).

One could argue, however, that from the 1940s onwards Polanyi's work was already situated within that organism. There is certainly documentary evidence that attests to this. He was, for example, sufficiently familiar with the work of Veblen that he could venture the gnomic assessment that "Veblen's secret was that he was a socialist, and the secret of secrets was that he wasn't" (Rotstein 45-14: 34). Although critical of Veblen's tendency "to discount the relevance of market laws for capitalism," he found much with which to agree, and went so far as to laud Veblen as "a prophet of the 'substantive' rebellion against the reign of the 'formal'" (Rotstein 24-6; Polanyi 48-6). One passage in Veblen's 1898 article, "Economics as a Study of Process," where the American Institutionalist argues that "there is no neatly isolable range of cultural phenomena that can be rigorously set apart under the head of economic institutions," elicited Polanyi's strong approval (27-8: 19–23). He also read Commons, and noted comparisons between his *Institutional Economics* and the work of Weber (as well as one important difference: that the emphasis in Commons is upon the "system," as against Weber's "spirit") (Polanyi 9-7).

Polanyi's invitation to Columbia University in 1947 was in part due to support from the Institutionalist economist Carter Goodrich (Polanyi 48-1; Goodrich 48-2; Neale 1990). At Columbia, the approach to economic analysis that he developed, which he dubbed "substantive economics," was based avowedly upon the method of institutional analysis (Polanyi 31-1 "Tool Box"). He saw his role as updating Institutionalism for the dawning age in which, he predicted, market behavior was bound to decline. "With the recession of market institutions from dominance," he wrote his student Abe Rotstein, somewhat cryptically (48-7),

> the substantive meaning reasserts itself in the guise of *institutionalism*. This is a "convergent" movement: the fringes of the market-system are hemmed and patched with the same *patterned* cloths (American institutionalism) as are displayed in the *whole cloth* of the non-market systems of the past and, although maybe to a lesser extent, of the future (institutional analysis of the Weberian type as developed in my "Semantics").

The "convergence" of which he speaks, Polanyi explains elsewhere, was between American Institutionalism and its European historical and sociological cousins, exemplified by Weber and Henri Pirenne. As the market economy receded, he believed, "the scope of its theory and method is reduced and institutionalism automatically comes to the fore." American Institutionalism "as conceived by Veblen, Mitchell or Clark, and historical Institutionalism of the Weberian type are converging towards a general theory of economic institutions, the main methodological instrument of which is institutional analysis" (Polanyi 31-1 "Report").

Antecedents of Embeddedness: Anthropology

The fourth and final seam from which Polanyi mined materials for his theory of the embedded economy was anthropology. It was fortuitous that he reached intellectual maturity precisely when economic anthropology was coming of age. The 1920s alone witnessed the publication of the *magna opera* of Richard Thurnwald, Bronislaw Malinowski, Raymond Firth, Marcel Mauss and Wilhelm Koppers, as well as Robert Lowie's *Primitive Society* and A. R. Radcliffe Browne's *The Andaman Islanders.* The ethnographic findings contained in these works and the theoretical generalizations drawn from them rippled far beyond the discipline. They were seen as debunking the utilitarian myth of *homo œconomicus,* a creature motivated by self-interest, desirous only to maximize "utility" and guided rigidly by the rational calculation of opportunity costs. In his synthetic account of economics in "primitive communities," Thurnwald (1932a) identified a characteristic feature as the absence of any desire to make profits either from production or exchange and the concomitant "harmonization of all aspects of life into a complete whole." The economic activity of the "primitive peoples" (*Naturvölker*) he surveyed (1932b: 46) possessed a spirit that contrasted with market society: it was geared to the "act" rather than to "acquisition." Many did not know commodity exchange and those that did held it at arm's length, through "silent trade," in which agreement on prices and quantities is reached without either party communicating directly with its counterpart—a phenomenon that Polanyi pursued further in the writings of the anthropologist Bódog Somló, as well as in Heredotus. Another anthropologist whose work attracted him was Malinowski's friend and student Raymond Firth. As summarized by Richard Tawney in his preface to Firth's *Primitive Economics of the New Zealand Maori* (1929: xv), the book dealt a swinging blow to that monster, *homo œconomicus*, for whom every effort is a "cost" the incurring of which is motivated only by the individual's desire to satisfy their wants. It depicted Maori economic activity not as occurring within a separate sphere, suitably set apart for study by economists, but enmeshed within "a framework set by the family, the tribe, the class system, the institution of property, the powers and duties of chiefs." To isolate it from these social institutions, Tawney concluded (1929: xi), would be "to give a quite abstract and misleading picture even of the economic aspects of Maori society."

Polanyi was inspired by his anthropological studies to pursue several interrelated lines of inquiry, in particular into the role of cultural beliefs in structuring economic behavior, and the institutions that guided economic behavior in non-market societies. He gleaned particular satisfaction from Malinowski's *Argonauts of the Western Pacific,* which was regarded as having debunked the myth of economic man by revealing "the communistic tendencies" of the Trobriand Islanders. Whether or not the Trobriand Islanders knew egotism, their reproduction and stability depended crucially upon a sense of community, to which self-interested economic behavior posed a threat. In his notes, Polanyi (10-8) inserts an exclamation mark next to the Polish anthropologist's observation that "giving for the sake of giving is one of the most important features of Trobriand sociology, and from its very general and fundamental nature, I submit that it is a universal feature of all primitive societies." Malinowski's Trobrianders appeared to be more concerned to fulfill moral obligations than to maximize gain; they may have valued material goods but chiefly in order to safeguard their social standing or social assets.

What thrilled Polanyi in the emerging ethnographic evidence was that the lack of a primary orientation to material gain displayed by "primitive" people was evidently a function of the structure of their society, and this opened a window onto new ways of construing "the economy" that were radically different to the contemporary capitalist norm. In the Pacific islands investigated by Firth and Malinowski "purely economic" institutions did not exist; nor did "the economy" assume the form of a separate and distinct sphere. Rather, economic structures (division of labor, patterns of distribution, etc.) were over-determined by non-economic values and institutions: "community" absorbed "economy"; it directed it, or infused it with its values, rather than being governed by it as in liberal capitalism. In this sense the economic systems of "primitive" societies were invisible: they were submerged in the totality of social relationships.

Generalizing from the ethnography of the aforementioned authors, as well as Radcliffe-Brown and Margaret Mead, Polanyi (1947: 99) concluded that

> the legend of the individualistic psychology of primitive man is exploded. Neither crude egotism, nor a propensity to barter or exchange, nor a tendency to cater chiefly for himself is in evidence. . . . As a rule, the individual in primitive society is not threatened by starvation unless the community as a whole is in a like predicament. It is the absence of the threat of individual starvation which makes primitive society, in a sense, more humane than nineteenth century society, and at the same time less economic.

In this summation he is pushing the point further than his sources had done. Malinowski's scotching of the legend of *homo economicus* was tempered by his own tendency to accept the utilitarian depiction of society as consisting of utility-maximizing individuals, and he relativized his findings on the prevalence of altruistic behaviour with observations that the Trobriander's motivation in giving included ambition and vanity—that, indeed, "whenever the native can evade his obligations without the loss of prestige, or without the prospective loss of gain, he does so, exactly as a civilized business man would do" (in Kuper 1996: 24–25). But Polanyi, more than Malinowski, was deploying the new ethnographic data towards general theoretical ends. That "primitive" people lacked a primary orientation to material gain, he reasoned, was evidently a function of the structure of their society, and this recognition opened a window onto new ways of envisaging the relationship between society and economy.

Karl Polanyi on Embeddedness[4]

Polanyi did not use "embeddedness" only in passing, as some have suggested (Krippner 2001: 779; Barber 1995). In his masterwork, *The*

Great Transformation, admittedly, it makes only the occasional appearance. Yet it does crop up repeatedly in his published books and articles from the post-war period, and even more frequently in his unpublished notes and manuscripts. We do not know what inspired him to deploy "embeddedness" to refer to the interaction between economic and other social institutions. Perhaps he noticed the definition of "institution" penned by the American Institutionalist economist Walton Hamilton in 1932. An institution, wrote Hamilton (in Neale 1987: 1178), "connotes a way of thought or action of some prevalence or permance, which is embedded in the habits of a group or the customs of a people." More likely, Polanyi noticed its usage by Richard Thurnwald. Indeed, some credit Thurnwald as the originator of the concept. As Jens Beckert points out (2009: 40), citing Firth (1972: 473), Thurnwald used the term embedded (*eingebettet*) in his *Die menschliche Gesellschaft*. However, Firth and Beckert overlook the fact that Thurnwald's usage is quite unlike Polanyi's. For the German anthropologist it denotes the fact that *individual* economic activity is rarely isolated but is instead, as a rule, plugged into the broader economic circuits of the *community*. Used thus, embeddedness is roughly synonymous with "economic cooperation" or "division of labor." Thurnwald (1932b: 44–45) did possess a developed conception of the "sozialpsychische Verflochtenheit" (social-psychological interwovenness) of economic life—a kindred concept to Polanyi's "embeddedness"—but he did not, to my knowledge, refer to that relationship with the term "eingebettet." If Polanyi did borrow the term from Thurnwald, he subjected it to two alterations. First, for him, the "ground" in which individual behavior is embedded is not the cooperative economy but society as a whole. Thus, in his notes on reading *Coming of Age in Samoa* in the mid-1930s (7-9), he pens the term "embeddedness" against this paraphrase of a passage in Mead: "The emphasis was never upon what an individual did, neither upon his skill nor upon the size of his catch or harvest, but always upon its place in a larger *social* situation." Second, and crucially, he expands the referent of embeddedness from individual behavior to the relationship between ensembles of social relationships (economy, society).

As regards Polanyi's first public use of the term, this was, to my knowledge, in a 1934 essay (2002: 239) that explains that no system of labor (*Arbeitsverfassung*) can be understood without first making sense of "the social system in which it is embedded." Later in the same decade he wrote (18-8) that in all systems other than modern market society "economic life is embedded in social relations." In these early incarnations his usage is Marxian-Tönniesian. (If anything, it is closer to Tönnies in that it locates the font of alienation and disembeddedness in the separation of politics and economics rather than in the separation of labor from productive property.) The context was formed by the ongoing crisis of the inter-war decades, which, Polanyi believed (45-2: 11), was caused essentially by the sundering of the "unity of society" under the impact of the separation of economics and politics induced by the market system. Later, as he was to explain to Rotstein (45-2: 11), he shifted away from that theory while retaining the concept of embeddedness—albeit now in a Weberian-Tönniesian mold. A case can be made that already in *The Great Transformation* (TGT; 1944) the concept of "disembedded economy" came to rely upon a Weberian notion: that economic behavior in capitalism is driven by particular types of psychological motivation, hunger and gain. However, this perspective was not original to Weber—among others, Polanyi's lifelong idol, Robert Owen, subscribed to it too. Either way, the nub of the argument in TGT is that a society in which individual drives motivate economic behavior will be atomized, a *Gesellschaft*, in contrast to societies in which economic behavior is steered by irreducibly social-cultural motivations such as status, religion, and morality.

Polanyi's classic formulations on embeddedness arrived in a series of texts written between 1947 and 1957: "Our Obsolete Market Economy," "Aristotle Discovers the Economy" and *The Livelihood of Man*. In these he equates societies based on "status" or "*Gemeinschaft*" with those in which "the economy is embedded in non-economic institutions." Policy in such societies is geared to satisfying socially-determined needs; their individual members tend to suppress egotistical behavior in favor of their role within the collective whole. In Trobriand society, for example, "the production and distribution of material goods [was] embedded in social relations of a noneconomic kind" and neither labor nor distribution was undertaken "for economic motives, i.e., for the sake of gain or payment or for fear of otherwise going hungry as an individual" (1977: 52). In pre-colonial West Africa the "slave trade was embedded in the medley of their practically sovereign bodies"—i.e., territorial states (42-2; see also Polanyi 1966: 106). These regimes are contrasted to those based on "*contractus*" or "*Gesellschaft*," in which the sphere of economic exchange is "institutionally separate and motivationally distinct" (Polanyi 1968a: 84). In the latter, the economy is governed by laws of its own and "motivated in the last resort by two simple incentives, fear of hunger and hope of gain" (1977: 52).

This entailed an inversion of the historical norm: instead of the economy being enmeshed within society, social relationships "*were now embedded in the economic system*" (Polanyi 1968a: 84, emphasis in original).

Given the cross-cutting intellectual and political currents upon which it draws, it is no surprise that Polanyi's use of the term embeddedness can appear indistinct, or even beset by contradiction. At the most general level, it is true, its meaning is clear. If economic relations are embedded within society, priority within the policy process, in Matthew Watson's (2005: 97) paraphrase of Polanyi, "is given to the oikonomic needs of social provisioning. The individual within such a society [is one who] is willing to subordinate self-interest to a broader vision of the social good." Where, conversely, social relations are embedded within "the market," priority within the policy process

> is given to the chrematistic needs of personal acquisitiveness. Individuals within such a society are subjected to socialization pressures that [encourage them to] respond solely to their own wants, irrespective of the standards of justice that are infringed while satisfying those wants. In short, they are individuals who act as *homo oeconomicus.*[5]

But beyond this basic framework, a number of difficulties arise. There exists, for example, an ambiguity as to whether the counter-movement successfully "embeds" the market economy. There are passages in TGT that imply that it can so do but that, given the inherent tension between protective measures and a market system any such victory would be pyrrhic; yet elsewhere in the same book, and more so towards the end of his life, his use of the term tends to drift towards the commonplace that "the economy is embedded in institutions" and that because markets depend upon non-economic conditions they can

never be completely self-regulating (Rotstein 45-3: 6). At a methodological level there exists some uncertainty as to whether the dis/
embedded economy is a descriptive empirical term or an "ideal type"
(a structural-analytical concept for the purposes of comparison). In
this, the Polanyian ambiguity directly follows its Tönniesian predecessor. *Gemeinschaft* and *Gesellschaft* can be interpreted in one of two
ways. It can be taken to refer to different types of society—one, based
on contract and interest, the other, on feeling and custom. Alternatively, the dichotomy can be applied to the customary and contractual
relations that exist symbiotically in every society. The social relationships characteristic of *Gesellschaft*, in the interpretation of the philosopher and saint, Edith Stein,

> need to be informed and sustained by relationships characteristic of
> *Gemeinschaft*. Individuals come together in the forms of association char-
> acteristic of *Gesellschaft* for their own purposes, treating other individuals
> as instruments for the achievement of the purposes of the association. But
> nonetheless, they bring with them to these new relationships habits of
> living together with others that do not allow them to treat others *only* as
> such instruments. And in the course of their working together with others
> further sympathies are engendered that motivate the treatment of those
> others in ways characteristic of *Gemeinschaft* rather than *Gesellschaft*.

No association, she concludes, "no matter how well organized, no
matter how faultless a social mechanism, could continue to function,
if it were no more than the norms and values of *Gemeinschaft* require
it to be."[6] In a similar fashion, Polanyi's "embeddedness" can be
understood either as a methodological axiom that holds that *all*
economic behavior is enmeshed in non-economic institutions, or as a
theoretical proposition that refers to differences in the degree of that
"enmeshment" (see Gemici 2008). The contradiction between these
two meanings is not irreconcilable, but confusion would have been
avoided had Polanyi highlighted the semantic difference.

If the term is used in the empirical sense, further ambiguities
emerge when one turns to examine what societies come under which
bracket. Polanyi left no room for doubt that 19th-century Britain
exemplified the "disembedded" end of the spectrum with the Trobri-
and Islanders, Dahomey and Stalin's Russia at the other, yet his student
Terence Hopkins, in a contribution to *Trade and Market in the Early
Empires* (1957: 299), saw things otherwise. He concurs that embed-

dedness is a matter of degree, with one extreme being represented by "economies whose constituent actions are patterned through their occurrence in non-economic roles." But at the other end of the spectrum he finds economies "organized through such economic institutions as fluctuating prices *and centralized planning.*"

On the question of the Soviet Union it seems to me that the student's grip was firmer than the master's. Stalin's Russia was a far cry from the Trobriands: in most respects a typical late-industrializing society of the early 20th century, it used state power as a lever for implementing land reform, marshaling resources and concentrating capital in its drive to catch up, economically and militarily, with the advanced powers. Military competition from a position of backwardness during an epoch of world-market disintegration stamped it with its characteristic "war-economic" form: relative autarky, an emphasis on heavy industry and a high savings ratio. Stalin's revolution, in this light, entailed the conversion of the Soviet state, under the whip of geopolitical competition, into an agent of accumulation, presiding over a no-holds-barred exploitation of nature, peasants and workers. Far from being embedded in social custom, labor-power in 1930s Russia more closely resembled a commodity than did its counterpart in Western democracies. (As Keynes remarked (1936: 269), it was only in authoritarian societies like 1930s Russia in which "sudden, substantial, all-round changes could be decreed, that a flexible wage-policy could function with success.") This was not a society in which "politics" dominated "economics" but one in which decisions at the apex of power were subordinated to the imperatives of global competition and these were passed downwards through the state-controlled transmission mechanisms. It is the case that the mobilization of society behind the accumulation drive occurred by way of an unprecedented empowerment of a "political" organ, the party state, but this was simultaneously experiencing a process of "economization." For the Communist Party, as the Soviet historian Moshe Lewin has described (1985: 32), this process involved its cells being refunctioned as

> brokers in the service of their branch of the economy, sometimes even of just one enterprise. . . . The economy was declared to be the most important "front" . . . In this way the country's cultural, artistic, and other activi-

ties were "economized." Everyone, from writers to judges and procurators, had to contribute to the battle for the productivity of labor, the quality of industrial products, or the building of dams.

Institutions such as the traditional peasant commune and factory committees that offered genuine protection against the diktat of capital accumulation were subordinated to the state or destroyed. From this vantage point it is ironic, Wolfgang Streeck has observed (1999: 208–209), that the Stalinist "economy-*cum*-state" bore an uncanny resemblance in its core dynamic to free market capitalism—that self-regulating market that "Karl Polanyi suggested was driven to subordinate the social order entirely to rational-economic objectives," and to marginalize any and all "social institutions capable of representing a logic other than that of economic accumulation."

Further Adventures of a Concept

"Embeddedness" has come a long way since Polanyi coined the term. It exercises a general appeal for those who are dissatisfied with the narrow focus of orthodox economics, serving as a doorway to explorations of the relationship between economic behavior and the social integument. In economic sociology it has become a key conceptual tool with which to explain those social and psycho-social features of human behavior that are ignored or marginalized in orthodox economic analysis—for example, relations of trust, which lubricate market transactions, or those such as fraud and malfeasance, which represent distortions of the market ideal. It is deployed as "a categorical instrument," in Beckert's formulation (2007), "for describing those ordering processes that lead to a reduction of the uncertainty of the action situation and the social structuring of decisions in market contexts." In the New Institutional Economics it has found favor as shorthand for the ways in which the choices of individuals are conditioned by the institutional context in which they find themselves (e.g., Menard and Shirley 2005). From these theoretical beginnings it has migrated into the realm of policy debate. Broadly speaking one can discern, with Gillian Hart, three distinct "pathways out of Polanyi." The first is the use of the term "embeddedness" to shore up the argument that the "developmental state" was the decisive factor in the East Asian "miracles"—against the neoliberal explanation that they were market-led. The second, a neo-Weberian perspective, is deployed in the projection of a "kinder, gentler" capitalism that is associated in particular with the World Bank during the transition from Washington to post-Washington consensus. The other "asks a more Marxist set of questions that have to do with the slippages and contradictions that emerge within the 'neo-liberal thrust' of the 1980s and 1990s" (Hart 2004).

The term's primary portal into economic sociology and the New Institutional Economics was through an essay by a neo-Weberian economic sociologist, Mark Granovetter, in 1985. Granovetter's article brought embeddedness its current prominence but at the cost of considerable confusion. If Polanyi's usage influenced him at all it was subconsciously, for he recruits the concept to a quite different purpose, and did not intend his usage to be seen as a reappropriation (Granovetter 2004). His aim was to chart a course between two "extreme" positions: the utilitarian, "undersocialized" conception of man, which plays down the influence upon economic behavior of non-economic norms and institutions, and the "oversocialized" conception, represented by the argument of Polanyi and others "that the behaviour and institutions to be analyzed are so constrained by ongoing social relations that to construe them as independent is a grievous misunderstanding" (Granovetter 1985: 481–482). In what one may charitably assume to have been a slip of the pen, at different stages in the argument he identifies both the Polanyian "extreme" and his own middle course as "*the* embeddedness approach" (Granovetter 1985: 481, 487).

Granovetter (1985, 1992) reserves his sharpest criticisms of Polanyi for the postulation of a rupture between pre-modern embedded societies and disembedded market society. For him, economic behavior in market societies is rooted in socialized networks: all societies are "embedded." Sometimes known as the "network approach"—because embeddedness is taken to denote "the way social and economic activities are mixed up with networks of social relations" (Granovetter 2004)—Granovetter's case is that explanation of the behavior of market actors should privilege structures of social networks and the positions individuals hold within them rather than ethical commitments or institutional arrangements. This approach, he suggests (1985: 504), can serve to broaden the basis of rational choice theory: what may appear to be non-rational behaviour or the automatic following of cultural rules may be seen to be a perfectly sensible individual calculation when "situational constraints, especially those of embeddedness, are fully appreciated."

As Greta Krippner and Anthony Alvarez (2007) have pointed out, Granovetter is not so much engaging in a critique of Polanyi as advancing a wholly different concept. Whereas Polanyi's conception of embeddedness is, at bottom, a critique of the analytically autonomous economy that is the hallmark of the neoclassical approach, Granovetter's "is focused squarely on the problem of atomism, insisting on the intrinsically relational nature of all social action, including action in economic contexts." Yet, in so doing, he "leaves intact the notion of an analytically autonomous economy criticized forcefully by Polanyi." Others concur with Krippner and Alvarez' critique. Beckert (2009: 42), for example, describes Granovetter's approach as one that isolates "a single aspect of markets—networks of ongoing social relations—as constituting the proper domain of economic sociology," as contrasted with Polanyi's institutional approach, according to which "markets are not networks of structurally equivalent producers but rather fully social institutions, reflecting a complex alchemy of politics, culture, and ideology." Similarly, the neo-Polanyians Maucourant and Michele Cangiani remark that Granovetter's concept refers to the fact that economic agents are always already socialized, and to the connectedness of individuals in social networks, and not to the institutional arrangement of the economic system as a whole. His approach is not concerned with the larger social systems in which economies are located but instead

> remains individualistic and micro-sociological. He settles for a generalisation of "*embeddedness*", understood in his own way, which minimises the difference between the "*market system*" and the other *institutional organisations* of the economy.[7]

Over the last twenty years "embeddedness" has taken on a life of its own. Its proliferation would appear to suggest that it fulfills a useful role, yet the directions it has followed have been semantically various to such an extent that, as Granovetter (2004) recently remarked in explanation of why he himself rarely uses it any longer, "it has become almost meaningless, stretched to mean almost anything, so that it therefore means nothing." Its critics argue that it was always problematic, for it encourages the misleading view that there exists a dichotomy between social relations, grounded in trust and reciprocity, and market relations, based upon free exchange between rational egotists. In this regard, Greta Krippner (2004) has astutely remarked, the term is paradoxical: "the basic intuition that markets are socially embedded has led economic sociologists to take the market itself for granted." Those who follow Granovetter in isolating the "network" aspect of markets neglect the underlying social content. It is, she goes on, an approach that obscures the fact that

> congealed into every market exchange is a history of struggle and contestation that has produced actors with certain understandings of themselves and the world which predispose them to exchange under a certain set of social rules and not another. In this sense, the state, culture and politics are *contained* in every market act.

By directing attention to the layers of social behavior outside the market, the concept of embeddedness desociologizes the market itself. The Granovetterian approach reinforces the notion—which Krippner (2001: 799) locates in Parsonsian sociology but others (e.g., Clarke 1982) have identified as originating with Weber—that "economy" is usefully counterposed to "society," as separate spheres.

Does this critique apply to Polanyi himself? John Lie (1991) has suggested that it does, and provocatively describes Polanyi's concept of market exchange as "disembedded." From his heterodox—not to say heretical—perspective, Polanyi offers a moral critique of the sociologically empty market concept of neoclassical economics without probing its weakness by way of investigating "the concrete social relations of those who buy and sell." The weak point of Polanyi's model, he argues, is its equation of market exchange with commoditization, for this renders invisible the underlying social relations through which commodity exchange is organized.

In Krippner's view (in Beckert 2009), by contrast, Polanyi is not susceptible to this criticism, for he does not theorize markets as networks of structurally equivalent producers but rather as "fully social institutions, reflecting a complex alchemy of politics, culture, and ideology." Others agree, arguing that Polanyi's conceptual apparatus does not divide social life in market society into reified spheres; his point concerns, rather, the separate institutionalization of economic and political activity. Moreover, he uses embeddedness not only as an analytical term but also to allude to the political goal of ensuring a stable democratic society through the regulation of markets in land, labor and money. The term's reference point, Beckert has argued (2009), is not the economy as such but

> the larger social systems in which all economies are located . . . In *The Great Transformation* Polanyi did not aim to understand the functioning of market exchange in order to explain the social preconditions for market efficiency; he was concerned with what happens to social order and political freedom when economic exchange is organized chiefly through self-regulating markets.

It follows that a sociological theory of the economy that claims Polanyi as its inspiration cannot limit itself to examining the preconditions for designing economic institutions adapted to "efficiency" but must also attend to the effects of the organization of the economic system on society at large.

Neo-Polanyian Interpretations

Amongst neo-Polanyians no consensus exists with respect to the meaning and appropriate usage of "embeddedness." Probably the most influential position has been advanced by the political economist Fred Block. With detailed reference to the development of Polanyi's ideas propaedeutic to TGT, Block argues that because he was exiting from his most Marxian phase as he began to write TGT a clash of conceptual frameworks exists in that book that generated conceptual ambiguity. One lens in TGT, a survival from Polanyi's Marxian period, frames its subject as the logic of market forces that disembed economy from society. Coupled with this is another, much more original, lens through which Polanyi begins to glimpse something startlingly new. By observing that for most of their history market societies are constituted by two opposing movements, with the strength of protection effectively re-embedding the economy, he begins to see that there can be no such thing as a disembedded economy: a pure market economy is an illusion that may be pursued but never attained. It therefore makes no sense to speak of the "logic" of the market economy, for economic processes cannot but result from a mix of cultural, political and economic forces. From these observations Block infers that the non-Marxian Polanyi should be hailed as the originator of the notion of the "always embedded economy," the recognition that functioning market societies must maintain some threshold level of embeddedness—of interrelation with the other social-structural and cultural-structural elements of society—or else risk social and economic disaster; that, in Block's phrase (2001; cf. Barber 1995), "markets must construct elaborate rule and institutional structures to limit the individual pursuit of gain or risk degenerating into a Hobbesian war of all against all." Given that a moral and institutional framework is invariably present, this approach directs attention towards the different degrees of "marketness" and of "embeddedness" in different economic structures (Block 1991). In what ways are transactions and contracts embedded in social relations such as family ties, friendships or long-term supplier-contractor relations? To what extent do non-economic goals such as moral or spiritual commitments shape economic behavior? Such questions may then guide comparative research into the social and moral underpinnings of market behavior in different states and regions—a project that Block himself (e.g., 2008) has pursued in his subsequent research.

Block's interpretation is influential but has not lacked its critics. In Krippner's judgment (2001: 788, 799), Block subverts Polanyi's vision of market society because he operates with a framework that counterposes a "stripped down version of the market" to the social economy, thereby reinforcing the asocial market construct that has long blighted economic sociology. Others have focused upon Block's concept of the "always embedded economy." That there is a sense in which all economies, including those in which markets are comparatively "free," are "embedded" is non-contentious. As Ron Stanfield has put it (1986: 107),

> The economy is always instituted by a socialization process which moulds individual character toward the ethical, aesthetical, and instrumental norms, standards, and practices which are needed to participate in the

economy. This much is true of all social economies in that all must integrate economic activity by means of systems of communication and sanction. These systems inform individuals as to the behaviour expected of them and of others, and of the rewards and penalties that they can apply to others or expect to be applied to themselves in cases where expected behaviour is or is not forthcoming.

At this level of abstraction it is difficult to dispute the institutional and normative embeddedness of free market capitalism. Of course, in such a society the market requires an array of institutional supports: property rights, forms of law, means of enforcement of contracts, etc. But surely Polanyi was not simply making the commonplace points that economic behavior is always woven into legal, political, customary and ideological fabrics, or that the stability and predictability of markets depend upon their connections to wider webs of social relations? Given, to mention only a few examples, the traditions of sociological thought and the Scottish and German Historical Schools, with their explorations of the market economy's institutional preconditions, that would represent one of the more tiresome attempts to reinvent an 18th-century wheel. This "was a point that Adam Smith devoted his life to making," as one economist has put it (McCloskey 2009), knocking for six the notion that the "always embedded" thesis is original to Polanyi. No, say Block's critics, his reading obscures the freshness and theoretical richness of Polanyi's case. The novelty of the market economy is that its institutional embedding involves its diremption from non-economic institutions in manner that negates both social control over economic institutions and moral behavior within them. The connectedness between the moral, motivational and structural aspects of the term has been well expressed by Matthew Watson (2005: 153).

> Embeddedness, for Polanyi, is the social control of economic relations through institutional means, where a link can be drawn between embeddedness and the social obligation to act in a morally dutiful manner. Insofar as "the market" imposes purely functional character traits on individuals, the moral dimension of economic activity is increasingly dissolved.

To grasp this, one has to step a little way into Polanyi's mental universe. It is not enough to envision the market economy as embedded in norms of individual liberty, egalitarianism and pluralism. He recognizes these but perceives at a deeper motivational level the norms of acquisitiveness and self-interest that they sanction. These norms that undergird the market economy are reprehensible: they atomize society and dissolve its moral fabric, spawning egotism and anomie. To say that the liberal market is "embedded" in the sense of "instituted," then, does not negate its "disembeddedness" at other levels. The term does not denote the economy's separation from society but from non-economic institutions, a separation that produces a rift between individual and society and a resulting moral degeneration. Polanyi's argument here has been likened by Peter McMylor to Alasdair MacIntyre's understanding of liberal ethics: that liberalism cannot do without a moral discourse and is in the abstract sense "ethically embedded," but is best grasped as an *incoherent* moral tradition because it arises from within a compartmentalized social order (see MacIntyre 2007; McMylor 2003, 1994).

What Block's critics emphasize, against the "always embedded" concept, is the uniqueness of the modern market society. It is an exceptional social order because its customs and values are so powerfully shaped by the imperatives that pulse from a distinct market sphere. The self-regulating market, as Stanfield describes (1995: 116), has its own "logic (calculated self-gain), process of control (bargaining and competition), and teleological momentum (economic progress conceived solely as expanding commodity production)." Such an economy is necessarily superordinate to society. In it,

> family life must be geared to socializing effective market competitors and culture must legitimate, even celebrate, the calculated selfishness that can alone drive the competitive process and lend any meaning to the relative prices it establishes. Culture must define success as pecuniary achievement and promote an ideology of scarcity that creates the moral imperative of calculated maximization. The family unit and social relationships must be restricted so as not to interfere with the mobility necessary for effective market participation.

This is why it does make sense to speak of a disembedded economy, and even to conceive of it as one in which society is embedded. It is a system that, in the words of Cangiani and Maucourant (2008, emphases in original), remains *disembedded*, precisely as a result of its *general institutional characteristics*; hence it is by nature autonomous and constitutes the fundamental constraint in the development of society. Thus, it is society which tends to be, as Polanyi says, *embedded* in its economy.

This is a wholly different interpretation from Block's. It situates Polanyi's concept closer to that of Marxists, who view the rise of the market economy less as the outcome of than as the primary cause of that broad set of legal and cultural changes characteristic of "modernity," which included the generalization of contractually based economic behavior, the emergence of norms associated with absolute property rights, and separate legal systems geared to enforcing those rights.

Conclusion

Karl Polanyi's research into the "embedding" of economic life in social systems has become a touchstone for economic sociologists, but the usefulness of the concept has been called into question even as its usage has proliferated. In this essay I have explored some of the ambiguities. Embeddedness can be interpreted as the simple thesis that economic action is, always and everywhere, conditioned by non-economic institutions. In Granovetter's hands, it came to refer to the dependence of market behavior upon networks of individuals, as contrasted with the focus upon the relationship between functionally differentiated institutional complexes within an overall social system that characterizes Polanyi's usage. Ironically, "embeddedness" only became recognized as a pivotal Polanyian concept as the result of interest in a quite alien idea, Granovetter's. Given that the dominant usage of the term is so unlike Polanyi's, the fact that Polanyi is widely cited as its originator is the cause of not a little confusion. Some avowedly Polanyian scholars (e.g., Boyer and Hollingsworth 1999: 444–445) use his sense and the Granovetterian recoinage interchangeably, seemingly unaware of their dissimilarity.

Yet, even without Granovetter's intervention, Polanyi's term is far from straightforward. One interpretive problem has been a lack of awareness as to sources upon which Polanyi drew when developing the concept. In the above, I have delineated what I believe to be the chief sources, drawing attention to areas of overlap and of tension. Polanyi is a major sociologist and institutional economist, and if this essay has made a small contribution to developing an improved understanding of his formative influences and methodology, it has performed a worthwhile task.

Notes

1. Etzioni (1987: 204). On similarities to Parsons, see Hopkins (1957).
2. Kari Polanyi-Levitt, telephone conversation with the author, 06.10.2007 and email to the author, 29.10.2007.
3. For example, Neale (1990), Stanfield (1986), Mayhew (1989), Waller and Jennings (1991), Carroll and Stanfield (2003), Rodrigues (2004), Özveren (2005), Barthélemy and Nieddu (2007), and Davis (2008).
4. This and the following paragraphs draw upon Dale (2010).
5. Polanyi, expertly paraphrased by Watson (2005: 97).
6. As paraphrased by Macintyre (2006: 127).
7. Cangiani and Maucourant (2008). Emphases in original. See also Randles (2007: 148) and Harvey et al. (2007: 4–5).

References: Documents from the the Archive of the Karl Polanyi Institute for Political Economy, Concordia University

[Numerals in the form "1-11" refer to box and folder numbers respectively.]

7-9, Karl Polanyi: "Origins of Institutions."
9-7, Karl Polanyi: Notes on readings, 1936–1946.
10-8, Karl Polanyi: 1934–46, "Notes on Malinowski."
18-8, Karl Polanyi: "The Fascist Virus."
24-6, Abraham Rotstein: Drafts, 1951–1960.
27-8, Karl Polanyi: "Thorstein Veblen: 'Economics as a Study of Process,' 1898."
31-1, Karl Polanyi, "Report on term paper no. 2."
31-1, Karl Polanyi: Lecture—"The Tool Box of Institutional Analysis"—Columbia University, New York—Outline and report, 1947–1953.
31-15, Karl Polanyi: Research Proposal No.1; 37-2, "Lecture—'Methodology—The Methodological Problems Connected with the Question of Capitalism in Antiquity'," n.d.
42-2, Karl Polanyi (1961) "Dahomey"—Notes.
42-9, Karl Polanyi: "A Note on the Translation of Menger's 'Grundsaetze'," n.d.
45-2 Abraham Rotstein (1956) "Notes of Weekend I with Karl Polanyi."
45-3, Abraham Rotstein (1956) "Notes of Weekend II with Karl Polanyi."

45-14, Abraham Rotstein (1957) "Notes of Weekend XIX with Karl Polanyi."
48-1, Correspondence: Karl Polanyi to Carter Goodrich 20.11.46.
48-2, Correspondence: Telegram 28.5.47 from Goodrich to Polanyi.
48-6, Correspondence: Karl Polanyi to Abe Rotstein 25.8.51.
48-7, Correspondence: Karl Polanyi to Abe Rotstein 19.4.52.

References: Published Texts

Barber, B. (1995). "All Economies Are Embedded: The Career of a Concept, and Beyond." *Social Research* 62(2): 387–413.

Barthélemy, D., and M. Nieddu. (2007). "Non-Trade Concerns in Agricultural and Environmental Economics: How J.R. Commons and Karl Polanyi Can Help Us." *Journal of Economic Issues* 41(2): 519–556.

Beckert, J. (2007). "The Great Transformation of Embeddedness: Karl Polanyi and the New Economic Sociology." In *MPIfG Discussion Paper 07/1.* Cologne: Max Planck Institute for the Study of Societies.

——. (2009). "The Great Transformation of Embeddedness: Karl Polanyi and the New Economic Sociology." In *Market and Society: The Great Transformation Today.* Eds. Chris Hann and Keith Hart. Cambridge University Press.

Block, F. (1991). "Contradictions of Self-Regulating Markets." In *The Legacy of Karl Polanyi; Market, State and Society at the End of the Twentieth Century.* Eds. Marguerite Mendell and Daniel Salée. Macmillan.

——. (2001). "Karl Polanyi and the Writing of *The Great Transformation.*" Paper presented at Eighth International Karl Polanyi Conference, Mexico City, November.

——. (2008). "Swimming Against the Current: The Rise of a Hidden Developmental State in the United States." *Politics & Society* 36(2): 169–206.

Boyer, R., and J. R. Hollingsworth. (1999). "Conclusion." In *Contemporary Capitalism: The Embeddedness of Institutions.* Eds. Hollingsworth and Boyer. Cambridge: Cambridge University Press.

Cangiani, M., and J. Maucourant. (2008). "Introduction." In *Essais de Karl Polanyi.* Eds. Cangiani and Maucourant. Seuil.

Cangiani, M. et al. (2005). "Die Polarität: Menschliche Freiheit— marktwirtschaftliche Institutionen. Zu den Grundlagen von Karl Polanyi's Denken." In *Chronik der großen Transformation.* Eds. Cangiani et al. Band 3, Marburg: Metropolis.

Carroll, M., and R. Stanfield. (2003). "Social Capital, Karl Polanyi, and American Social and Institutional Economics." *Journal of Economic Issues* 37(2): 397–404.

Clarke, S. (1982). *Marx, Marginalism and Modern Sociology: From Adam Smith to Max Weber.* Houndmills: Macmillan.

Dale, G. (2010). *Karl Polanyi: The Limits of the Market.* Polity Press.

Davis, A. (2008). "Endogenous Institutions and the Politics of Property: Comparing and Contrasting Douglass North and Karl Polanyi in the Case of Finance." *Journal of Economic Issues* 42(4): 1101–1122.

Etzioni, A. (1987). *The Moral Dimension: Toward a New Economics.* New York: Free Press.

Firth, R. (1972). "Methodological Issues in Economic Anthropology." *Man* 7(3): 467–475.

Gemici, K. (2008). "Karl Polanyi and the Antinomies of Embeddedness." *Socio-Economic Review* 6(1): 5–33.

Granovetter, M. (1985). "Economic Action and Social Structure: The Problem of Embeddedness." *American Journal of Sociology* 91(3): 481–510.

———. (1992). "The Nature of Economic Relations." In *Understanding Economic Process.* Ed. Sutti Ortiz. Lanham: University Press of America.

———. (2004). "Opening Remarks on Embeddedness." In Greta Krippner et al., Eds. "Polanyi Symposium: A Conversation on Embeddedness." *Socio-Economic Review* 2(1): 109–135.

Halperin, R. (1988). *Economies Across Cultures: Towards a Comparative Science of the Economy.* Houndmills: Macmillan.

Hart, G. (2004). "The Career of the Concept of Embeddedness." In Greta Krippner et al., Eds. "Polanyi Symposium: A Conversation on Embeddedness." *Socio-Economic Review* 2(1): 109–135.

Harvey, M. et al. (2007). "Working With and Beyond Polanyian Perspectives." In *Karl Polanyi: New Perspectives on the Place of the Economy in Society.* Eds. Mark Harvey et al. Manchester: Manchester University Press.

Hopkins, T. (1957). "Sociology and the Substantive View of the Economy." In *Trade and Market in the Early Empires: Economies in History and Theory.* Eds. Karl Polanyi et al. New York: Free Press.

Keynes, J. M. (1936). *The General Theory of Employment, Interest and Money.* London: Macmillan.

Krippner, G. (2001). "The Elusive Market: Embeddedness and the Paradigm of Economic Sociology." *Theory and Society* 30: 775–810.

———. (2004). "Opening Remarks on Embeddedness." In Greta Krippner et al., Eds. "Polanyi Symposium: A Conversation on Embeddedness." *Socio-Economic Review* 2(1): 109–135.

Krippner, G., and A. Alvarez. (2007). "Embeddedness and the Intellectual Projects of Economic Sociology." *Annual Review of Sociology* 33: 105–128.

Kuper, A. (1996). *Anthropology and Anthropologists: The Modern British School,* 3rd edition. London: Routledge.

Lewin, M. (1985). *The Making of the Soviet System; Essays in the Social History of Interwar Russia.* London: Methuen.

Lie, J. (1991). "Embedding Polanyi's Market Society." *Sociological Perspectives* 34(2): 219–235.

Liebersohn, H. (1988). *Fate and Utopia in German Sociology, 1870—1923.* Cambridge: MIT Press.

MacIntyre, A. (2006). *Edith Stein: A Philosophical Prologue, 1913—1922.* Lanham: Rowman & Littlefield.

———. ([1981] 2007). *After Virtue.* London: Duckworth.

Marx, K. (1973). *Grundrisse.* Harmondsworth: Penguin.

Maucourant, J. (2002). "Polanyi on Institutions and Money: An Interpretation Suggested by a Reading of Commons, Mitchell and Veblen." In *Economy and Society: Money, Capitalism and Transition.* Eds. Fikret Adaman and Pat Devine. Montreal: Black Rose.

Mayhew, A. (1987). "The Beginnings of Institutionalism." *Journal of Economic Issues* 21(3).

———. (1989). "Polanyi's Double Movement and Veblen on the Army of the Commonweal." *Journal of Economic Issues* 23(2): 971–998.

McCloskey, D. (2009). *Bourgeois Towns: How Capitalism Became Virtuous, 1300–1776,* deirdremccloskey.org/docs/towns2.doc, accessed 7 February 2009.

McMylor, P. (1994). *Alasdair MacIntyre: Critic of Modernity.* London: Routledge.

———. (2003). "Moral Philosophy and Economic Sociology: What MacIntyre Learnt from Polanyi." *International Review of Sociology—Revue Internationale de Sociologie* 13(2): 393–407.

Menard, C., and M. Shirley. (2005). "Introduction." In *Handbook of New Institutional Economics.* Eds. Claude Menard and Mary Shirley. Cheltenham: Edwar Elgar.

Nafissi, M. (2005). *Ancient Athens and Modern Ideology; Value, Theory and Evidence in Historical Sciences.* London: Institute of Classical Studies.

Nau, H. H. Ed. (1998). *Gustav Schmoller. Historisch-ethische Nationalökonomie als Kulturwissenschaft. Ausgewaehlte methodologische Schriften.* Metropolis.

Neale, W. (1987). "Institutions." *Journal of Economic Issues* 21: 1177–1206.

———. (1990). "Karl Polanyi and American Institutionalism: A Strange Case of Convergence." In *The Life and Work of Karl Polanyi.* Ed. Kari Polanyi-Levitt. Montreal: Black Rose.

Özveren, E. (2005). "Polanyi, Chayanov, and Lessons for the Study of the Informal Sector." *Journal of Economic Issues* 39(3): 765–776.

———. (2007). "Karl Polanyi and Return of the 'Primitive' in Institutional Economics." *Journal of Economic Issues* 41(3): 783–808.

Peukert, H. (2001). "Bridging Old and New Institutional Economics: Gustav Schmoller and Douglass C. North, Seen with Old Institutionalists' Eyes." *European Journal of Law and Economics* 11(2): 91–130.

Polanyi, K. (1947). "On the Belief in Economic Determinism." *Sociological Review* 39(1).

———. (1957). *The Great Transformation: The Political and Economic Origins of Our Time.* Boston: Beacon Press.

———. (1966). *Dahomey and the Slave Trade; An Analysis of an Archaic Economy.* Seattle: University of Washington Press.

———. (1968a). *Primitive, Archaic and Modern Economies.* Boston: Beacon Press.

———. (1968b). "Karl Bücher." In *International Encyclopedia of the Social Sciences.* Ed. David Sills. vol. 2, Macmillan.

———. (1977). *The Livelihood of Man.* New York: Academic Press.

———. ([1934] 2002). "Lancashire als Menschheitsfrage." In *Chronik der großen Transformation.* Eds. Michele Cangiani and Claus Thomasberger. Band 1, Marburg: Metropolis.

Randles, S. (2007). "Issues for a Neo-Polanyian Research Agenda in Economic Sociology." In *Karl Polanyi: New Perspectives on the Place of the Economy in Society.* Eds. Mark Harvey et al. Manchester: Manchester University Press.

Rehmann, J. (1998). *Max Weber: Modernisierung als passive Revolution. Kontextstudien zu Politik, Philosophie und Religion im Übergang zum Fordismus.* Hamburg: Argument.

Rodrigues, J. (2004). "Endogenous Preferences and Embeddedness: A Reappraisal of Karl Polanyi." *Journal of Economic Issues* 38(1): 189–200.

Savage, S. (1977). "Talcott Parsons and the Structural-Functionalist Theory of the Economy." In *Sociological Theories of the Economy.* Ed. Barry Hindess. London: Macmillan.

Stanfield, R. (1986). *The Economic Thought of Karl Polanyi; Lives and Livelihood.* Houndmills: Macmillan.

———. (1995). *Economics, Power and Culture: Essays in the Development of Radical Institutionalism.* Macmillan.

Streeck, W. (1999). "Beneficial Constraints: On the Economic Limits of Rational Voluntarism." In *Contemporary Capitalism; The Embeddedness of Institutions.* Eds. J. Rogers Hollingsworth and Robert Boyer. Cambridge University Press.

Tawney, R. H. (1929). "Preface to Raymond Firth." In *Primitive Economics of the New Zealand Maori.* London: Routledge.

Therborn, G. (1976). *Science, Class & Society: On the Formation of Sociology & Historical Materialism.* London: New Left Books.

Thurnwald, R. (1932a). *Economics in Primitive Communities.* London.

———. (1932b). *Die menschliche Gesellschaft, Band 3: Werden, Wandel und Gestaltung der Wirtschaft.* Berlin: Walter de Gruyter.

Tönnies, F. ([1921] 1974). *Karl Marx: His Life and Teaching.* Michigan State University Press.

——. ([1887] 1988). *Community and Society*. New Brunswick: Transaction.
Waller, W., and A. Jennings. (1991). "A Feminist Institutionalist Reconsideration of Karl Polanyi." *Journal of Economic Issues* 25(2): 485–497.
Watson, M. (2005). *Foundations of International Political Economy*. Houndmills: Palgrave.
Weber, M. (1964). *The Theory of Social and Economic Organization*. New York: Free Press.

Social Ecological Economics: Understanding the Past to See the Future

By CLIVE L. SPASH*

ABSTRACT. The attempt to provide insight into the interactions between the economy and the environment has been an on-going struggle for many decades. The rise of Ecological Economics can be seen as a positive step towards integrating social and natural science understanding by a movement that aims to go beyond the confines of mainstream economics towards a progressive political economy of the environment. However, this vision has not been shared by all those who have associated themselves with Ecological Economics and there has been conflict. An historical analysis is presented that shows the role of mainstream theory in delimiting the field of environmental research. The argument is put forward that rather than employing a purely mechanistic objective empirical methodology there is a need for an integrating interdisciplinarity heterodox economic approach. In order to distinguish this approach—from the more mainstream multidisciplinary linking of unreconstituted ecological and economic models—the name Social Ecological Economics is put forward as expressing the essential socio-economic character of the needed work ahead.

*Clive L. Spash holds the Chair of Public Policy and Governance in the Department of Socio-Economics, WU Vienna University of Economics and Business, Nordbergstr. 15/4/B-UZA 4, 1090 Wien, and is a Professor II in the Department of International Environment and Development Studies (Noragric), Norwegian University of Life Sciences. E-mail clive.spash@umb.no. Professor Spash is an economist who specializes in environmental problems. His recent works include a controversial paper on carbon trading (Spash 2010), a co-edited volume on Post-Keynesian and Ecological Economics (Holt, Pressman, and Spash 2010), and a 4-volume collection of papers defining the field of Ecological Economics (Spash 2009a). For more information go to www.clivespash.org.

American Journal of Economics and Sociology, Vol. 70, No. 2 (April, 2011).

Introduction

Ecological Economics has developed as a modern movement since the late 1980s (see Spash 1999). This movement has gathered together a variety of perspectives and interests concerned to address the modern environmental crisis. A crisis because environmental degradation—species loss, long range transport of air pollutants, contamination of soil and water, introduction of synthetic chemicals, desertification, deforestation—has only belatedly been recognized as integrally linked to the way the economy is run.

In economics, the appearance of environmental problems has for long been minimal and attention largely left to sub-disciplinary specialists (e.g., agricultural, resource and environmental economists) easily sidelined and disregarded by both mainstream micro and macro economists. In micro economics, core theoretical ideas have set the stage in terms of price theory for over a century (see Lee 2009: 2–3), providing a restricted orthodox worldview.[1] In macro economics, the type of subjects that dominate (e.g., money supply, unemployment and inflation) have seemed divorced from environmental problems. This has meant economists working on the environment could easily be dismissed as having consigned themselves to irrelevance. Even amongst heterodox schools (e.g., post-Keynesians, critical institution-alists, neo-Marxists), where a voice might have been more readily expected to be heard, there has been little or no attention. Economists of all schools have generally been able to ignore the evidence of environmental problems as having anything to do with their work. Yet in more recent times this seems to have been changing.

Since the early 1990s a range of Nobel economic prize winners (e.g., Arrow, Kahneman, Ostrom, Sen, Solow, Stiglitz) have been found imparting their wisdom on environmental matters,[2] and some have even associated with ecological economists (e.g., Arrow, Ostrom, Sen).[3] This appears to indicate a new engagement by economists with environmental issues and a newfound respect for the field of research. Thus, the magazine *The Economist* has moved from relegating occasional environmental articles to its science section to running regular features and leaders. An economist may now apparently study and publish on environmental topics while maintaining some collegiate standing. Indeed, specialists in the area appear, in neoclassical economic terms, as rather cunning speculators who foresaw the potential personal returns of an early investment.

That the environment is now a headline economic issue goes hand-in-hand with the fact that controlling pollution is big business. The high political profile given to human induced climate change and neo-liberal support for multi-billion dollar carbon trading markets have made this very clear. For example, the European emissions trading scheme had an estimated worth of $US51 billion in 2007 (European Commission 2008: 21) and $US80 billion in 2008 (Kantner 2008). The market in carbon offsets is also a growth industry (European Commission 2008). As potentially the largest commodity market ever created, carbon trading has stimulated considerable interest in the financial markets and amongst banks and corporations (Spash 2010). All this provides an incentive for the newfound environmental interest within the economic establishment.

Unfortunately, increased popularity does not necessarily indicate serious engagement with the subject matter, even from the most hopeful sources. For example, Amartya Sen appears a thoughtful writer on economics who has expressed ideas critical of orthodox economics and offered insights on development,[4] poverty and gender issues. In a rather overlooked book, he highlighted the role and importance of ethics in economics (Sen 1987). All this fits well with arguments for value pluralism as found in Ecological Economics (Gowdy and Erickson 2005). Yet he gave a plenary at the International Society for Ecological Economics (ISEE) conference in 2006 that was not only disappointing, in offering little of substance specifically on the environment, but also finished up expressing support for the monistic global cost-benefit analysis of the report by Stern (2006) on human induced climate change. He later endorsed the published report. This support would seem in stark contrast to his ideas on economic development as opportunity, writings on problems with welfarism in economics, and general criticisms of using growth as a measure of well-being. Sen, unlike some in his audience, was apparently unconcerned by, or perhaps unaware of, Stern's underlying expected utility model, standard discounting approaches and use of GDP growth as means for justifying human action, or inaction, on this major environmental issue (see critique by Spash 2007). At the ISEE conference he seemed oblivious to any debates in Ecological Economics of direct relevance to his own work, or the ways in which his own work might relate to environmental issues.

That eminent figures in the economic establishment talk to but not about the environment is seriously problematic and brings into question the new rhetoric of environmental concern amongst economists. Indeed, there is a continued neglect of the environment as anything to do with the core of economics as a subject. This can be explained by considering two alternative ways in which economists address environmental issues. First is the treatment of environmental problems as special cases of more general theoretical constructs in mainstream economics. This allows (both mainstream and heterodox) economists who are embedded in an establishment discourse to maintain their own preoccupations without needing to pay much attention to the specifics raised by environmental problems (e.g., transforming to a low carbon economy becomes green jobs, which are just an aspect of macroeconomic employment policy). This has been the preferred approach for most economists. Second is the recognition that serious attention to environmental reality leads to the need for a totally new way of thinking based in political economy and interdisciplinary learning. As will be shown, this is the raison d'être of Ecological Economics. Thus, work by ISEE Presidents Bina Agarwal (2001), Joan Martinez-Alier (2002), Richard Norgaard (1994) and John Gowdy (1994) has addressed the social and political as much as the economic, while emphasizing the need to learn from interactions with ecosystems. A perhaps inevitable struggle has then been on-going between this Social Ecological Economics approach and those engaged in legitimizing economics as an objective technical means for engineering society, where the environment is something external to the economy.

This paper explores that struggle and some of the resulting confusion it has created for understanding the meaning and content of Ecological Economics.[5] The central contention of the current paper is that the institutionalized power of mainstream theory has played an important role in delimiting the field of environmental research. As Lee (2009: 7) states: "The mainstream explanation focuses on how asocial, ahistorical individuals choose among scarce resources to meet competing ends given unlimited wants and explains it using fictitious concepts and a deductivist, closed-system methodology." Adopting that approach, in part or whole, then has serious implications for the conduct and relevance of Ecological Economics.

Understanding the discourse surrounding the work that has been appearing as Ecological Economics involves more than merely focussing on the academic technical debates. This requires historical analysis, exploration of conflicts and probing of the ideological and methodological differences. The overarching objective of the project, of which this paper is a part, is to enable a better classification of relevant work and indeed explain why some is inappropriately classified while other, dispersed across a range of fields, could easily be included within the bounds of relevance. More than one paper is necessary to take such a project to completion.

The current paper provides an historical exploration of the community of scholars grouped around Ecological Economics and probes their motives and interests in order to start clarifying areas of ideological and methodological unity and division. The next section looks at the rise of environmental concern leading to the development of economic thinking in the area. This sketches the claim to deep historical roots for Ecological Economics, but clearly identifies the modern movement as arising from late 20th-century environmentalism. Environmental economics is then seen as an earlier failed attempt to create a community challenging mainstream economic thinking. This background shows how Ecological Economics was born into a divided and contested world. The next section then explores specific divisions and conflict in the recent history of Ecological Economics. Examples of scholarly interactions are employed to explain how the movement became partially entrapped by an orthodox economic dialogue. This historical analysis emphasizes the role of individuals in developing and propagating ideas amongst a community of scholars and other interested people. Rather than denying the relevance of divisions the aim is to clarify their role in creating the current community. I then outline some ideological and methodological developments relating to specific subject areas and so form a vision of the heterodox foundations of Ecological Economics. This section is an initial attempt to bring the intellectual ideas more to the fore and has no pretense to being an in-depth analysis of the debates or their validity. The ideas proposed are part of the needed on-going discussion as to the appropriate intellectual pursuits of Ecological Economics. The overall aim is to reveal the "interwoven, interdependent narrative of ideas and community," as Lee (2009: 11) puts it. The paper concludes that if this movement is to make a substantive difference then it must pursue Social Ecological Economics as an heterodox interdisciplinary movement in political economy.

Roots of the Modern Movement

Ecological economics engages with a range of topics that recur across time and have been debated since the ancient Greeks. As such the subject matter includes the limits to wealth creation, the meaning of the "good life," how to achieve well-being individually and socially, ethics and behavior, the epistemology of value, and the psychological and social impact of ostentatious consumption. Threads of reasoning and ideas that are represented in the modern subject can be identified in a range of 18th- and 19th-century sources and call upon many topics discarded or ignored by mainstream economists, including: the writings on social motivation of Adam Smith ([1759] 1982), population and poverty in Malthus ([1798] 1986), Jevons ([1865] 1965) on non-renewable energy dependence, John Stuart Mill's (1848) steady-state economy, Marx (1867) on exploitation, class conflict and capital accumulation, and the evolutionary institutional analysis and "conspicuous consumption" of Veblen ([1899] 1991). The Romantic critique of economics is also relevant and most notably the writings of Ruskin ([1862] 1907). In Ecological Economics some limited forays have been made into this historical context (e.g., Becker et al. 2005; Christensen 1989; Smith 1980; Spash 1999), but most notably with respect to the energy-environment interface in the work by Martinez-Alier (1990).

While the subconscious roots may run deep, the conscious ones lie directly in the 1960s and 1970s, although a few economists during the 1940s and 1950s did express ideas in form and substance that are still current in Ecological Economics. Most notable is K. William Kapp, who dedicated himself to researching the relationship between economics and the environment. He also explored the relationship between social and natural sciences, the need for knowledge integration and meaning of interdisciplinarity (Kapp 1961). He wrote on history of thought and methodology (Kapp and Kapp 1963), and produced extensive empirically based institutional analyses of environmental problems (Kapp 1950, 1978). Indeed the reason he is largely unknown is that his critique was so far ahead of its time in breadth and depth. Ciriacy-Wantrup's (1952) work on conservation, land and resource use is also noteworthy, not least for developing the concept of a safe-minimum standard. More generally, there is the work on modern industrial economies of Polanyi (1944) and Galbraith ([1958] 1969, [1967] 2007) covering the rise of self-regulating market economies and the corporation, respectively. Both at points link their thesis explicitly to environmental degradation. Like Kapp, these authors offer critical institutional analysis of the economic process. So, while few contributed at this time, some powerful ideas emerged that remain highly relevant to our understanding of environmental problems.

The Emergence of Environmentalism

In the 1960s a more general and popular awakening to environmental problems arrived with books such as Rachael Carson's ([1962] 1987) *Silent Spring* on agro-chemical pollution and Paul Ehrlich's (1968) *Population Bomb*. The issue of economic growth was also placed on the agenda (Boulding 1966; Mishan 1969). In popular culture, the hippie movement raised the ideal of harmony with Nature, dematerialization and alternative lifestyles (from self-sufficiency to communes). However, the popular environmental literature really took off in the 1970s and only then spread into economic debates. Topics expanded from population growth (Ehrlich and Holdren 1971), to general limits to economic growth (Meadows et al. 1972), to questioning the means of production (Schumacher 1973) and social impacts of growth (Hirsch 1977). Radical environmentalism was being born (Abbey 1975), and an associated protest movement became institutionalized in non-governmental organizations from Friends of the Earth and Greenpeace to Earth First and Sea Shepherd.

In economics the major factor that helped concentrate minds on environmental issues was the energy crisis (Commoner 1976; Tanzer 1974). While this crisis was created by oil producers restricting supply, leading to price increases, the general idea of economic dependence on finite non-renewable resources was brought back on the agenda after having been neglected since the 1800s. There was inevitably also a backlash against environmental concern and defensive arguments from mainstream economists. For example, Beckerman not only attacked those raising concerns over finite natural resources (Beckerman 1974), but also Kapp's environmental work (see the reply to Beckerman by Kapp 1978: 305–318).

Such economists were, and remain, out of tune with public perception and the growing awareness of pollution as a techno-industrial threat to life on Earth. The link of DDT to non-human and human birth defects was a starter. Similar consequences were feared due to nuclear fallout from weapons testing. In 1959, contamination of the food chain became evident when radioactive deposits were found in wheat and milk in the northern United States. The result was to move testing underground, although France and China persisted with above ground testing and global pollution (e.g., Simpson et al. 1981). The new nuclear power industry, which supplied weapons grade plutonium, provided another environmental concern. The threat of accidents and pollution became increasingly real from the reactor scare at Three Mile Island in the USA to the radioactive releases from the UK's reprocessing plant at Windscale (renamed Sellafield in a political rebranding exercise). Fears of a major reactor accident were ultimately realized with the catastrophe at Chernobyl in 1986 and the resulting global nuclear fallout.

The increasing geographical scope of pollution threats also slowly became accepted elsewhere. In the 1970s scientists debated the idea that air pollutants from coal fired power stations could be transported internationally. This was contested into the 1980s and persistently denied by countries (e.g., UK and Germany) responsible for large scale emission of sulphur dioxide and nitrous oxides, that is until damages became evident domestically, e.g., tree loss in the Black Forest, Germany. Confirming the sources of acidic deposition impacting Scandinavian ecosystems became a political issue and an international research project, leading to the 1979 United Nations Convention on Long-Range Transboundary Air Pollution. Meanwhile, the aircraft industry's proposal for large fleets of supersonic aircraft, as the future for international travel, raised the specter of polluting the upper atmosphere and affecting global climate. This received some analytical attention from economists (d'Arge 1975). Another global pollution problem to get some economists' consideration was the depletion of stratospheric ozone connected to the use of aerosol propellants, mainly chlorofluorocarbons at the time (Cumberland, Hibbs, and Hoch 1982). In a few decades pollution had moved from being regarded as localized smog from domestic fires to international and global with numerous sources and seriously threatening consequences—including genetic mutation and irreversible damage to life-supporting ecosystems and their functioning.

The Rise and Fall of Environmental Economics

Environmental economics arose, along with the growth in public awareness, as a direct response to such problems (see, for example, Kneese 1971). By the late 1960s, the promise of material wealth for all and post World War II optimism in the abilities of science and technology were faltering. Boulding (1966) characterized the economy as being run like the Wild West, populated by cowboys who exploited resources, chucked their waste on the ground and rode away to infinite horizons—where lay the promise of fresh resources and new environments to exploit and degrade—this was contrast with Earth as a closed system like a spaceship. Economic growth was seen as positively misleading in terms of the consequences for human society (Mishan 1969). The challenge was for a new approach to economics.

Environmental economics then appeared both innovative and progressive, if not downright revolutionary. For example, Bohm and Kneese (1971: ix–x) introduced their edited volume, *The Economics of the Environment*, stating that this was "a profession rethinking, extending, and revising its concepts, and finding new applications for them." They drew a parallel with "the ferment in the profession when the Keynesian revolution was in progress" and claimed history was in the making. The reality was a little different.

Any serious challenge by such key figures of the time that might have been posed to orthodox economic methodology, its theoretical models, or even its non-environmental preoccupations was muted. Indeed, besides some passing rhetorical comments, time was mostly devoted to developing mainstream economic thought and applying this to environmental issues. Materials balance theory brought in the laws of thermodynamics, but for compatibility with the mainstream this needed to fit within a general equilibrium framework (Kneese, Ayres, and d'Arge 1970). Pollution was seen as all pervasive (Hunt and d'Arge 1973), but this needed to fit within an optimal control framework (d'Arge and Kogiku 1973). The environment was seen to involve a range of values neglected by and outside of economics (Krutilla 1967), but these had to fit within cost-benefit analysis and a welfare theoretic framework (Kneese 1984).

Despite this, innovation certainly did occur. Environmental valuation in cost-benefit analysis introduced new methods such as travel cost, hedonic pricing and contingent valuation. The travel cost method was the earliest to be more fully developed (Clawson and Knetsch 1966), while contingent valuation followed later, opening a whole new research agenda (Cummings, Brookshire, and Schulze 1986). Primary data collection from face to face interviews gave results that questioned the economic model of human psychology and motivation, and for some created interdisciplinary interactions (Spash 2008a). The theory behind values expanded from pure use to option, existence and bequest values (Krutilla 1967; Krutilla and Fisher 1978). This contributed to discussions over the ethical basis of economics (Kneese and Schulze 1985; Schulze and Brookshire 1982; Schulze, Brookshire and Sandler 1981). Climate change and the treatment of future generations were also topics on the valuation agenda (d'Arge 1979), which raised ethical concerns (d'Arge, Schulze, and Brookshire 1982; Spash and d'Arge 1989).

However, working inside orthodox economics—preference utilitarianism, optimal control modeling, discounting, a monistic value system, and mathematics as a doctrine of rigor—heavily constrained criticism, innovation and the ability to address environmental and social problems. For example, in the early 1980s a key workshop on contingent valuation was run by Cummings, Brookshire, and Schulze

(1986), bringing together a range of people including psychologists (e.g., later Nobel prize winner Daniel Kahneman). Yet, those advocating the use of attitude-behavior models from social psychology were extremely critical of their reception: "We certainly underestimated the barriers to interdisciplinary communication. Our proposal that economists consider the attitudes-behaviour literature has met with indifference or hostility. CBS are no exception" (Bishop and Heberlein 1986: 141).

A second example is the experience of Jack Knetsch. Despite being a pioneer of travel cost and hedonic pricing, Knetsch has also been highly critical of valuation practice (e.g., Knetsch 1994, 2005), and in particular its failure to learn from empirical evidence with respect to loss-gain differences (Knetsch 1985, 1989; Knetsch and Sinden 1984). His work with Kahneman provoked strong and defensive reactions. This was especially so for their paper on embedding (Kahneman and Knetsch 1992b), which refers to willingness to pay under contingent valuation as the purchase of moral satisfaction rather than an exchange value. Getting the paper published in the main environmental economics journal proved problematic and it received some special critical treatment.[6]

These examples indicate the roots of dissension that would lead to Ecological Economics. While some economists posed, but never answered, various questions, others followed arguments to their logical ends. Those ends raised issues that just could not be addressed within the orthodox economic frame. The entire thrust of the work towards a new and challenging research agenda seemed to be denied. For example, long range transport of multiple air pollutants from dispersed sources is a major topic of environmental concern. Yet environmental economists have persisted in teaching a core model that characterizes pollution as a local problem between two actors, easily corrected as a one-off market failure (Spash 2010), or worse, as optimal due to transactions costs (a problem in their economic logic noted early on by Mishan 1971). By the mid-1980s university education in the area was mainly limited to North America where the approach to topics was controlled and the curriculum restricted (e.g., post graduate education excluding methodology and history of thought). In this atmosphere Ecological Economics emerged as a challenge to what had become a captured orthodox economics of the environment.

The Rise of Ecological Economics and Conflict

Those economists voicing strong environmental critiques in the 1970s generally found themselves and their ideas marginalized within a decade. The criticisms were just too revolutionary. Kapp (1970a, 1970b) was pointing out the basic failure of a system that pushes costs onto others and characterizes them as "externalities," as if these were minor aberrations from outside an otherwise perfectly efficient system. Georgescu-Roegen (1971) wrote a major thesis on the importance of entropy for the economy that basically concluded that economic growth was infeasible over the long run and as a result policy needed fundamental reform. His reasoning led to questioning human society from the size of population and the pressure placed upon systems, to the time allowed for change and the rate at which human systems impose change. Economic systems were then inseparable from ethical judgments, both concerning others currently living and future generations. Herman Daly (1977, 1992) came to the conclusion that the best option in the face of entropy laws and critiques of growth was to aim for a steady-state economy. All three suffered marginalization, derision of their ideas and neglect.

Understanding the treatment of such economists requires being aware of how orthodoxy operates and defends itself against potential threats from heterodoxy. As Lee (2009: 6) has defined heterodoxy there are those heretical economists who are tolerated because they use many of the same tools and models and whose ideas have led to theoretical advances in the orthodoxy, e.g., Knetsch. Then there are blasphemous economists whose ideas are a rejection of and challenge to the orthodoxy, e.g., Kapp, Geogescu-Roegen, Daly. They are non-brethren and their persecution is a legitimate act in defense of the orthodoxy. Economists who are lauded as part of the establishment (e.g., Nobel prize winners) often have some heretical ideas, but they are not blasphemers because they still believe in the fundamental core ideas of the orthodoxy, they protect and defend that core and hold back from pursuing the logic of their ideas to revolutionary ends.

The arrival of Ecological Economics in the late 1980s offered the potential of picking up on the more radical literature and thinkers. That at least became the hope of socio-economists, for if the field were no different from the mainstream sub-fields of resource and environmental economics the entire exercise of galvanizing a new community would be a rather pointless repetition of what had gone before. History pointed in the direction of a more blasphemous heterodox economics of the environment that dared to reject neoclassical economics in *totalitus*. However, developing an heterodox interdisciplinary research field with a distinct methodology and approach to society-economy-environment interactions was not on everyone's agenda and has involved conflict.

In an in-depth study, involving interviews with several noted ecological economists, Røpke (2004, 2005) found the international movement started by forming an uneasy alliance of divergent ecological and economic opinions on the basis of some very broad common concerns. In general terms, the unifying positions might have been no more than the environment matters to the economy, the environment is being degraded, ecology has important messages for economics that are being neglected. Ecologists came forward who were passionate about connecting ecological understanding with socio-economics in order to better address environmental problems in the public arena. Any economist prepared to talk to an ecologist concerning the environment was a bonus. These ecologists then appear to have been largely (often willfully) ignorant of differences between types of economist, and many remain so. Yet such ecologists filled key roles running the ISEE and its journal.

The result was substantial involvement by economists supporting core neoclassical methodology and ideology. This was further encouraged by the strategy for popular recognition and headline breaking articles in *Science* or *Nature*. The bigger the name in the field the better for getting the environmental message across, and as far as economists are concerned that would clearly favor the orthodoxy. A core group of ecologists—including Bob Costanza, Brian Walker, Paul Ehrlich, David Pimentel and Carl Folke—chose to associate with mainstream economic theorists such as Ken Arrow, Karl-Goran Maler and Partha Dasgupta. The ISEE's journal, originally controlled by

Costanza, had mainstream economists placed on its board and increasingly published much falling well within neoclassical thought, including the mechanistic equilibrium models and preference utilitarianism that so constrained the earlier endeavors of the more heterodox environmental economists.

David Pearce, a noted UK mainstream environmental economist and advocate of all pervasive monetary valuation, was an early Associate Editor of the journal who became increasingly hostile to anything heterodox. He is particularly remembered for a 1996 plenary to the inaugural European Society for Ecological Economics (ESEE) Conference in Saint Quentin en Yvelines where he questioned the reason for Ecological Economics as anything distinct from neoclassical thought (Røpke 2005: 271), and went on to point at Charles Perrings and rhetorically questioned his presence. Pearce was not separated from the journal for another two years.

Perrings, later an ISEE president, has himself pursued abstract modeling in the mode of resource economics (Perrings 1987). This confines Ecological Economics to optimal control models despite all the ensuing contradictions of squeezing and remolding concepts to make them fit the method (see his collected works, Perrings 1997, and the review by Spash 2000). This can be seen as following a line of reasoning—common amongst mainstream economists—that equates rigor with mathematical formalism; an argument flawed even within mathematics itself (see Dow 2003). So mainstream economic approaches were from the outset brought into Ecological Economics, although the aim for many had been explicitly to move away from this orthodoxy (e.g., Söderbaum 1999, 2008).

The potential for divisiveness was apparent to some early on. In 1990 the Swedish Beijer Institute was rebranded under the title Ecological Economics with a Board mixing orthodox economists (Dasgupta, Maler, Pearce, Zylicz) and ecologists (Ehrlich, Holling) with one heterodox economist (Daly). The Institute was headed by Maler, the Board chaired by Dasgupta and two research programs were directed by Perrings and Costanza. As has been documented by Røpke (2005: 272) the decisions made by Dasgupta soon drove Daly to resign, which allowed the Beijer to concentrate on methods from traditional mainstream economics with models linked to ecology. The attempt to capture what was fast becoming a successful new field relates to power in academia and the potential for wider political influence. As Daly (quoted by Røpke 2005: 272) has stated with respect to his experience at the Beijer: "I felt it was a kind of take-over—here is something called Ecological Economics, it is beginning to get a little following, it might get in the way some day, let's just take it over."

As the field has matured these divisions have remained strong and resurfaced on occasion. In 2002 the incoming journal Editor, Cutler Cleveland, expelled from the Board the more heterodox European representatives (including an Associate Editor, and both the founding and then current ESEE Presidents). This went unnoticed by most people. The ISEE executive at the time refused to take any counter action and preferred to brush over the incident in the name of avoiding open conflict.

In 2004 a more public controversy occurred concerning the award of the ISEE prize in the name of Kenneth Boulding. The recipients were Dasgupta and Maler. In the Society newsletter (distributed at the biennial conference) Perrings, then ISEE President, rejoiced in this as signifying a change towards the approach of the Beijer Institute, i.e., mainstream economic formalism. However, the award came as something of a shock to many when announced at the opening session of the biennial ISEE conference. It was debated and contested by the membership at the Society's business meeting (Røpke 2005: 284–285; Söderbaum 2007: 212–213). Neither Dasgupta nor Maler had previously engaged with the wider community (e.g., despite being European residents, never attending the European conferences) nor been (nor are) members of ISEE. Their work was felt by many to be incongruent with the developing field and Røpke (2004: 309) notes Maler's dislike of socio-economics. Obviously those making this award had a different perspective[7] from that of the concerned ISEE membership, and their active involvement with the Beijer Institute appears a unifying factor.

Such occurrences will not surprise those familiar with the book *A History of Heterodox Economics* by Lee (2009). There he explains that scientific knowledge develops within a community that defines how work is conducted, what is valid and who is part of the community of scholars. In self-definition an academic community selects the goal-dependent central issues of research and those designated as colleagues are meant to work on broadly the same or supportive issues. Scientific knowledge is then produced by an elaborate intellectual and social organization embedded in educational systems, academic departments and research institutes. There is a system of dependency and interdependence. As Lee (2009: 12) notes:

> scientists that do not "fit" into this structure of dependency, do not produce the right kind of knowledge, can be marginalized and excluded from the community, but still exist within the field or they can be cleansed from the field altogether.

The attempts at cleansing are apparent in Ecological Economics.

At the same time a lack of clarity as to how heterodox the movement should be has permitted a confusing array of literature to appear under the title of Ecological Economics. For example, consider environmental valuation. Measurement and value issues have been high on the agenda of Ecological Economics, in part because of the various attempts to get old wine into new bottles to attract economic and political support for action. For some, mainly ecologists and conservation biologists, large monetary numbers regardless of their theoretical foundation have been lauded a success. For others, physical numeraires of environmental impact are sought and ecological footprints proposed. Yet others believe environmental economists were basically right all along and we just need more cost-benefit type studies extending into ecosystems services (e.g., Daily 1997). Treating ecosystems as if some artifact for trading in a market is highly problematic on many grounds (Spash 2008b). In addition, ecologists, or economists, simply plucking monetary numbers from the air to claim importance for ecosystems actually undermines an alternative theoretically grounded research agenda. Hence a mix, or muddle, of literature has appeared, none of which learns from past experience in economics or addresses the basic problem of developing a coherent theory of value. Pluralism is then sometimes misleadingly referenced as the reason for tolerating such diversity, but this is to misconceive the requirements for advancing knowledge, which require coherence not contradiction.

The Basis for an Heterodox Ecological Economics

There is then a need to go beyond the historical analysis to begin exploring ideology, methodology and why the movement needs to be heterodox in order to address society-economy-environment interactions. A comprehensive in-depth account would require at least a dedicated paper and need to cover much ground. A recent attempt to define the field in this way extends to four volumes and includes a hundred papers (Spash 2009a). The aim here is merely to indicate the strength of argument from a few key perspectives and point to the essential need for moving away from mainstream economics if environmental problems are to be taken seriously, and indeed if economics is to be taken seriously.

Learning from Ecology and the Biological Sciences

There is a dynamic and evolving interaction between human activity and the environment that is central to understanding the development of economic systems. Mainstream thought is resistant to the idea of economic systems as dynamic evolving structures, something recognized long ago by Veblen (1898). Physics rather than biology has been the dominant comparator and methodological influence. In contrast, a methodology is necessary that moves away from a simple belief in mechanistic cause-effect relationships as explaining social interactions, something that was criticized by both Kapp (1978: 281–301) and Georgescu-Roegen (1979). Interactions with ecology have then revived interest in biological concepts and metaphors within Ecological Economics.

Most prominent amongst the biological/ecological concepts are ideas of sustainability, resilience and co-evolutionary development (Gowdy 1994; Norgaard 1981, 1987, 1988). In an evolving system concepts of equilibrium are abstractions for convenience to describe specific states on a path of change. Managing and attempting to maintain systems in perceived equilibrium states can then prove disastrous, e.g., preventing small fires in forests eventually resulting in large scale catastrophic fires. Ecosystems understanding has developed in terms of cycles of energy and materials organization, accumulation, destruction and release. Interestingly, in the current context,

Holling (who pioneered this approach) at one point drew a parallel with work by Schumpeter on creative destruction (Holling 1986). Whether such comparisons are appropriate or not, the ideas clearly cannot fit within orthodox theory, which is built upon concepts of stasis, equilibrium and self-correction.

Yet, employing biological analogies is no guarantee of a more enlightened economics, as shown by Gowdy (1987). In the 1970s economists of the Chicago School, such as Becker, Hirshleifer and Tullock, made use of Wilson's (1975) sociobiology to effectively revive Social Darwinism. A natural science basis was given to their political ideology, which was then justified as consistent with universal assumptions for human behavior. Despite the evolutionary rhetoric, static equilibrium thinking was maintained. Others actually advocated a type of "economic ecology" where animals foraging become consumers optimizing, predators are like firms and population growth is investment (Rapport and Turner 1977).

There is also a darker side justifying a rejection of connections between economics and biology. In the early 1900s, the rise of Social Darwinism led to the justification of racism, sexism, and elitism as somehow scientifically ordained. The concept is forever tainted by the fascists use of Eugenics to justify the gas chamber for millions and similar reasoning behind more recent "ethnic cleansing." Thus, biological metaphors in the social sciences remain highly unpopular in many circles along with constructs such as Eugenics and Sociobiology (Mokyr 1991: 132). Caution would certainly seem the order of the day.

Caution is also required due to the tendency to take ecological concepts as new overarching goals that are universally applicable and from there make a jump to policy conclusions. The unquestioning faith expressed in new guiding principles (e.g., sustainability, resilience) then bears a parallel with the belief in natural laws by economists, during the late 1700s and early 1800s, who wished to match the apparent progress of the natural sciences in discovering universal truths. Sustaining something, or increasing its resilience, does not answer the fundamental questions of why and what for.

There are clearly alternative approaches in ecology and biology, as there are in economics, some helpful, others not so. Ecology in some guises is an optimizing and maximizing discipline with deterministic mathematical equilibrium models. In other guises it is a dynamic questioning discipline that pushes the boundaries of accepted knowledge. Modeling can be part of the latter, although in a rather different fashion than the former approach assumes (e.g., Holling 1986). Thus, that a core group of ecologists writing on environmental policy issues have worked within the rhetoric of the economic orthodoxy is perhaps unsurprising. However, some have done so despite their own work being of the dynamic questioning type and appearing fundamentally at odds with mainstream theory.

In general, treating environmental issues as just a technical or modeling problem for economic and ecological scientists to solve is far too reductionist and mechanistic. For example, this leads to denying human agency, unpredictability, partial ignorance and social indeterminacy. Hodgson (1993) argues economists should pay attention to the non-reductionist forms of modern biology, rather than the atomistic and mechanistic alternatives of Richard Dawkins, George Williams and Edward Wilson. A biological metaphor then offers the potential for debating a variety of issues including: complexity, levels of abstraction, appropriate units of analysis, irreversibility, non-marginal and qualitative change, and non-optimizing behavior.

Redefining the Objective of the Economy

Modern economics has become dominated and obsessed with two goals: growth and efficiency. Ecology challenges orthodox economics by contributing the realization of alternative requirements arising from the non-human world. Thus, concepts such as sustainability and resilience have appeared as strong independent goals not achieved by economic efficiency (e.g., Common and Perrings 1992). That efficiency has come to dominate economics as a goal is interesting in itself and is ideologically driven (Bromley 1990). The insufficiency of such a goal is often remarked upon by economists themselves, before venturing to set everything else to one side and proceeding to make policy recommendations on the sole basis of supposed efficiency analysis. Efficiency is in fact a sub-goal of growth, justified as the means to maximize desired outputs, namely goods and services for consumption, by avoiding resource wastage.

Ecological Economics emphasizes the limits to material and energy throughput and the problems then posed by the modern economic obsession with increasing consumption. The idea of limits is firmly related to the literature arising from thermodynamics and energy use with its implications for the physical functioning of systems (Georgescu-Roegen 1971). The critique of consumption has connected consumer manipulation by corporations (Galbraith [1967] 2007; Kapp 1978: 224–247) to the psychological and social roles material consumption plays in a modern market economy (Reisch and Røpke 2004; Røpke 1999). The psychological treadmill of material throughput then raises concerns over how to address the scale of growth, which is something ignored in the mainstream literature where efficient allocation dominates regardless of scale (Daly 1991, 1992). Yet the growth goal remains despite its inadequacies. Signals of failure are clear in the persistence of distributional inequity, global poverty and the imposition of pollution and environmental degradation on the poor.

In addition growth has been shown to fail as a means to happiness even for the rich. Easterlin (1974, 1995, 2003) has shown that, within a country at a given point in time, the richer are on average happier, but higher living level norms ("keeping up with the Joneses") mean increased income over time does not increase happiness. Easterlin (1995) offers evidence from the USA, nine European countries and Japan. More recently, he argues the expected utility from pecuniary gains is undermined as opposed to those from nonpecuniary domains—such as friends, family life and health—where hedonic adaptation and social comparison are less important.

> Once it is recognised that individuals are unaware of some of the forces shaping their choices, it can be no longer argued that they will successfully maximize their well-being. (Easterlin 2003: 11181)

This is a conclusion guaranteed to upset the political ideologies of orthodox economics with its rhetoric of the sovereign consumer and minimalist government. Thus, Easterlin should really be less surprised by the neglect of the evidence he and others have brought forth.

Such self-reported happiness research suggests less material consumption and a search for alternative hedonic satisfiers. A tension, common to Green political thought, then appears between appealing to better sources of experiential pleasure and identifying that such pleasures are in fact not the prime source of a good and meaningful life. O'Neill (2006) takes issue with the hedonic account of welfare because the focus is upon isolation of pleasures for the individual rather than the pattern of a life and its experiences. There is more to life than being a hedonist and to be a pure hedonist is to be nothing more than bestial. This is a denial of the human potential and richness of human relationships.

Besides the relationship of humans to each other across time and space there is the question of our relationship with the non-human world around us and the encroaching replacement of natural systems with human artifacts. This exposes how economics has rather missed the point by focusing on substitutability and the belief, or presumption, that man-made capital can be substituted for other inputs—Nature defined as "land" or capital—(Holland 1997). That economic growth creates harms, as well as goods, is heavily downplayed in mainstream economics while their incommensurability is totally denied.

These various insights have direct relevance for how economic growth is perceived to operate as a means for improving the human condition and why we need new operational goals. Economics might, for example, be redefined as achieving sustained human well-being on the basis of the maintained health and functioning of Earth's ecosystems or, more radically, how to create and maintain systems that fulfil the needs of a meaningful and worthwhile life for all moral agents (human and non-human). The critiques call for a transition in the economy away from material and energy consumption but the more radical position also calls for the abandonment of hedonism and so a fundamental redesign of the modus operandi of modern economic systems. In either case the orthodoxy is a block not an aid. Future research in Social Ecological Economics requires opening up a series of closed boxes in the orthodox cellar and dusting off the contents—what contributes to well-being, is well-being an appropriate goal, what are the aspirations of human society, who is to be taken into account, how should human society conduct its affairs from individual behavior to institutional design?

Expanding Understanding of Human Behavior and Motivation

Rejecting atomistic and mechanistic explanations as universal truths leads to opening up the black box of the individual. Rather than regarding the human as some essentially irreducible atomic structure that should remain unquestioned, the realm of human motivation is brought into question as requiring further analysis. Psychology can then offer tremendous potential for insight into behavior, but only if economists are prepared to learn from rather than dominate the subject (Earl 2005). Dropping the focus on self-interested utility maximization leads to a rich array of possibilities. Lexicographic preferences no longer appear as a strange exception to the rule of gross substitution but a relatively normal approach to choice, which may be motivated by non-utilitarian ethics, strong uncertainty, or satisficing behaviour. Needs can be differentiated from positional affluence. Social norms provide a link between individual and societal motivators and connect with the role of institutions as explored by classical or critical institutional economists (as opposed to the neoclassical "new" institutional economists). Social organizations are then seen to involve perceptions as to power, trust and control that impact how people respond to requests and incentives for behavioral change.

Taking Environmental Values and Ethics Seriously

Economic value theory is derived from Benthamite utilitarianism converted into preference theory—a move that supposedly divorces choice from ethics. In fact the basic philosophy remains utilitarian but now preference utilitarian as opposed to Bentham's theory of total utility.[8] What is found within the practice of environmental cost-benefit analysis is an implicit value theory based upon consequences telling what is right and the value of outcomes being measured in money as a shorthand for welfare based upon individual preferences. More than this, while preference theory and "new" welfare economics claim to be based only upon ordinal preferences, the way in which money is used to aggregate and make decisions means it is being implicitly converted into a cardinal measure for interpersonal comparisons of well-being.

Yet those producing policy information hardly seem to be paying attention to economic theory. The rise of transferring money numbers across time and space indicates a tendency to choose approaches on the basis of political convenience (see Spash and Vatn 2006). The danger here is that numbers become merely artificial means to an end and any means of justification will suffice. This is a form of new environmental pragmatism that has become evident in recent times (Spash 2009b). Rather than pursue the more difficult task of developing theoretically justified alternatives the tendency is to borrow mainstream tools with little attention to mainstream methodology, ideology or their implications. This is exactly why neither social ecological economists nor neoclassical economists gave any credence to the studies driven by ecologists for valuing ecosystems and the world. Ecologists themselves have then lost sight of their own expressed values, e.g., summarized by Naess (1973, 1984) as deep ecology. Concern for Nature, and the plural values that involves, is not expressible within the context of preference utilitarianism (Spash 2008b). Here is where neoclassical theory is fundamentally rejected because of its persistent monism, reducing everything, including all ethical and moral issues, to a single numeraire.

A key area in which such monism controls and distracts the discourse is in the treatment of future generations (Spash 1993, 2002). The justifications for using a single discount rate have been taken seriously and at high levels. Within mainstream rhetoric, discount rates are meant to be observable objective determinants of how society should treat the future. Unable to move outside the narrow confines of mathematical formalism, economists, from Nobel prize winners down (e.g., Arrow et al. 1996a), then write off the future on the basis that they are being empirical and objective. That is, they claim, how future generations should be treated can be determined by observing a few factors such as rates of return on capital and consumption growth. The result is a fruitless waste of time arguing over the appropriate rates rather than addressing the fundamental issue, which is fair and just treatment of the unborn, and what should determine undertaking or denying actions with long-term impacts.

Taking Institutions Seriously

Well-being in society, and social decision processes, require institutions that allow for the expression of different types of values. This may be described as the need for value articulating institutions (Vatn 2005). Indeed the general hope amongst the various institutional options that might be developed is for a more inclusive participatory approach to governance that would allow deeper environmental values than those prevalent in daily Western life to come to the fore.

Such issues of public policy and governance have been placed outside of mainstream economics in a deliberate attempt to make economics appear "objective." Yet the role of power in society cannot be removed from the analysis and merely remains hidden. This then makes economic analysis highly misleading because policies applied in reality play directly to vested interest groups (such as multinational corporations) that are not part of the analysis. Account must be taken of government power and how the institutions of governance are structured. The textbook approach of assuming state intervention is minimal, markets perfectly efficient and consumers sovereign produces highly misleading recommendations, or worse, attempts to make the world perform like the model. Realizing that markets are socially constructed institutions means taking responsibility for market design and functioning rather than pretending markets can be left to themselves.

The ways in which our institutions conduct their policy discourse is then something that affects the direction in which society heads. For example, the science-policy interface has run into serious problems in several areas of public policy (from nuclear power to genetic modification to climate change). The approach to uncertainty as weak—where probabilities and future states are known or knowable—conflicts with the strong uncertainty confronted in reality (e.g., the type of uncertainty noted by Keynes [1921] 1988). Once again mainstream economics seems unable to offer much and instead attempts to reduce all strong uncertainty to weak uncertainty (Spash 2002). Hence the rise of post normal science (Funtowicz and Ravetz 1990) as one means by which to rethink the science-policy interface and engage the technocentric establishment with wider public values (van der Sluijs et al. 2005). This implies challenging existing institutions and creating new ones.

Conclusions

The subconscious roots of Ecological Economics run deep into the past but the modern community arose from the ashes of heterodox environmental economics. Environmental economists were taken along with the political turmoil of the 1960s but failed to realize the revolutionary potential they once saw in their field. That failure was a reflection of the power that lies in orthodox economics to control debate, forgive heretics and expell blasphemers.

Ecological Economics as a modern movement started at the basic level of trying to combine models from two disciplines, an approach popular in America. While linking ecology and economics was an interesting initial step, the narrow confines of model interactions and multidisciplinary collaboration failed to advance the movement beyond the orthodox. In addition, ecologists within the society advanced collaboration with orthodox economists who had little interest in the heterodox agenda. Orthodox economists were also placed in positions of power within the society. None of this aided the development of the new movement in providing an alternative research agenda. Instead, some adopted orthodox economic models and methods despite the conflict this creates with the realization that the environment and the economy are intertwined and neither can be meaningfully analyzed independent of the societal context. Unfortunately, the importance of social, political, ethical and institutional factors is something that ecologists are not trained to detect and orthodox economists are trained to neglect.

In Europe, where the tradition of political economy is stronger, the range of social science interactions has encouraged interdisciplinarity. In the ESEE, then, the field has in part become established as an heterodox socio-economic school of thought bridging the science-policy interface. Consistent with the historical roots, the aim of this heterodox community is very much to be able to address policy problems and environmental issues, not to sustain theoretical constructs for their own sake. At the same time "scientific" standards of accumulating knowledge and understanding are seen as necessary for progress and theoretical consistency.

This is not to deny the potential for different factions to coexist within Ecological Economics whether in Europe or elsewhere. The question is the extent to which differences are tolerated within the frame of a pluralist methodology. There need to be some core shared ideological and methodological positions in creating the community of scholars that is Ecological Economics. That means identifying where differences are fundamentally divisive and create incoherence. This paper argues, on the basis of the history behind the movement, that an heterodox economic approach is necessary both for unity and meaning. That means excluding the incompatible orthodox and moving ahead with alternative theories and practice.

The inability of mainstream economists to engage with the ideas of Social Ecological Economics is both ideological and methodological. Such economists typically have various characteristics, for example, championing self-regulating market approaches, accepting the basic tenets of neoclassical theory, regarding humans within the narrow behavioral model of homo œconomicus. Under this system of thought, economics is believed to gain rigor from using abstract mathematical models regardless of their empirical basis or policy relevance. This is despite claims of scientific empiricism and prediction as providing validity. In practice primary data collection is rare, theory is conducted without application or hypothesis testing and evidence contradicting theory is ignored or explained away. In the extreme, arguments that persist are redefined for incorporation within the existing theory by borrowing the language of other disciplines while neutering the concepts for the sake of conformity with existing belief structures and overall ideological positions. All this mitigates the potential for learning from problem and policy oriented interdisciplinary research.

For Social Ecological Economists interactions with ecology and biology have raised the profile of evolution in relation to economics. How we understand the world is vastly different if we treat it as a deterministic mechanical system or a chaotic evolving biological system. The future becomes uncertain in a strong sense, which denies our ability to predict. This describes the large divide between reality and the technocentric ideological dream, and macroeconomic hope, that enough capital might be accumulated, via compound interest, to enable a leisure society. A politically untenable reality is then that Western economies actually reached satisfaction of basic needs long ago, but have persisted with expanding the scale of material and energy consumption, which degrades the environment, while failing to address declines in human social and psychological well-being or increases in the inequitable distribution of resources.

Differences and divisions have in many ways become clearer due to the developing alternative research agendas. The desire to combine different heterodox schools of thought—ecological, critical institutional, evolutionary, post-Keynesian—is in direct contrast to the drive for recognition within and by orthodox economics. Rather than paying attention to methodological and ideological positions, some high profile ecologists and conservation biologists have aligned themselves with those who hold mainstream positions, and appear to have political power. Those taking this line may regard themselves as being pragmatic, in the sense of achieving an end by the easiest available means, but actually have created problems for those trying to be far more grounded in terms of changing economic thinking. Indeed, much of the ecosystems services valuation work, for example, merely buys into an existing political economy in which no substantive effort is on the agenda for challenging the idea that material and energy growth can continue ad infinitum. At the same time this work undercuts alternative efforts—increased public participation and empowerment of the disenfranchised—not least by pretending that producing simple money numbers is a politically adequate response to global environmental problems. This argument by environmental pragmatists both fails to achieve its aims and causes much damage along the way.

Thus, some clearer lines need to be drawn between what is progressive in Ecological Economics, what lacks credibility and where incoherence is preventing the advancement of ideas. Social Ecological Economics is then envisaged as a community of scholars developing a distinct ideological vision and specific methodological agenda. Ideologically there is a commitment to: environmental problems requiring behavioral and systemic change, continued economic growth through material and energy consumption being unsustainable and politically divisive, poverty and distribution as major economic concerns, a need for balancing power (e.g., individual, group, government, corporate) at different spatial scales (from the local to international), a central role for ethical debate, envisioning markets as social constructs with numerous flaws, political economy, design of alternative institutions, public participation, empowerment and engagement as necessary to address the science-policy interface, recognizing the importance of "others" (both human and non-human). Methodologically distinct characteristics include: value pluralism, acknowledging incommensurability, interdisciplinarity, empiricism using quantitative and qualitative methods, rejection of mechanistic reductionist approaches, rejection of mathematical formalism and its claimed rigor, acceptance of strong uncertainty (i.e., ignorance and social indeterminacy). Only some of the constitutive elements have been touched upon in this paper, which serves as an introduction to stimulate debate. That debate is essential for self-understanding. If Ecological Economics is to have a meaningful future the community must show greater awareness of where it has come from as well as the methodological and ideological challenges ahead.

Notes

1. The terms mainstream and orthodox are used interchangeably to designated economists adhering to the basic textbook versions of economic theory. Neoclassical economists are equated with both terms. No strict definition is attempted in this paper and the boundaries of such classifications are notoriously fuzzy. Still the core conceptual foundations are clear and distinct from those of heterodox economics (see Lawson 2005). For more on the definition of neoclassical and heterodox economics see Lee (2009), especially Chapter 1.

2. Prior to the award in 2009 being given to Ostrom (see note 3), Kahneman was perhaps the most consistent, having been associated with the work of environmental economist Jack Knetsch from his time in Vancouver at the University of British Columbia 1978–1993 (Kahneman and Knetsch 1992b). He also contributed to early debates on contingent valuation (see Cummings, Brookshire, and Schulze 1986). Arrow and Solow were involved on opposite sides of the *Exxon Valdez* oil spill legal case for compensation and the ensuing National Oceanic and Atmospheric Administration panel on the use of the contingent valuation method for natural resource damage assessment (Arrow et al. 1993). Sen (1995) also wrote commenting on contingent valua-

tion. Arrow and Stiglitz were authors for the Intergovernmental Panel on Climate Change third assessment report (Arrow et al. 1996a, 1996b).

3. In some senses Eleanor Ostrom is an exception in terms of her level of engagement on resource and environmental problems, having been consistently focused on common property resource management in her work and actually being a member of the Society for Ecological Economics. A trained political scientist, she has taken a more critical institutional economics approach.

4. He has been attributed with inspiring the multiple criteria approach of the Human Development Index (HDI). Note, this actually ignores environmental factors.

5. Some sections of this paper are based on the general introduction to volume one of Spash (2009a).

6. After a protracted review process the article appeared simultaneously with a critique (Smith 1992), commissioned by the editor, and a reply by the authors (Kahneman and Knetsch 1992a). When a second critique was published the editor (Ron Cummings) refused the authors an opportunity to reply despite their concerns that they be allowed to defend their work. Jack Knetsch (personal communication June 2004 and January 2006). Ironically this soon became the most highly cited article in the journal and remains so by far.

7. Three ecologists Rapport D. J. (Canada) Chair, Brian Walker (Australia), Buzz Holling (USA); one environmental scientist Kerry Turner (UK) and two economists Clem Tisdell (Australia) and Charles Perrings (UK now USA) ISEE President at the time of the award.

8. Polanyi (1944: 119) states that Bentham actually failed to make the link between value and utility.

References

Abbey, E. (1975). *The Monkey Wrench Gang*. New York: Avon Books.

Agarwal, B. (2001). Participatory Exclusions, Community Forestry, and Gender: An Analysis for South Asia and a Conceptual Framework. *World Development* 29(10): 1623–1648.

Arrow, K. J., W. R. Cline, K.-G. Maler, M. Munasinghe, R. Squitieri, and J. E. Stiglitz. (1996a). Intertemporal Equity, Discounting, and Economic Efficiency. In *Economic and Social Dimensions of Climate Change*. Eds. J. P. Bruce, L. Hoesung, and E. F. Haites. Cambridge: Cambridge University Press: 125–144.

Arrow, K. J., J. Parikh, G. Pillet, M. Grubb, E. Haites, J. C. Hourcade, K. Parikh, and F. Yamin. (1996b). Decision-Making Frameworks for Addressing Climate Change. In *Economic and Social Dimensions of Climate Change*. Eds. J. P. Bruce, L. Hoesung, and E. F. Haites. Cambridge: Cambridge University Press: 53–77.

Arrow, K., R. Solow, P. R. Portney, E. Leamer, R. Radner, and H. Schuman. (1993). Natural Resource Damage Assessment Under the Oil Pollution Act of 1990. *Federal Register* 58(10): 4601–4614.

Becker, C., M. Faber, K. Hertel, and R. Manstetten. (2005). Malthus vs. Wordsworth: Perspectives on Humankind, Nature and Economy. A Contribution to the Histroy and the Foundations of Ecological Economics. *Ecological Economics* 53: 299–310.

Beckerman, W. (1974). *In Defence of Economic Growth*. London: Jonathan Cape.

Bishop, R. C., and T. A. Heberlein. (1986). Does Contingent Valuation Work? In *Valuing Environmental Goods: An Assessment of the Contingent Valuation Method*. Eds. R. G. Cummings, D. S. Brookshire, and W. D. Schulze. Totowa, NJ: Rowman & Allanheld: 123–147.

Bohm, P., and A. V. Kneese, Eds. (1971). *The Economics of Environment*. London: Macmillan.

Boulding, K. E. (1966). The Economics of the Coming Spaceship Earth. In *Environmental Quality in a Growing Economy: Essays from the Sixth RFF Forum*. Ed. H. Jarrett. Baltimore: John Hopkins University Press: 3–14.

Bromley, D. W. (1990). The Ideology of Efficiency: Searching for a Theory of Policy Analysis. *Journal of Environmental Economics and Management* 19: 86–107.

Carson, R. ([1962] 1987). *Silent Spring*. Boston: Houghton Mifflin.

Christensen, P. P. (1989). Historical Roots for Ecological Economics: Biophysical Versus Allocative Approaches. *Ecological Economics* 1(February): 17–36.

Ciriacy-Wantrup, S. V. (1952). *Resource Conservation: Economics and Policies*. Berkeley: University of California Press.

Clawson, M., and J. L. Knetsch. (1966). *Economics of Outdoor Recreation*. Baltimore and London: John Hopkins University Press.

Common, M., and C. Perrings. (1992). Towards an Ecological Economics of Sustainability. *Ecological Economics* 6: 7–34.

Commoner, B. (1976). *The Poverty of Power: Energy and the Economic Crisis*. London: Jonathan Cape.

Cumberland, J. H., J. R. Hibbs, and I. Hoch, Eds. (1982). *The Economics of Managing Chlorofluorocarbons: Stratospheric Ozone and Climate Issues*. Baltimore, Maryland: Johns Hopkins University Press.

Cummings, R. G., D. S. Brookshire, and W. D. Schulze, Eds. (1986). *Valuing Environmental Goods: An Assessment of the Contingent Valuation Method*. Totowa, NJ: Rowman & Allanheld.

d'Arge, R. C. (1975). Economic and Social Measures of Biologic and Climatic Change. 6. Washington, DC, US Department of Transportation, Climate Impact Assessment Program. 699.

———. (1979). *Climate and Economic Activity.* Proceedings of the World Climate Conference, Geneva, WMO Report.

d'Arge, R. C., and K. C. Kogiku. (1973). Economic Growth and the Environment. *Review of Economic Studies* 40: 61–78.

d'Arge, R. C., W. D. Schulze, and D. S. Brookshire. (1982). Carbon Dioxide and Intergenerational Choice. *American Economic Association Papers and Proceedings* 72(2): 251–256.

Daily, G. C., Ed. (1997). *Nature's Services: Societal Dependence on Natural Ecosystems.* Washington, DC: Island Press.

Daly, H. E. (1977). *Steady-State Economics.* San Francisco, CA: W H Freeman.

———. (1991). Towards an Environmental Macroeconomics. *Land Economics* 67(2): 255–259.

———. (1992). *Steady-State Economics: Second Edition with New Essays.* London: Earthscan.

Dow, S. C. (2003). Understanding the Relationship Between Mathematics and Economics. *Journal of Post Keynesian Economics* 25(4): 547–560.

Earl, P. E. (2005). Economics and Psychology in the Twenty-First Century. *Cambridge Journal of Economics* 29(6): 909–926.

Easterlin, R. A. (1974). "Does Economic Growth Improve the Human Lot?": Some Empirical Evidence. In *Nations and Households in Economic Growth: Essays in Honor of Moses Abramovitz.* Eds. P. A. David and M. W. Reder. New York: Academic Press: 98–125.

———. (1995). Will Raising the Income for All Increase the Happiness for All? *Journal of Economic Behavior & Organization* 27(1): 35–47.

———. (2003). Explaining Happiness. *PNAS* 100(19): 11176–11183.

Ehrlich, P. R. (1968). *The Population Bomb.* New York: Ballantine Books.

Ehrlich, P. R., and J. P. Holdren. (1971). Impact of Population Growth. *Science* 171(3977): 1212–1217.

European Commission. (2008). EU Action Against Climate Change: EU Emissions Trading, European Commission. http://ec.europa.eu/environment/climat/pdf/brochures/ets_en.pdf, 6 February, 2008.

Funtowicz, S. O., and J. R. Ravetz. (1990). *Uncertainty and Quality in Science for Policy.* Dordrecht, The Netherlands: Kluwer Academic Publishers.

Galbraith, J. K. ([1958] 1969). *The Affluent Society.* Boston: Houghton Mifflin.

———. ([1967] 2007). *The New Industrial Estate.* Princeton and Oxford: Princeton University Press.

Georgescu-Roegen, N. (1971). *The Entropy Law and the Economic Process.* Cambridge, MA: Harvard University Press.

———. (1979). Methods in Economic Science. *Journal of Economic Issues* XIII(2).

Gowdy, J. M. (1987). Bio-Economics: Social Economy Versus the Chicago School. *International Journal of Social Economics* 14(1): 32–42.

———. (1994). *Coevolutionary Economics: The Economy, Society and the Environment.* Dordrecht: Kluwer Academic Publishers.

Gowdy, J. M., and J. D. Erickson. (2005). The Approach of Ecological Economics. *Cambridge Journal of Economics* 29(2): 207–222.

Hirsch, F. (1977). *Social Limits to Growth.* London: Routledge and Kegan Paul Ltd.

Hodgson, G. M. (1993). Why the Problem of Reductionism in Biology Has Implications for Economics. *World Futures* 37: 69–90.

Holland, A. (1997). Substitutability: Why Strong Sustainability is Weak and Absurdly Strong Sustainability is Not Absurd. In *Valuing Nature? Economics, Ethics and the Environment.* Ed. J. Foster. London: Routledge: 119–134.

Holling, C. S. (1986). The Resilience of Terrestrial Ecosystems: Local Surprise and Global Change. In *Sustainable Development of the Biosphere.* Eds. W. C. Clark and R. E. Munn. Cambridge: Cambridge University Press: 292–317.

Holt, R. P. F., S. Pressman, and C. L. Spash, Eds. (2010). *Post Keynesian and Ecological Economics: Confronting Environmental Issues.* Cheltenham: Edward Elgar.

Hunt, E. K., and R. C. d'Arge. (1973). On Lemmings and Other Acquisitive Animals: Propositions on Consumption. *Journal of Economic Issues* 7(June): 337–353.

Jevons, W. S. ([1865] 1965). *The Coal Question: An Inquiry Concerning the Progress of the Nation and the Probable Exhaustion of Our Coal-Mines.* New York: Augustus M Kelley.

Kahneman, D., and J. L. Knetsch. (1992a). Contingent Valuation and the Value of Public-Goods: Reply. *Journal of Environmental Economics and Management* 22(1): 90–94.

———. (1992b). Valuing Public Goods: The Purchase of Moral Satisfaction. *Journal of Environmental Economics and Management* 22(1): 57–70.

Kantner, J. (2008). Clean Carbon Copy Not Enough for US. *Australian Financial Review* 12 December.

Kapp, K. W. (1950). *The Social Costs of Private Enterprise.* New York: Shocken.

———. (1961). *Toward a Science of Man in Society: A Positive Approach to the Integration of Social Knowledge.* The Hague: Martinus Nijhoff.

———. (1970a). Environmental Disruption and Social Costs: Challenge to Economics. *Kyklos* 23(4): 833–848.

———. (1970b). Environmental Disruption: General Issues and Methodological Problems. *Social Science Information* 9(4): 15–32.

———. (1978). *The Social Costs of Business Enterprise,* 3rd edition. Nottingham: Spokesman.

Kapp, K. W., and L. L. Kapp. (1963). *History of Economic Thought: A Book of Readings.* New York: Barnes & Noble.

Keynes, J. M. ([1921] 1988). *A Treatise on Probability.* London: Macmillan and Co.

Kneese, A. V. (1971). Background for the Economic Analysis of Environmental Pollution. *Swedish Journal of Economics* 73(1): 1–24.

——. (1984). *Measuring the Benefits of Clean Air and Water.* Washington, DC: Resources for the Future.

Kneese, A. V., R. U. Ayres, and R. C. d'Arge. (1970). *Economics and the Environment: A Materials Balance Approach.* Washington, DC: Resources for the Future.

Kneese, A. V., and W. D. Schulze. (1985). Ethics and Environmental Economics. In *Handbook of Natural Resource and Energy Economics.* Eds. A. V. Kneese and J. L. Sweeney. Amsterdam, The Netherlands: Elsevier. I: 191–220.

Knetsch, J. L. (1985). Values, Biases and Entitlements. *Annals of Regional Science* 19(2): 1–9.

——. (1989). The Endowment Effect and Evidence of Non-Reversible Indifference Curves. *American Economic Review* 79(5): 1277–1284.

——. (1994). Environmental Valuation: Some Problems of Wrong Questions and Misleading Answers. *Environmental Values* 3(4): 351–368.

——. (2005). Gains, Losses, and the US EPA Economic Analyses Guidelines: A Hazardous Product? *Environmental & Resource Economics* 32(1): 91–112.

Knetsch, J. L., and J. A. Sinden. (1984). Willingness to Pay and Compensation Demanded: Experimental Evidence of an Unexpected Disparity in Measures of Value. *Quarterly Journal of Economics* 99(3): 507–521.

Krutilla, J. V. (1967). Conservation Reconsidered. *American Economic Review* (September): 777–786.

Krutilla, J. V., and A. C. Fisher. (1978). *The Economics of Natural Environments: Studies in the Valuation of Commodity and Amenity Resources.* Baltimore, MD: Johns Hopkins University Press.

Lawson, T. (2005). The Nature of Heterodox Economics. *Cambridge Journal of Economics* 30(4): 483–505.

Lee, F. (2009). *A Histroy of Heterodox Economics: Challenging the Mainstream in the Twentieth Century.* London: Routledge.

Malthus, T. R. ([1798] 1986). *An Essay on the Principle of Population.* London: Pickering & Chatto Publishers Ltd.

Martinez-Alier, J. (1990). *Ecological Economics: Energy, Environment and Society.* Oxford, UK: Basil Blackwell.

——. (2002). *The Environmentalism of the Poor: A Study of Ecological Conflicts and Valuation.* Cheltenham: Edward Elgar.

Marx, K. (1867). *Das Kapital. Krtiik der Polotischen Oekonomie. Buch I: Dar Producktionsprocess des Kapitals.* Hamburg: Verlag von Otto Meissner.

Meadows, D. H., D. L. Meadows, J. Randers, and W. W. Behrens, III. (1972). *The Limits to Growth.* London: Pan.

Mill, J. S. (1848). *Principles of Political Economy, with Some of Their Applications to Social Philosophy.* London: John W. Parker.

Mishan, E. J. (1969). *Growth: The Price We Pay.* London: Staples Press.

——. (1971). Pangloss on Pollution. *Swedish Journal of Economics* 73(1): 113–120.

Mokyr, J. (1991). Evolutionary Biology, Technological Change and Economic History. *Bulletin of Economic Research* 43(2): 127–149.

Naess, A. (1973). Shallow and Deep, Long-Range Ecology Movement: Summary. *Inquiry: An Interdisciplinary Journal of Philosophy* 16(1): 95–100.

——. (1984). A Defence of the Deep Ecology Movement. *Environmental Ethics* 6(4): 265–270.

Norgaard, R. B. (1981). Sociosystem and Ecosystem Coevolution in the Amazon. *Journal of Environmental Economics and Management* 8: 238–254.

——. (1987). Economics as Mechanics and the Demise of Biological Diversity. *Ecological Modelling* 38(1–2): 107–121.

——. (1988). Sustainable Development: A Co-Evolutionary View. *Futures* (December): 606–662.

——. (1994). *Development Betrayed: The End of Progress and a Coevolutionary Revisioning of the Future.* London: Routledge.

O'Neill, J. F. (2006). Citizenship, Well-Being and Sustainability: Epicurus or Aristotle? *Analyse & Kritik* 28(2): 158–172.

Perrings, C. (1987). *Economy and Environment.* Cambridge, UK: Cambridge University Press.

——. (1997). *Economics of Ecological Resources: Selected Essays.* Cheltenham: Edward Elgar.

Polanyi, K. (1944). *The Great Transformation.* New York/Toronto: Rinehart & Company Inc.

Rapport, D. J., and J. E. Turner. (1977). Economics Models in Ecology. *Science* 195(Jan–March): 367–373.

Reisch, L. A., and I. Røpke. (2004). *The Ecological Economics of Consumption.* Cheltenham: Edward Elgar.

Røpke, I. (1999). The Dynamics of Willingness to Consume. *Ecological Economics* 28(3): 399–420.

——. (2004). The Early History of Modern Ecological Economics. *Ecological Economics* 50(3–4): 293–314.

——. (2005). Trends in the Development of Ecological Economics from the Late 1980s to the Early 2000s. *Ecological Economics* 55(2): 262–290.

Ruskin, J. ([1862] 1907). *'Unto This Last': Four Essays on the First Principles of Political Economy.* London: George Routledge & Sons Limited.

Schulze, W. D., and D. S. Brookshire. (1982). Intergenerational Ethics and the Depletion of Fossil Fuels. In *Coal Models and Their Use in Government Planning.* Eds. J. Quirk, K. Terasawa and D. Whipple. New York: Praeger: 159–178.

Schulze, W. D., D. S. Brookshire, and T. Sandler. (1981). The Social Rate of Discount for Nuclear Waste Storage: Economics or Ethics. *Natural Resources Journal* 21(4): 811–832.

Schumacher, E. F. (1973). *Small is Beautiful: A Study of Economics as if People Mattered.* London: Sphere Books.

Sen, A. (1995). Environmental Evaluation and Social Choice: Contingent Valuation and the Market Analogy. *Japanese Economic Review* 46(1): 23–37.

Sen, A. K. (1987). *On Ethics and Economics.* Oxford, UK: Basil Blackwell.

Simpson, R. E., F. G. D. Shuman, E. J. Baratta, and J. T. Tanner. (1981). Projected Dose Commitment from Fallout Contamination in Milk Resulting from the 1976 Chinese Atmospheric Nuclear Weapons Test. *Health Physics* 40: 741–744.

Smith, A. ([1759] 1982). *The Theory of Moral Sentiments.* Indianapolis: Liberty Fund.

Smith, G. A. (1980). The Teleological View of Wealth: A Historical Perspective. In *Economics, Ecology, Ethics: Essays Towards a Steady-State Economy.* Ed. H. E. Daly. New York and San Fransico: W. H. Freeman & Co.: 215–237.

Smith, V. K. (1992). Arbitrary Values, Good Causes, and Premature Verdicts. *Journal of Environmental Economics and Management* 22(1): 71–89.

Söderbaum, P. (1999). Values, Ideology and Politics in Ecological Economics. *Ecological Economics* 28(2): 161–170.

——. (2007). Towards Sustainability Economics: Principles and Values. *Journal of Bioeconomics* 9: 205–225.

——. (2008). *Understanding Sustainability Economics: Towards Pluralism in Economics.* London: Earthscan.

Spash, C. L. (1993). Economics, Ethics, and Long-Term Environmental Damages. *Environmental Ethics* 15(2): 117–132.

——. (1999). The Development of Environmental Thinking in Economics. *Environmental Values* 8(4): 413–435.

——. (2000). Review of "Economics of Ecological Resources" by Charles Perrings. *Environmental Values* 10(1): 125–126.

——. (2002). *Greenhouse Economics: Value and Ethics.* London: Routledge.

——. (2007). The Economics of Climate Change Impacts à la Stern: Novel and Nuanced or Rhetorically Restricted? *Ecological Economics* 63(4): 706–713.

——. (2008a). Contingent Valuation as a Research Method: Environmental Values and Human Behaviour. In *The Cambridge Handbook of Psychology and Economic Behaviour.* Ed. A. Lewis. Cambridge: Cambridge University Press: 429–453.

——. (2008b). How Much is that Ecosystem in the Window? The One with the Bio-Diverse Trail. *Environmental Values* 17(2): 259–284.

——. (2009a). *Ecological Economics: Critical Concepts in the Environment,* 4 Volumes. Routledge Major Work. London: Routledge.

———. (2009b). The New Environmental Pragmatisits, Pluralism and Sustainability. *Environmental Values* 18(3): 253–256.

———. (2010). The Brave New World of Carbon Trading. *New Political Economy* 15(2): 169–195.

Spash, C. L., and R. C. d'Arge. (1989). The Greenhouse Effect and Intergenerational Transfers. *Energy Policy* (April): 88–95.

Spash, C. L., and A. Vatn. (2006). Transferring Environmental Value Estimates: Issues and Alternatives. *Ecological Economics* 60(2): 379–388.

Stern, N. (2006). *Stern Review on the Economics of Climate Change.* London: UK Government Economic Service. www.sternreview.org.uk.

Tanzer, M. (1974). *The Energy Crisis: World Struggle for Power and Wealth.* New York: Monthly Review Press.

van der Sluijs, J. P., M. Craye, S. Funtowicz, P. Kloprogge, J. Ravetz, and J. Risbey. (2005). Combining Quantitative and Qualitative Measures of Uncertainty in Model-Based Environmental Assessment: The NUSAP System. *Risk Analysis* 25(2): 481–492.

Vatn, A. (2005). *Institutions and the Environment.* Cheltenham: Edward Elgar.

Veblen, T. ([1899] 1991). *The Theory of the Leisure Class.* Fairfield, NJ: Augustus M Kelley.

Veblen, T. B. (1898). Why Economics is Not an Evolutionary Science? *Quarterly Journal of Economics* 12(July): 373–397.

Wilson, E. O. (1975). *Sociobiology.* Cambridge, MA: Harvard University Press.

Would You Barter with God? Why Holy Debts and Not Profane Markets Created Money

By Alla Semenova*

ABSTRACT. Attempting to revitalize the substantive approach to economics in the tradition of K. Polanyi, this paper revives the neglected substantive theory of money's origins by Bernhard Laum and thus disputes the formal approaches that see the origins of money in the context of trade. A wide range of evidence, from archeological to etymological, is utilized to demonstrate that relations between men and God, carried out through the intermediary of state-religious authorities, played a causal role in the genesis of the ox-unit of value and account, and, further, in the origins of money, and, subsequently, coinage. The substantive state-religious approach presented in this paper is also compared and contrasted to the Chartalist perspective on money's origins. It is concluded that the substantive approach presented in this paper differs from the more formal approaches (e.g., Metallism) because it does not rely upon a projection of modern institutions and habits of thought (e.g., a medium of exchange; monetary taxation) into ancient societies.

Introduction

This article begins by examining the significance of the ox-unit of value and account in the ancient Greek world. While the ox-unit is commonly acknowledged as one of the earliest (if not *the* earliest) units of value and account in ancient Greek societies, there are

*Alla Semenova is a Visiting Instructor in Economics at Dickinson College. The author is thankful to John F. Henry and Mark Peacock for providing feedback on an earlier version of this paper. The author thanks two anonymous referees for very helpful comments and suggestions that improved this paper. The paper itself was inspired by L. Randall Wray's approach to money. All the remaining mistakes are the author's. Direct correspondence to: Alla Semenova, Department of Economics Dickinson College, PO Box 1773, Carlisle, PA 17013; e-mail: semenova@dickinson.edu

American Journal of Economics and Sociology, Vol. 70, No. 2 (April, 2011).

competing interpretations regarding the origins of this unit. Correspondingly, there are competing perspectives on the origins of a mere notion (or idea) of valuing objects in terms of other objects. Highlighting the marginality of trade in ancient Greece, this paper disputes the common interpretation that the origins of the ox-unit must be sought in barter exchange. As an alternative, this article revives Bernhard Laum's neglected contribution towards the theory of money's origins. One of the key propositions of Laum's thesis is that the origins of the ox-unit must be located in non-commercial "state"— religious practices and institutions of ancient Greek societies. To locate such origins, this article examines the ancient Greek rituals of sacrificial offerings to deities. It is argued that by specifying the precise quality, type and quantity of oxen to be sacrificed, ancient Greek religion provided the first instance of a unit of value established and guaranteed by the "state." Further, this article examines the ancient Greek rituals of communal sacrificial meals to demonstrate how the ox-unit of value gave rise to the first form of money embodied in sacrificial bull's flesh that was centrally (re)distributed among the ritual participants. Next, it is explained how temple-issued coinage emerged as a symbolic representation of roasted bull's flesh, thus making the latter "currency" obsolete. This article concludes that money emerged as a means of "recompense" administered by the "temple-state" to its subjects. Finally, the "state"-religious mechanism of money's origins presented in this article is contrasted to the traditional Chartalist perspective of money's introduction by the state. While in the latter money emerges as a token that extinguishes a population's debt to the state, the "state"-religious approach expounded in this article views money as a token via which the *state* extinguishes its "debt" to the underlying population.

The Ox-Unit of Value and Account

In the early history of the Graeco-Roman culture, oxen were commonly used as a unit of value and account (Desmonde 1962: 109; Burns 1927: 6–8; Seaford 2004; Angell 1929). Homeric epics (ca. 9th–8th cc. BC) where values "are invariably expressed in terms of oxen" serve as one of the earliest written testimonies to this (Desmonde 1962: 109; see also Seaford 2004: 30).[1] For example, the arms of Diomedes were declared worth nine oxen, while those of Glaucos were proclaimed equivalent to one hundred. "Female slaves skilled in crafts sold for four oxen, and the three-legged pot was worth twelve" (Desmonde 1962: 109). When metallic *coinage* appeared in ancient Lydia and Greece (ca. 7th–6th cc. BC),[2] "it was common to talk of a given coin being worth so many oxen, not the ox being worth so many coins" (Angell 1929: 59). Further, the ox-unit of value became the unit of account in which various fines and payments were denominated in the earliest laws of the Graeco-Roman world, such as the laws of Draco (ca. 620 BC)[3] (Desmonde 1962: 110; Quiggin [1949] 1963: 271; Einzig [1949] 1966: 223). The testimony of language can also be evoked here. As is well documented (Laum 1924a; Quiggin [1949] 1963; Desmonde 1962; Grierson 1977; Seaford 2004) many modern terms pertaining to monetary and financial matters have been derived from the use of cattle as a unit of value and account in the early times. To begin with, everyone is familiar with the derivation of the term "pecuniary" from Latin *pecus* denoting cattle. Another example is the term "fee," presumably derived from Gothic *faihu* meaning cattle. The term "capital" derived from *capitale* originally designating cattle counted by the head (Desmonde 1962: 110). And, finally, some have suggested that the term "collateral" might have derived from Greek *kōlakterai* originally referring to the receivers of bull's limbs during the ancient Greek rituals of communal sacrificial meals, and later designating Athenian financial officials (Seaford 2004: 79). Lastly, the earliest Greek word for coinage, *nomisma*, derived from *nemein* meaning to "distribute" and referring originally to the ordered distribution of roasted bull's flesh during the rituals of communal sacrificial meals (Seaford 2004: 49–50; von Reden [1995] 2003: 177). These and numerous other examples attest to the fact that the ox served as "a recognized traditional and conventional" unit of value and account prior to and after the introduction of coinage in Lydia and Greece (Angell 1929: 60). Importantly, the use of the ox-unit persisted long after the introduction of metal use and the invention of coinage (Einzig [1949] 1966: 223).

While the role of oxen as one of the earliest units of value and account is generally acknowledged, views differ as to the *origin* of this role. Where did the idea of valuing objects in terms of cattle (in particular, oxen) come from? Or, one could raise a more fundamental question: what is the origin of a mere *notion* or *idea* of valuing one object in terms of another? How did the *notion* or *idea* of a unit of value and account come into being (Grierson 1977)? The conventional answer to this question is that barter gave rise to the notion and use of a unit of value. Within this barter-based perspective, there are two distinct mechanisms explaining how exactly this could have taken place. In the first mechanism, "[t]he difficulties of pure barter were first overcome by the expression of values [of commodities] in terms of some common prized object *before* that object or any other object served as a medium of exchange, *and* the qualities which fitted the commodity to serve as a common denominator of values would *not* necessarily fit it to serve as a given medium of exchange" (Gregory 1933: 603, emphases added).[4] In this way, "price-lists" could be established and commodities of equal value could be exchanged against each other. In the second mechanism, the logical precedence of a unit of value for the carrying out of commodity exchanges is ignored. Instead, it is proclaimed that "a favorite medium of barter" became a unit of value. The ox was "the old unit of barter," wrote Ridgeway (1892: 6), which explains its further use as the (oldest) unit of value and account (1892: 6). Notably, this position is supported by Karl Menger ([1909] 2002), who argued that Homeric valuation of goods in terms of cattle *derived* from the primary role of cattle as objects of barter in Homeric Greece (1909 [2002]: 59):

> At the time of Homer, barter was already highly developed among the Greeks, and in the acquisition of substantial items of wealth, as even today on many barter markets, the larger of the domestic animals must have been preferably accepted in payment; *that is why* he [Homer] could value their heroes' arms in cattle, even though his assessments could not claim meticulous exactness. ([1909] 2002: 59, emphases added)[5]

The barter-based view is contrasted by the state-religious approach, the advocates of which would argue that the ox-unit of value and account derived from the use of oxen in state-religious practices (Laum 1924a; Desmonde 1962; Seaford 2004). Likewise, it is argued that the mere notion of a unit of value and account was developed in the context of socially-embedded state-religious institutions. Because the institution of trade, both foreign and domestic, played a marginal role in archaic Greek and Lydian societies, it would be unlikely that the ox-unit derived from the practice of exchanging commodities (Laum 1924a; Desmonde 1962; Grierson 1977; von Reden [1995] 2003; Kurke 1999; Seaford 2004). For the marginality of trade in ancient Lydia and Greece, Homeric epics (ca. 9th–8th century BC) provide a good testimony (Laum 1924a; Grierson 1977; von Reden 1995 [2003]; Seaford 2004).

The Marginality of Trade in Homeric Societies

As noted by Seaford (2004), in Homeric epics references to trade hardly ever occur in the main narrative and are almost always "confined to asides" (2004: 27). References to local trade are almost non-existent, while foreign commerce is usually confined to traffic in slaves (2004: 27). Among modern scholars, this aspect of Homeric societies has also been emphasized by von Reden ([1995] 2003), while Grierson (1977) stressed this point two decades earlier:

> In [Homeric] epic, sale is by definition an exchange between strangers. As Finley observed, not once is there a sale transaction which involves either two Greeks or two Trojans. This is supported by the semantic field of the word *pernêmi* and its derivatives *pratêr* and *prasis*. In all its occurrences *pernêmi* denotes transactions abroad; and it always describes the purchase or ransom of a captive. (von Reden [1995] 2003: 67)

> Virtually the only buying and selling in Homer, apart from jewelry and similar foreign luxuries, is that of slaves, and *pernēmi*, the early word for selling, seems to be confined to the selling of captives from abroad, so that scholars have doubted if it had any wider sense at all. (Grierson 1977: 27)

Thus, similar to Grierson (1977), von Reden ([1995] 2003) draws attention to the early term for "selling"—*pernêmi*—stressing its wider connotations of provisioning and voyage rather than that of commercial exchange. The term *pernêmi* "is probably related to the word *peraô* and *poros*, which never assumed clearly commercial meanings but retained more precisely the connotations of voyage and provisioning" ([1995] 2003: 67).

The marginality of market commodity-exchange is conspicuous in Homeric "transactions," and, instead, numerous references are made to (centralized) allocations of prizes, rewards, and booty; gift-exchange, payment of ransom, bride-price, payment of compensation, etc. (Seaford 2004: 23–26). Likewise, Homeric goods are rarely described as commodities exchanged impersonally in the market place. Rather, they are the objects that embody personal relationships and are exchanged as gifts, or redistributed as booty, or given away as rewards or prizes. "Exchange of *things*, not of people, and *not* to create interpersonal links but for the sake of the things"—writes Seaford (2004)—occurs rarely in Homeric epics (2004: 2, emphases added). Considering the marginality of market exchange and trade in general, and taking into account the prevalence of centralized redistribution and reciprocity as the dominant modes of integration in archaic Greece and Lydia (2004: 27), the ox-unit of value and account could not have derived from market exchange, and its origins must be sought elsewhere.

The State-Religious Context for the Origins of the Ox-Unit of Value and Account

Accounting for the marginal sphere occupied by trade in ancient Lydia and Greece, the use of the ox-unit must have derived from a non-market context. In fact, Bernhard Laum (1924a, 1924b, 1925a, 1925b) was among the first scholars to question the conventional theory that the ox-unit of value derived from a market exchange of commodities. Rather, in his work *Heiliges Geld* (*Holy Money*) Laum (1924a) suggested that "the evolution of cattle as a unit of value originated in their religious use" (Laum 1924a: 17, in Burns 1927: 6, ft. 1; see also Einzig [1949] 1966: 369–370; Peacock 2010).[6]

Far from the market, the (re)distributive economies of ancient Greek and Lydian societies were shaped by religion and its normative character. This applies to both "chieftain" societies reflected (though indirectly) in Homeric epics and the archaic Greek city-states. While the process of transformation of the largely "chieftain" societies reflected in Homeric epics into the archaic Greek city-states is beyond the scope of this article, the point is that temples came to be "among the very first manifestations of the polis" (Seaford [1994] 2003: 197). As we know from archeological evidence, from 8th century BC onwards (the period when the archaic Greek city-state came to emerge), the leader's dwelling place was "replaced by, or transformed into" a temple—a center of giving to the deity ([1994] 2003: 197).[7] With the state and religious authorities generally "inter-related in the closest and most ancient bonds" (Burns 1927: 81), "no distinction between State and Church [temple]" (Barker [1918] 1925: 8) could practically be made. Religion "was not another life"—wrote Barker ([1918] 1925)— but "an aspect of the political life of a political society" ([1918] 1925: 8). The pre-eminence of state religion in civic matters was signified by the Priest-King, the head of the archaic Greek and Lydian city-state; and a well-defined hierarchy of priests and other state-religious authorities (Desmonde 1962: 61). Thus, it was the economics of state religion rather than market exchange that provided an organizational framework for the archaic Greek and Lydian societies.

The well-being of the archaic city demanded that its protective divinity be pacified by public gift-offerings (Laum 1924a: 28, in Burns 1927: 7). Here, the ox served as "the most prestigious and important sacrificial animal" (Peacock 2010: 10). Importantly, the types, quality and quantity of oxen used as religious offerings were subject to thorough regulation by the state-religious authorities (Laum 1924a: 28, in Burns 1927: 6, ft. 1). The ox brought to deities had to be "of a very definite type and character," conforming to "painstakingly described rules" (Desmonde 1962: 115). Considering the thorough regulation by the state-religious authorities of the type, quality and quantity of oxen offered, Laum (1924a) suggested that the ox-unit served as the first unit of value and account, a unit established and guaranteed by the state (Laum 1924a: 40, in Burns 1927: 7, ft. 1). As Einzig ([1949] 1966) wrote in summary of Laum's (1924a) argument, ". . . the State authority in Ancient Greece and elsewhere laid down rules determining the precise quality of animals suitable for sacrifice and guaranteed this quality, thereby providing early instances of State-guaranteed units of value" (Einzig [1949] 1966: 372).

Thus, it was in the relationship between humans and deities, mediated through the temple, that the ox-unit of value was developed. But what was the precise nature of this relationship? On the surface, the relationship between man and his gods consisted of offerings to deities[8] in return for which certain blessings were expected, such as favorable weather conditions and good harvests, protection from sickness, safety from foreign invasions. Alternatively, as suggested by Einzig ([1949] 1966), offerings could have been made to deities "in *payment* for blessings *already received*" ([1949] 1966: 371, emphases added). It may be tempting to conceive of this relationship between man and God as an exchange akin to that in the market place, where God's blessings are traded for livestock. For example, Desmonde's (1962) characterization of the ox-unit as "*a medium of exchange* in the relationship between humans and deity" (Desmonde 1962: 115, emphases added), or as a "fixed unit . . . of payment in an *exchange* between man and god" (1962: 115, emphasis added) is suggestive that the relationship between man and deities is perceived as a trade relationship. "[T]he practice of making sacrifices to deity was to a large extent a form of *barter* between man and his gods", wrote Einzig ([1949] 1966) while summarizing Laum's (1924a) contribution (Einzig [1949] 1966: 371, emphasis added). If this interpretation is plausible, and the relationship between men and deities could be considered as a form of barter exchange, then sacred rather than profane exchange gave rise to the ox-unit of value. But would the archaic man barter with God?

As Desmonde (1962) himself admitted in another passage, the personal relationship between man and God was "similar to the *reciprocities* among individuals" (Desmonde 1962: 114, emphasis added). Likewise, questioning his previous argument, Einzig ([1949] 1966) asserted that "there was no question of any barter between man and god" ([1949] 1966: 372) because, as Laum (1924a) himself admitted, "man only returned to god a small proportion of the goods received from him" ([1949] 1966: 372). In a similar vein, Finley (1965) argued against a barter-based interpretation of the relationship between man and God, emphasizing that an act of giving was "in an essential sense always the first half of a *reciprocal* action, the other half of which was a counter-gift" (Finley 1965: 62, emphasis added). Therefore, rather than making payments for blessings received (or to be received in the future), a mortal could express his gratitude for the blessings obtained (or expected) from the deities through the acts of reciprocation. This transforms the relationship between humans and deities into a reciprocal gift-exchange rather than that of barter. Finally, as Polanyi (1957) emphasized, "reciprocity demands adequacy of response, not mathematical equality" of the goods or services reciprocated (Polanyi 1957: 73). Therefore, as summarized by Einzig ([1949] 1966), the "exchange" between man and God cannot be interpreted as a barter relationship "unless it is assumed that the difference between value received and given was made up in prayers and various forms of rites designed to please the deity who, on a strictly commercial basis, came second best out of the bargain" ([1949] 1966: 372).

Further arguments could be made against a commercial interpretation of sacrifice. The presence of an *obligation* to make sacrifices to deities is one of them: "for if people have an obligation to make sacrifices to the gods, humans cannot be deemed equal partners in a 'free relationship of exchange'" (Peacock 2010: 13). Already in Homer, mortals are not free to refuse sacrificial interactions with deities (2010: 13). The presence of a sacrificial obligation suggests that humans not only wish to thank their deities for goods and blessings received (or to be received in the future), but "people also make sacrifices to honour the gods, as is their due" (2010: 13).

Finally, considering the normative character of state-religion prescribing a precise quality and quantity of sacrificial objects, while at the same time determining an exact timing of offerings (Desmonde 1962), the relationship between humans and deities, carried out through an intermediary of state-religious authorities, could be analyzed as a debt relationship. While this relationship could appear as a reciprocal gift-exchange to the archaic Greek men, the inherent nature of this relationship, mediated through the temple authorities, was that of a centrally imposed debt relationship, in which a man was God's debtor. Within this debt relationship, a definitive unit of value and account was adopted for the repayment of debts to deities. The ox, as the most important sacrificial offering in archaic Lydia and Greece, whose quality and type was rigidly regulated by state-religious authorities, thus performed a monetary function of a unit of value and account in which "debts" to deities could be extinguished (Laum 1924a: 40, in Burns 1927: 7, ft. 1).

Another important context for the social use of the ox-unit of value and account was the payment of fees to priests for the services they performed at religious rituals and elsewhere. Because livestock (such as oxen) served as the most important and prestigious category of sacrificial offerings to deities, they naturally became the means of payment to priests (Laum 1924a: 43, in Burns 1927: 7, ft. 1). It was in this state-religious context, therefore, rather than in the market place, as Laum (1924a) had argued, that oxen were first used in *payments* between *man* and *man* (Einzig [1949] 1966: 373). Gradually, the range of commodities offered as sacrifices to deities and in payment to priests began to increase, and it was necessary to establish equivalency ratios, so that fees and sacrifices previously expressed and paid in terms of oxen could be reckoned in terms of other commodities. For this purpose, these other commodities became evaluated in terms of the already existent ox-unit of value and account ([1949] 1966: 373).

It bears noting that Homeric epics contain important evidence in support of Laum's (1924a) overall thesis that the idea and practice of valuing "commodities" in terms of cattle (such as oxen) originated in a religious context. In particular, what is so peculiar about Homeric valuation of things in terms of cattle ("worth a hundred cattle," "worth ninety cattle") is the correspondence between the numbers of cattle quoted as the value of various objects to the numbers of cattle sacrificed in Homeric sacrificial rituals (Seaford 2004: 61). More specifically, the numbers of oxen sacrificed are usually hundred, twenty, twelve, nine, four and one. But these units are *also* the customary units of value in the *Iliad* and *Odyssey* (Einzig [1949] 1966: 382; Seaford 2004: 61). This means that there is a distinct connection between the customized numbers of sacrificial victims *and* the specific quantities of oxen (the specific numbers of the ox-units) in terms of which the worth of various goods was estimated. Moreover, the above mentioned quantities of cattle would be "too large and cumbersome to be used as a medium of exchange, and so as a measure could not have derived from commerce" (Seaford 2004: 61). Rather, the numbers specified suggest that their suitability as a unit of value and account derived, at least partially, "from the sacrifice of set numbers of cattle of standard quality" (2004: 61). These numbers suggest that "valuations were relatively certain only when they mirrored sums . . . to which people were accustomed in sacrificial sphere" (Peacock 2010: 11). Notably, Laum (1924a) was the first to establish this connection between specific numbers of cattle sacrificed as offerings to deities *and* specific numbers of cattle-units in terms of which the worth of Homeric goods was reckoned (Seaford 2004: 61; Einzig [1949] 1966: 373).

The next section of this article will focus specifically on the sacrificial rituals of communal sacrificial meals that emerged in Homeric societies and gave rise to the ox-unit of value and account subsequently adopted by the Greek city-states.

The Rituals of Communal Sacrificial Meals

While the rituals of sacrificial offerings to deities served as a mechanism through which a surplus of goods was *collected* from the local population and made available to the state priest-kingship and priesthood, the quasi-"*redistributive*" part of the rite took place in the rituals of communal sacrificial meals. As "a universal feature of the city worship throughout Greece," a communal sacrificial meal was a ritualized repast in honor of a commonly-worshiped divinity (Desmonde 1962: 60). The ritual consisted of a public killing, roasting and eating of sacrificial animals (such as bulls), accompanied by liturgies and prayers. The priest-king, who presided over the ritualized repast, distributed the portions of a roasted bull to *all* the ritual participants, including deities. Importantly, *all* members of a community, even the slaves, had an equal right of participation in a public sacrificial repast. In fact, such participation was considered a *symbol* of citizenship (1962: 124, 60, 116).

It is important to emphasize the concept and the social role of this *symbolic* citizenship. Note that the slave population of the archaic Greek *pólis* did not hold a legal citizenship status, as such status was granted to free-born members of a community only (Martin [1966] 1996: 61). In this, the institution of citizenship further intensified the degree to which slaves were excluded from civic society. A participation in an all-inclusive communal sacrificial meal, on the other hand, allowed those excluded from citizenship and civic community, the slave population, to experience a sense of unity with it, *as if* they were full-fledged members of a civic society. Allowing an experience of a sense of communality, rather than a feeling of exclusion from a larger society, the ritualized public repast performed a harmonizing social function. Indeed, argued Desmonde (1962), generating a spirit of communality was an important social function of a communal sacrificial repast. Here, the priest-king himself, the members of the city priest-kingship and priesthood, citizens and slaves, *all* participated in a common meal, sharing the flesh of the same animal(s), sitting at the same table(s), in the same public space. The public meal thus fostered a spirit of a communal association, or *koinōmia*, thereby disguising the underlying social reality of antagonistic relationships between masters and slaves, and other dependents. Without doubt, the sacrificial meal performed a harmonizing social function creating a sense of a loving communion between the ruling elite and the lower classes (Desmonde 1962: 63).

At this point, it bears noting that the tradition of communal sacrificial meals existed long *before* the establishment of the archaic Greek city-state. For example, there are "six lengthy descriptions" of communal sacrificial meals in Homer (Seaford 2004: 40). From these descriptions we know that consumption involved an "egalitarian" participation of the whole group. In Homeric epics, this point is stressed by a formulaic sentence "they feasted, nor was anybody's hunger denied the equal feast" (2004: 40). This all-inclusive and harmonizing character of communal sacrificial meals has been recently emphasized by Seaford (2004):

> The ancient, regular, and highly ritualized slaughter and distribution of the animal ensures that everybody is given a share, that there is an "equal feast". Equal distribution to all and (especially) collective participation (*koinōnia*) are persistently emphasized in numerous later references to animal sacrifice performed by groups varying in size from the household to the whole city-state or even Greeks from different city-states at Panhellenic festivals. (2004: 41)

While "equal distribution to all" and collective participation (*koinōnia*) were among the vital features of communal sacrificial repasts, the principle of "equal distribution among all" did not preclude the existence of a "privileged share" or a "leading role" for a chieftain and later for a priest-king and members of the priesthood.

> . . . we find not only a privileged share or leading role for chieftain or leading men but also the principle of equal distribution among all. (2004: 24)

This is because the principle of "equal" share to all did not correspond to the principle of absolute equality. Rather, it was "proportionate" equality that was evoked, where one's "equal" share corresponded to one's social status (see Seaford 2004; von Reden 1995 [2003], Desmonde 1962). In this way, the portion received by each communicant expressed his worth and the degree of his esteem in the community (in accordance with the principle of "proportionate" rather than absolute equality). This explains the vital importance of the specific manner in which a sacrificial animal was allocated among ritual participants (Desmonde 1962: 115). Each person received a share deemed commensurate with his social status: "to the order of social rank there corresponded an order of rank in the apportionment of the roasted flesh" (1962: 116). An inscription from Attica ca. 330 BC, though belonging to a much later period, demonstrates the case in point very well. The inscription carefully describes the specific manner in which a bull's flesh was to be distributed, where the "just" portion allotted to each communicant was proportionate to his social status:

Five pieces each to the presidents
Five pieces each to the nine archons
One piece each to the treasurers of the goddess
One piece each to the managers of the feast
The customary portions to others.[9]

The "just shares" allocated to ritual participants differed not only in quantity, but in quality as well. The more "honored" parts of the sacrificial animal, such as the limbs, were customarily allotted to religious officials. Notably, the term *kolakretai* that was later used to designate Athenian financial officials, originally referred to the "receivers of limbs" suggesting a connection between sacred rituals and state finances (Desmonde 1962: 116; Seaford 2004: 79).

Finally, a right of participation in a sacrificial repast was perceived as a "*recompense*" received by the subjects for the goods and services rendered to the temple-state. Or, to put it differently, a portion of a sacrificial bull's flesh allotted to a communicant served as a priest-king's "*payment*" or "*compensation*" for the contributions rendered (Desmonde 1962: 116). Thus, we see a movement of surplus goods to the temple from "the public" (sacrificial offerings to deities), and a further redistribution of a portion of a surplus during the rituals of communal sacrificial meals. Moreover, a portion of the surplus given to a communicant serves as a temple's "recompense" or "payment" for his contributions. The portions of roasted bull's flesh allocated to communicants could likewise be viewed as "counter-gifts" offered by the temple to the contributing community within a social context of "reciprocity." The temple reciprocated "on behalf of the deities" in response to the "gifts to gods" given by the mortals. Recall that "reciprocity demands adequacy of response, not mathematical equality" of the goods reciprocated (Polanyi 1957: 73).

The vital importance of sacrificial distribution in Homeric and archaic Greek societies is confirmed by its notable impact on a range of Greek conceptions, vocabulary and institutions. To begin with, the ordered distribution of food was associated by Greeks with the beginning of civilization. Further, the Greek terminology for dividing urban space commonly employed the terminology of carving up an animal. When the archaic Greek city-state was established, full citizenship and entitlement to participation in the sacrificial repast seemed be one and the same (Seaford 2004: 49–50). What is more, etymological evidence suggests that the rituals of communal sacrificial meals became the foundation of the archaic and classical Greek judicial systems. The Greek word for law or convention, *nomos*, derived from *nemein* meaning "to distribute" "and so presumably at first meant distribution, then the principle of distribution" (2004: 49). *Nomos* originally meant "anything assigned, distributed, or dealt out" (Del Mar [1885] 1968: 335). While the terminology of *nomos* does not occur in Homer, *nemein* is frequently used in the context of distribution of food and drink. "And so it seems reasonable to infer"—writes Seaford (2004)—that *nomos* had its origins "in the widespread and economically fundamental practice of distributing *meat*" (Seaford 2004: 50; see also Del Mar [1885] 1968: 335; von Reden 1995: 177; Kurke 1999). Related terms for which a sacrificial origin has been inferred include *nemesis* (retribution), *isonomia* (equality of political rights), and *nomisdein* (acknowledge, consider) (Seaford 2004: 50). Finally, the early Greek word for money—*nomisma*—suggests a connection between the rituals of communal sacrificial meals and the origins of money and coinage.

From Holy Debts to *Nomos*: The State-Religious Origins of Money and Coinage

When Aristotle referred to money he called it *nomisma* (Seaford 2004: 143; von Reden [1995] 2003: 184–187; Del Mar [1885] 1968: 172).[10] To begin with, this suggests that in the classical period Greeks well understood that the value of money was conventional, based upon convention, usage, or law, rather than upon its *intrinsic* characteristics (von Reden [1995] 2003: 184–185; Seaford 2004: 5; Kurke 1999: 41–42; Del Mar [1885] 1968: 338, 172, ft. 2).[11]

> That is the reason why it is called money (*nomisma*), because it has not a natural but a conventional (*nomos*) existence, and because it is in our power to change it, and make it useless. (Aristotle, *Nichomachean Ethics*, Book 5)

Secondly, since *nomos* referred originally to the "just" apportionment of the flesh of a sacrificial animal during the rituals of communal sacrificial meals, and later came to designate "anything assigned, distributed, or dealt out" by convention, this suggests an important connection between the rituals of communal sacrificial meals and centralized redistribution in general, *and* the institution of money (*nomisma*).

Another piece of evidence in support of a connection between communal sacrificial meals and the origins of money *and also coinage* pertains to the iron spits commonly used in the ritualized repasts. Utilized for roasting a sacrificial animal, an iron spit, called *obelos*, was also used for distributing roasted portions of meat among the ritual participants. In the course of time, suggested Laum (1924a), sacrificial meat on an iron spit came to be known as "obelos." Notably, *obolos* is the name of the 6th century BC silver Greek coin. Another 6th century BC Greek coin of a larger denomination, *drachma*, originally meant a handful of six iron spits (or a handful of six *obeloe*) (Seaford 2004: 102). "The Greeks themselves were aware"—writes Seaford (2004)—"that their coin of low value the obol (*obolos*) took its name from the spit (*obelos*), and that 'drachma' meant originally a handful of (six) spits" (2004: 102).

A famous passage from *Etymologicum Magnum* describes the abrupt transition from iron spits to coins (*obolos* and *drachma*), carried out by King Pheidon of Argos on the island of Aegina in the first half of the 6th century BC:

> First of all men Pheidon of Argos struck money in Aegina; and having given them (his subjects) coin and abolished the spits, he dedicated them to Hera in Argos. But since at that time the spits used to fill the hand, that is the grasp, we, although we do not fill our hand with the six obols (spits) call it a *grasp full* (δραχμή) owing to the *grasping* of them. (cited in Ridgeway 1892: 214)

Notably, the above legendary dedication of iron spits in the temple of Hera in Argos was confirmed as factual when archeological excavations on the site of the temple ruins revealed a bundle of 180 iron spits (Quiggin [1949] 1963: 282; Burns 1927: 27). The exact reason for this dedication cannot be known with certainty. Most probably, however, the iron spits "were dedicated as specimens of obsolete currency which had been superseded by the coins" introduced by Pheidon, or as an "obsolete apparatus of the period before the introduction of coins which was no longer required" (Burns 1927: 27).

The use of the term *nomisma* in reference to money, the use of the terms *obolos* and *drachma* to designate some of the earliest Greek coins, the dedication of iron spits in the temple of Hera, the connection between "holy debts," religious rituals and the ox-unit of value and account, and the religious imagery on the earliest Greek and Lydian coins (such as a bull-image), among other pieces of evidence, suggested to Laum (1924a) that the coin "originated in the spitted portion of the flesh of the sacrificial bull" (Desmonde 1962: 117).

> This apparent transition from roasting spits to coins was, along with other terms that seem to embody the transition from the sacrificial to the financial, adduced by Laum as part of an argument to the effect that animal sacrifice was an important factor in the genesis of coinage. (Seaford 2004: 102)

More specifically, Laum (1924a) argued that "obelos," i.e., a spitted portion of a roasted bull's flesh distributed among the ritual participants as a "state's payment for [their] contributions" was the first form of money (Desmonde 1962: 15). *Coins*, when they first appeared, served as a symbolic representation of the spitted portions of the bull's flesh distributed among the communicants, coins served as a symbolic representation of "obelos." Coins superseded "obelos": the distribution of coins replaced the actual distribution of the sacrificial bull's meat. In this, we see a transition from the actual forms (a portion of roasted meat on a spit) to symbolic representations (a coin as a representation of the roasted meat).[12] Notably, because of a belief in magic (Hocart [1925] 1970), no distinction was made between a symbol (a coin) and that which the symbol represented (a sacrificial bull's flesh). Possessing a coin was equivalent to the actual sharing in the sacrificial flesh of a bull (1962: 134).

To conclude, coins began as religious *symbols*, each coin representing a piece of a sacrificial bull's flesh allotted to a communicant as a "reward," "recompense" or "payment" for the goods and services rendered to the temple-state (Desmonde 1962: 121). This means that the earliest coins did not begin as media of exchange in commerce, but functioned "in the same fashion as the portion of food distributed at the sacred meal" (1962: 125). In this, the earliest coins could also be regarded as "religious medals": similar to the allotment of "obelos," coins (or medals) were given by the priest-king to his subjects in a manner that reflected the degree of their worth and esteem in the community (1962: 125).

If a connection between communal sacrificial meals and the earliest coins is a plausible one, and a coin served as a representation of a sacrificial bull's meat, then we can explain why so many of the earliest Lydian and Greek coins bear the image of a bull or a bull's head on their surface (Gardner 1883; Barclay and Head 1968). This also explains why the earliest Lydian and Greek coins were struck within temple precincts, under direct auspices of the priests (Barclay and Head 1968: 7; Angell 1929: 96; Del Mar [1885] 1968: 162; Desmonde 1962: 113; Gardner 1883: 6; Seaford 2004). Further, because the earliest Lydian and Greek coins were not intended for commercial circulation, the image of a bull on a coin's surface did not serve as a guarantee of a coin's commercial value (Desmonde 1962: 125). Rather than economic, the value of the earliest Lydian and Greek coins was symbolic: a coin served as a symbol of one's contribution to the temple state. Coinage became a symbolic means of recompense by the priest-king to his subjects. Nor did the value of the earliest coins derive from their intrinsic characteristics: the earliest Lydian coins[13] were made of electrum, a natural alloy of gold and silver, the internal composition of which is highly variable by nature. This means that a coin's weight, purity and fineness, and, thus, its intrinsic value, could not be guaranteed (Grierson 1977: 7; see also Innes 1913).

> As to the electrum coins, which are the oldest coins known to us, their composition varies in the most extraordinary way. While some contain more than 60 per cent of gold, others known to be of the same origin contain more than 60 per cent of silver, and between these extremes, there is every degree of alloy, so that they could not possibly have a fixed intrinsic value. (Innes 1913: 379)

In the mid-6th century BC, silver coinage began to spread in mainland Greek states (Kurke 1999: 9). Yet the only metallurgical device for testing precious metals, known to us from the texts of the 6th and 5th centuries BC, is the "touchstone" (*basanos*) (1999: 42–45). But the touchstone is ineffective in testing silver, as it is inadequate in testing electrum (1999: 45, ft. 13). Thus, the evidence does not support the common interpretation that the value of the earliest coins derived from their intrinsic characteristics. Rather, metallurgical knowledge pertaining to intrinsic properties of precious metals (electrum, in the first place) was not sufficient to provide near accurate assessments of the coins' intrinsic value (see also Desmonde 1962: 121–122).

A Footnote on the Competing Interpretations of the Earliest Greek Coinage

Whereas Laum (1924a) argued that the earliest bull-type coins served as representations of sacrificial bull's flesh distributed at communal sacrificial meals, proponents of the exchange-based view maintain that bull-type coins represented previously existing units of barter. The earliest coins were "representations of the objects of barter of more primitive times," argued Ridgeway (1892: 314). In accordance with this interpretation, each coin type stood for a specific commodity previously used as a unit of barter, as indicated by a coin's stamp. In this way, a bull-type coin allegedly replaced the actual bull previously used as a unit of bartering. At the same time, the value of a coin ("worth one bull") was indicated by placing a symbol of a commodity (a bull) upon its surface. The coin image guaranteed that coin's weight and quality stood at parity with the object previously employed as a unit of barter. In this vein, Ridgeway (1892) argued that, for example, the value of an early Greek coin called *talent* was set equal to the value of a cow (or an ox)—"the oldest unit of barter" (1892: 387). Whereas a golden *talent* represented a cow, other coins represented other units of barter. For instance, the early Greek coins representing pots and kettles presumably replaced the actual pots and kettles previously employed as the objects of primitive barter. Another example is the famous tunny-fish electrum coin from Cyzicus (1892: 313–316). The image of a tunny fish on the coins of Cyzicus, is, according to Ridgeway (1892), "an indication that these coins superseded a primitive system in which the tunny formed a monetary unit, just as the Kettle and Pot counter-marks on the coins . . . point back to the days when real kettles formed the chief medium of exchange" (1892: 316).

Elaborating upon the question who issued the earliest Lydian and Greek coins, Ridgeway (1892) concluded that they "were very likely struck in the temples, which had vast reserves of precious metals" (1892: 215). However, *contrary* to Laum's thesis, Ridgeway (1892) believed that coins were issued by the temples in order to facilitate the needs of *trade*, which the temple authorities encouraged in every way and hosted on their premises. The argument is rooted in a proposition that merchants and traders took advantage of huge public gatherings at the temple premises during the times of temple feasts (1892: 215–216).

The advocates of the state-religious approach (Laum 1924a; Desmonde 1962; Seaford 2004), on the other hand, stress the marginality of both domestic and foreign trade in 7th–6th cc. BC Lydia and Greece, and establish the origins of money and coinage in the context of state-religious practices of centralized collection and redistribution. More specifically, the origins of the ox-unit of value and account are established in a context of a debt relationship between men and deities—a relationship mediated through the temple authorities. Further, it is pointed out how money emerged in the form of roasted bull's flesh (re)distributed among the participants of communal sacrificial meals. This money, called "obelos," served as a "reward," "recompense" or "payment" administered by the priest-king for in-kind contributions rendered by the underlying population.

The State-Religious and Chartalist Approaches: A Comparison

Notably, the above outlined state-religious mechanism of money's origins shares important similarities with the Chartalist perspective on money (Knapp [1905] 1924; Wray 1998; Goodhart 1998). To begin with, both the Chartalist and the state-religious perspectives share a common opposition to exchange-based interpretations of money's origins (accounts in the tradition of Karl Menger) (see Menger 1892, [1909] 2002). Both perspectives locate the origins of money in a context of a debt relationship between a central public authority and an underlying population. Importantly, both the Chartalist and the state-religious approaches establish the causal role of the state in the origins of money. In both approaches, money is *not* viewed as a commodity with an intrinsic value. Rather, money is perceived as a state's token whose value and general acceptance do not derive from its intrinsic composition. However, some differences remain. To begin with, the substantivist state-religious approach establishes the origins of the ox-unit of value and account in a context of a debt relationship between men and deities—a relationship mediated through the temple authorities—thus bringing in the causal role of religious institutions into the origins of money. Further, money in the form of roasted bull's flesh is introduced by the temple as a "reward" or "recompense" or "payment" for the contributions rendered by the underlying population. The actual distribution of roasted bull's flesh at the rituals of communal sacrificial meals is further replaced by a distribution of its symbolic representation in the form of a coin (with a bull-image imprinted upon its surface). While being a "reward" or a "recompense" bestowed by the temple, money is, at the same time, a "certificate" of one's contribution to the temple-state. In the traditional Chartalist mechanism, on the other hand, money is introduced as a means of "inducing" the population into making such contributions *in the first place*. While in the traditional Chartalist perspective money is a token that extinguishes a population's debt to the state, within the state-religious approach money serves as a token via which the *state* extinguishes its debt to the underlying population. While the traditional Chartalist perspective locates the origins of money by projecting modern habits of thought and modern institutions (such as monetary taxation) into ancient societies, the substantivist state-religious approach inquires into the actual modes of socio-economic integration of archaic societies, and establishes a mechanism of money's origins that would be embedded into the actual institutions and social practices of those societies. This is what makes this approach a substantive interdisciplinary inquiry into the origins of money.

Conclusions

The ox-unit is commonly acknowledged as one of the earliest units of value and account in the Graeco-Roman world and elsewhere. Reviving a neglected contribution by Bernhard Laum (1924a), a contribution that was never translated into English, this article argues that the origins of the ox-unit of value and account must be sought in the context of ancient Greek state-religious practices and institutions, rather than in the context of trade, whether foreign or domestic. More specifically, the origins of the ox-unit of value and account were established in a context of a debt relationship between men and deities, mediated through the temple authorities. The ox-unit of value and account further became the unit of "recompense" whereby the state-religious authorities compensated the underlying population for their contributions to the temple. It was argued that the earliest Greek money took the form of roasted bull's flesh, which was centrally (re)distributed during the rituals of communal sacrificial meals. Money in the form of roasted bull's flesh, which came to be known as "obelos," was perceived as one's "just share" allocated by the temple in accordance with one's social status and socially-established value of one's contributions to the temple. The "recompense" in the form of "obelos" was further superseded by its symbolic representation in the form of coins such as *obeloe* and *drachma*.

Overall, this article disputes the origins of money in the context of trade. Rather, a wide range of evidence, from archeological to etymological, is utilized to demonstrate that relations between men and deities, carried out through the intermediary of state-religious authorities, played a causal role in the genesis of the earliest unit of value and account, and, further, in the origins of money, and, subsequently, coinage. The state-religious approach presented in this article was also compared and contrasted to the traditional Chartalist perspective on money's origins. It was concluded that the state-religious approach is a substantive inquiry into the origins of money that does not rely upon a projection of modern institutions and habits of thought (monetary taxation; a medium of exchange) into ancient societies in order to establish the origins of money. Rather, the state-religious approach establishes the origins of money by embarking on a substantivist inquiry into the actual institutions and modes of socio-economic integration of ancient societies.

Notes

1. See Peacock (2010) for a review of arguments supporting the use of Homeric epics as a historical source to illuminate archaic Greek society.

2. The earliest electrum coinage of Lydia (Asia Minor) dates back to ca. 640–630 BC; the earliest Greek coins were struck in 595 BC on the island of Aegina; in 575 BC in Athens, and in 570 BC in Corinth (Davies 2002: 64–65).

3. Cattle served as a unit in which fines and rewards were fixed in Athens by Draco (circa 620 BC). One of the reforms implemented by Solon (circa 590 BC) was the computation of fines and rewards in terms of coined money instead of livestock (Einzig [1949] 1966: 223).

4. Quoted in Einzig ([1949] 1966): 356.

5. The "heroes' arms" that Menger ([1909] 2002) refers to are certainly the arms of Glaucos and Diomedes mentioned above.

6. Unfortunately, none of Laum's works on the origins of money has been translated into English, and in what follows I will rely on references to Laum's work collected from various sources such as Desmonde (1962), Einzig ([1949] 1966), Burns (1927), Seaford (2004), and Peacock (2010).

7. Prior to the 8th century BC, monumental temple buildings were very rare. Most offerings to deities were conducted either in the open or at the house of the chieftain (Seaford 2004: 63).

8. Oxen (and livestock in general) formed the most important and prestigious category of sacred offerings (Peacock 2010), but such offerings were not limited to livestock and included agricultural staples and handicrafts such as vessels and utensils (Desmonde 1962; Seaford 2004).

9. Yerkes (1952: 108), in Desmonde (1962: 105).

10. As is well known to classicists (see von Reden [1995] 2003; Kurke 1999; Seaford 2004; also see Peacock 2006), Aristotle discussed the origins,

functions and meanings of money and coinage in two different contexts and in two different works (von Reden [1995] 2003: 184). One context is related to wealth, commerce and profit (as discussed in Aristotle's *Politics*), while the other context deals with the origins of the *polis* (as in *Nicomachean Ethics*). The two different contexts for the origins and functions of money and coinage correspond to Aristotle's distinction between money as a commodity (*Politics*) and money as a political token (*Nicomachean Ethics*). Money as a token was "a means of unilateral payment in a system of generalized reciprocity" while money as a commodity served as a medium of exchange in commerce (von Reden [1995] 2003: 184). Aristotle evaluated the two functions of money "completely differently" ([1995] 2003: 184). In the passage below, von Reden ([1995] 2003) evaluates Aristotle's conception of money as a political means of payment necessary to achieve "distributive justice" in a community:

> Coinage as payment was necessary in order to achieve justice in the *koinônia* (community) of the *polis*. As a standard of value it made different sorts of need (*chreia*) commensurate and was thus a crucial instrument for creating just relationships in the community of people whose products or needs were of necessity different: . . . . ([1995] 2003: 184)

11. When coinage was introduced by the Greek city-states, its value was "fiduciary" or conventional: the value of a stamped coin was higher than the value of its melted metal component (Seaford 2004: 7–8, 136–146; Peacock 2006: 639–640, 2010: 18).

12. Another account of representation applies to tripods and cauldrons— vessels used for cooking sacrificial bull's meat. Providing a translation of Laum's (1924a) argument, Peacock (2010) writes that tripods and cauldrons were "part of a currency which emanates directly from the cattle currency, and, like the latter, is based in sacrifice. The difference with the pure cattle currency is that a symbol [cauldron or tripod] has taken the place of the real good [cattle]" (Peacock 2010: 18). Further, archeological evidence suggests that the phenomenon of representation applied to sacrificial offerings as well (Laum 1924a; Seaford 2004; Peacock 2010). We find sacrificial offerings in the form of miniature cauldrons (commonly made of bronze), "and hence symbols (the miniatures) of the symbols (actual cauldrons) of the real good (cattle) were used to represent cattle in sacrifice" (Peacock 2010: 17–18). Likewise, there are terracotta and wood figurines symbolizing cattle (and serving as substitutes for real animal sacrifices) (Peacock 2010: 16). Although such offerings are not mentioned in Homer, they "date back to the period in which he wrote, and increase greatly in number thereafter" (Peacock 2010: 16).

13. According to Grierson (1977: 7) the earliest electrum coins date back to the third quarter of the 7th century BC, though their exact timing is still a matter of dispute.

References

Angell, N. (1929). *The Story of Money.* New York: Frederick A. Stokes Company.

Barclay, V., and M. Head. (1968). "Greek Coins." In *Coins and Medals: Their Place in History and Art.* Ed. S. Lane-Poole. Chicago: Argonaut, Inc., Publishers.

Burns, A. R. (1927). *Money and Monetary Policy in Early Times.* London: Kegan Oaul, Trench, Trubner & Co., Ltd.; New York: Alfred A. Knopf.

Davies, G. (2002). *A History of Money from Ancient Times to the Present Day.* Cardiff: University of Wales Press.

Del Mar, A. ([1885] 1968). *A History of Money in Ancient Countries from the Earliest Times to the Present.* New York: Burt Franklin.

Desmonde, W. H. (1962). *Magic, Myth, and Money: The Origin of Money in Religious Ritual.* New York: Free Press of Glencoe, Inc.

Einzig, P. ([1949] 1966). *Primitive Money in its Ethnological, Historical and Economic Aspects.* London: Eyre and Spottiswoode.

Finley, M. I. (1965). *The World of Odysseus.* New York: Viking Press.

Gardner, P. (1883). *The Types of Greek Coins.* Cambridge: Cambridge University Press.

Goodhart, Ch. (1998). "The Two Concepts of Money: Implications for the Analysis of Optimal Currency Areas." *European Journal of Political Economy* 14(3): 407–432.

Gregory, T. E. (1933). "Money." In *Encyclopaedia of the Social Sciences.* Vol. X. Eds. R. A. Seligman and A. Johnson. New York: Macmillan Company.

Grierson, P. (1977). *The Origins of Money.* London: Athlone Press, University of London.

Hocart, A. M. ([1925] 1970). *The Life-Giving Myth and Other Essays.* London: Methuen & Co, Ltd.

Innes, A. Mitchell. (1913). "What is Money?" *Banking Law Journal* 31: 151–168.

Knapp, G. F. ([1905] 1924). *The State Theory of Money.* London: Macmillan and Co., Ltd.

Kurke, L. (1999). *Coins, Bodies, Games and Gold: The Politics of Meaning in Archaic Greece.* Princeton, NJ: Princeton University Press.

Laum, B. (1924a). *Heiliges Geld: Eine Historishe Untersuchung über den Sakralen Ursprung des Geldes.* Tübingen: Verlag von J.C.B.Mohr.

——. (1924b). "Die Banken im Alterum." In *Handwörterbuch der Staatswissensch.* Vol. II. Eds. L. Elster, A. Weber, and F. Wieser. Jena: G. Fischer.

——. (1925a). *Das Eisengeld der Spartaner.* Braunsberg O. P.: Verlag der Staatlichen Akademie.

———. (1925b). "Münzwesen." In *Handwörterbuch der Staatswissensch.* Vol. VI. Eds. L. Elster, A. Weber, and F. Wieser. Jena: G. Fischer.

Martin, T. R. (1996). *Ancient Greece: From Prehistoric to Hellenistic Times.* New Haven and London: Yale University Press.

Menger, K. (1892). "On the Origins of Money." *Economic Journal* 2: 239–255.

———. ([1909] 2002). "Money." In *Carl Menger and the Evolution of Payments Systems.* Eds. M. Latzer and S. W. Schmitz. Trans. L. B. Yeager and M. Streissler. Cheltenham, UK; Northampton, MA, USA: Edward Elgar.

Peacock, M. (2006). "The Origins of Money in Ancient Greece." *Cambridge Journal of Economics* 30: 637–650.

———. (2010). "The Political Economy of Homeric Society and the Origins of Money." Unpublished Manuscript. *Contributions for Political Economy* 29, forthcoming 2011.

Polanyi, K. (1957) "Aristotle Discovers the Economy." In *Trade and Markets in the Early Empires.* Eds. K. Polanyi, C. Arensberg, and H. Pearson. Glencoe, IL: Free Press.

Quiggin, A. Hingston. ([1949] 1963). *A Survey of Primitive Money: The Beginnings of Currency.* London: Methuen & Co. Ltd.

Ridgeway, W. (1892). *The Origin of Metallic Currency and Weight Standards.* Cambridge: At the University Press.

Seaford, R. ([1994] 2003). *Reciprocity and Ritual: Homer and Tragedy in the Developing City-State.* Oxford: Oxford University Press.

———. (2004). *Money and the Early Greek Mind: Homer, Philosophy, Tragedy.* Cambridge: Cambridge University Press.

von Reden, S. ([1995] 2003). *Exchange in Ancient Greece.* London: Gerald Duckworth & Co. Ltd.

Wray, L. R. (1998). *Understanding Modern Money: The Key to Full Employment and Price Stability.* Cheltenham (UK), and Northampton (MA, USA): Edward Elgar.

Yerkes, R. K. (1952). *Sacrifice in Greek and Roman Religion and Early Judaism.* New York: Scribner.

Human Capital: Theoretical and Empirical Insights

By Germana Bottone* and Vania Sena**

*There is nothing more difficult to plan, more
Doubtful of success, nor more dangerous to manage
Than the creation of a new system.
For the initiator has the enmity of all who would
Profit by the preservation of the old system, and
Merely lukewarm defenders in those who should gain
By the new one.*

N. Machiavelli (1513)

ABSTRACT. The purpose of this paper is twofold. First, we want to challenge the notion of "human capital" as "education, training and work experience" and suggest that it is the "quality of the workforce" that matters, here defined as the set of characteristics that allow workers to function in a specific institutional and historical context. Our main conclusion is that the quality of the workforce is affected by the institutional environment where the workers live and that therefore it can vary across countries and institutional contexts. Second, we want to show the empirical relevance of this last point by testing the extent to which the quality of institutions (here proxied by the governance indicators of Kaufmann et al. (2007)) can affect the quality of the workforce (proxied by the percentage of the working age population registered in a lifelong learning program). Our empirical analysis is conducted on a data-set of 11 European countries observed over the period 1996–2006. The results indicate that countries with better governance indicators are also endowed with a more qualified workforce.

*Corresponding Author. Institute for Studies and Economic Analyses, Piazza dell'Indipendenza, 4, 00185 Roma, Italia. E-mail: g.bottone@isae.it. The author is researcher in the field of Public Economics. Main interests: Institutional Economics, Heterodox Economics.

**Reader at Aston Business School, Aston University, Birmingham, B4 7ET, United Kingdom. v.sena@aston.ac.uk.

American Journal of Economics and Sociology, Vol. 70, No. 2 (April, 2011).

Introduction

In the mainstream economics the notion of "human capital" is a rather established one. Indeed, OECD provides the most complete definition as "all the attributes embodied in individuals that are relevant to economic activity" (OECD 1998). In spite of the fact there have been attempts within the mainstream literature to define the concept of "human capital" in a more sophisticated way, the literature in this area still thinks of "human capital" as the equivalent of physical capital, forgetting that even though there are some similarities between the two, the process of accumulation of knowledge is quite different from the process of accumulation of physical equipment.

The purpose of this paper is therefore twofold. First, we want to challenge the notion of "human capital" as "education, training and working experience" and suggest that it is the quality of the workforce that matters, defined as the set of capabilities that allow workers to function in a specific institutional and historical context. In other words, we suggest that the decision-making process that is behind the accumulation of human capital at an aggregate level (as it is described by mainstream economics) does not take into account the fact that individuals when deciding whether or not to invest in knowledge respond to the incentives provided by the institutional context. On the contrary, the expression "quality of the workforce" conveys the very basic idea that the capabilities a worker is endowed with are contextual to the environment (s)he is in. For example, a worker living today in a democracy cannot have the same characteristics of a "quality worker" living 50 years ago in a dictatorship. To support our argument we will use insights from both the Institutional and Evolutionary Economics; more specifically we will consider the work of Commons, Veblen, Ayres and of some more recent Institutionalists such as Hodgson, Lee and Muerga. The advantage of using this theoretical framework is that Institutional economists examine economic activity using simply what Frederic Lee (2002: 790) calls "common sense."[1]

Our main conclusion is that the quality of the workforce is affected by the institutional environment where the workers live and that therefore it can vary across countries and institutional contexts. Second, we want to show the empirical relevance of this last point by testing the extent to which the quality of institutions can affect the quality of the workforce. In our paper we consider the quality of the workforce to be a special type of active citizenship as defined by the European Commission (2002: 4); in other words, an active citizen is an individual who can contribute to all the aspects of social life and is also capable to find the right job and to make the necessary investments in education and training. Our proxy for the quality of the workforce is the country-level percentage of individuals involved in a lifelong learning program. Indicators of institutional qualities are sourced from the well-known Kaufmann et al. (2007) data-set on the quality of governance. Our empirical analysis is conducted on a data-set of 11 European countries observed over 1996–2006. The results confirm that institutional quality has an impact on the quality of the workforce as countries with better quality institutions are also the ones with the quality workforce.

The paper is organized as follows. The next section reviews the institutional economics literature on human capital and knowledge. This is followed by an examination of the concept of quality of workforce and its relationship with active citizenship. We then describe the data and the econometric model, after which the empirical results are presented. Finally some conclusions are offered.

Human Capital in an Institutional Economics Perspective

The classical definition of human capital is provided by the OECD (1998), which defines it as "The aggregation of investments, such as education and on the job training that improves the individual's productivity in the labour market." However, this notion is rather restrictive and not always realistic. Indeed, the investment in education does not necessarily produce private benefits to the worker in terms of higher wages[2] but it surely creates positive externalities for the society as whole. Not surprisingly then, every society is willing to invest in education in order to take advantage of its benefits. Moreover, the investment in education can create long-term benefits as "The structures of physical, human and social capital constrain future production and wealth is always and everywhere a 'residuum of past activities'" (Mises L. 1996: 506).

However, the possibility that education and knowldege in general can generate positive externalities is not a totally new contribution of modern economic theory. Indeed the Old Institutional Economics, in general, recognized the importance of knowledge (embodied in individuals) for the progress of societies, but refrained from labeling it "human capital." This is hardly surprising: the Old Institutional Economics[3] rejected the association of the word "capital" (meaning "stock, wealth and goods") with phenonema that are not economic but are grounded in the cultural fabric of the society. Frank Fetter[4] was one of the staunchest writers against the use of the term capital.

> Physical objects of value are not capital, being sufficiently designated as goods, wealth or agents. (Fetter 1930: 190)

He gives also an interesting historical derivation of the word capital (Fetter 1930):

> Thus the business as a whole might be thought of either as the sum or fund of purchasing power invested, or as the mass of goods which, although not bought with borrowed funds, embodied the owner's business fund.
> These two types of capital concepts are so distinctive in essential thought and practical application that confusion inevitably resulted from the use of one word to designate both. This confusion occurred not later than the early years of the seventeenth century, when Cotgrave defined capital in 1611 as "wealth, worth; a stock, a man's principal, or chief, substance." Here the idea of "worth," implying a valuation, is thoroughly mixed with that of substance, no doubt in the sense of material things in possession. "Capital" thus used is a superfluous and confusing synonym of wealth, goods and stock. (Frank Fetter 1930: 187)

Schumpeter (1954) rejected the use of an expression such as "human capital" and insisted that the word "capital" should be applied exclusively to financial assets. During the 1960s and 1970s, a vivacious debate started on both sides of the Atlantic on the meaning of the word "capital" (so-called Cambridge controversies; see also Harcourt 1982). Since then, economists have tried to define the term "capital" more correctly. Joan Robinson (1979) explicitly wrote that the term capital should to be used only when referring to financial assets. Neverthless, the word "capital" is still used to denote the stock (or reserve) of any productive factor. This happens because in the current economic culture "even social or cultural problems may be resolved and explained by market forces, valued and exchanged in monetary terms, and invested like financial capital" (Hodgson 2001: 130).

The connection between the two terms "human" and "capital" is, however, particularly odd. The expression "human capital" is rather ambiguous; indeed it is not clear whether it refers to the number of workers that are the inputs in an aggregate production function or the attributes embodied in workers that allow them to be more productive. Also these attributes are particularly difficult to specify. Not surprisingly then there is no agreed empirical measure of workers' human capital where the main proxies have been education, training and working experience.

Therefore, we follow the institutional economics literature and prefer to think of human capital as the knowledge embodied in workers acquired from both formal and informal institutions. In our view, knowledge is the main instrument that helps individuals to develop what we call "contextual" capabilities, that is the capabilities necessary to individuals to function in the environment where they live. Indeed, the power and freedom that knowledge can give to individuals, except for the unusual and genial discoveries, can be used only if the institutions allow so.

This view of knowledge as the product of the interaction of formal and informal institutions is obviously consistent with the definition that the old institutionalists gave of knowledge. Consider first Commons. Commons (1964) described labor as the main factor that contributes to the creation of the wealth of the nation. He warned that human beings, and not money or commodities, are the real measure of prosperity of a nation. He always used the term "labor" and never the expression "human capital." While studying the local labor market in Wisconsin, Commons first noticed that education can generate positive externalities the whole society can take advantage from. In fact, he emphasized the role that education has both in preventing mental degradation, irregular work, pauperism and in creating self-reliant individuals. Given the importance of education, he also questioned the way the provision of education was arranged. In his opinion, firms are not well positioned to be the providers of education. Indeed, he claims that firms had created a separation between the "brain" and the "hands" (Commons J. R. 1964: 369) of low-skilled workers, as they need only workmanship: "What is the part that industrial education should perform in preventing vagrancy, irregular employment, and pauperism? Before we can answer the question, we need to know what kind of industrial education we mean, and what kind of industry it is that needs this education" (Commons J. R. 1964: 363).

His answer was that society needs *universal* education so that "every boy and girl become a business man . . . an intelligent worker . . . a citizen . . . and must protect his health. All these requirements are common to all occupations, yet no occupation of modern industry teaches them" (Commons 1964: 379). Universal education, according to Commons, contributes to create better citizens and not to acquire job-specific skills that can be learnt while on the job. Indeed, he observed that workers can become more capable (while learning on the job) in manual jobs and therefore they can move across different jobs and earn higher wages as time goes by.

However, the main contribution of institutional economists is the recognition that the behavior of individuals cannot simply be explained by the laws of economic rationality but it is the result of the interaction of the individuals with social norms and institutions. Therefore their action may be defined as social action (Muerga 2007). For instance, Commons (1934: 74) suggested individuals are not "*globules of desire*" but "*institutionalized minds*"; they learn the customs and the behavior that is considered acceptable by the society. In short, they are not passive beings pursuing exclusively their private interest, but they act following laws and social rules (customs and habits) as well. In Commons' words: *Individuals begin as babies. They learn the custom of language, of cooperation with other individuals, of working towards common ends, of negotiations to eliminate conflicts of interest, of subordination to the working rules of the many concerns of which they are members* (1934: 73).

The most important institutional economist, Thorstein Veblen (1919), wrote that the production function is not only a function of capital and labor, but also of the knowledge accumulated over time and passed on from generation to generation. However, he also suggested that, at any point in time, the stock of knowledge available to a society is a product of its institutions:

> But habits of thought are the outcome of habits of life. Whether it is intentionally directed to the education of individuals or not, the discipline of daily life acts to alter or reinforce the received institutions under which men live. (Veblen 1901: 121)

Moreover, Veblen, for the first time, introduces the dicotomy between progressive and ceremonial habits where ceremonial habits refer to all those habits that resist to any change to maintain established privileges. This idea will be used later on by Clarence Ayres (1962) to show the importance of tecnological change against ceremonial habits. He opposed the convention to explain the notion of value in terms of price system, equilibrium and "utility" and introduced the notion of "social medium": i.e., the environment where an individual lives and where his/her utility is determined.[5] According to Ayres (1962: vi), the evolutionary process of human beings has been driven by two main forces: *one, progressive, dynamic, productive of cumulative change; the other counter-progressive, static, inhibitory of change* (xiv). In *Toward a Reasonable Society* (1961), he explained the coexistence of scientific (objective) knowledge and socially accepted values rooted in traditions, beliefs, and customs. He considered technology to be a progressive force, which induces individuals to use new instruments. Ceremonial institutions prevent technological change and create barriers such as social stratification, conventions, customs and ideology (Ayres 1962). The accumulation of knowledge is therefore important not only for individuals but for the society as a whole because it nurtures progressive forces.

The kind of knowledge described by old institutionalists is very different from the specific knowledge advocated by the knowledge-based economy in order to improve labor productivity (Gagnon M. A. 2007). We may say briefly that knowledge is the whole set of information individuals learn from institutional context. People are rational in the sense that they act in the most effective way given the institutional context they are in.[6] Because of the shortcomings of the traditional mainstream economic literature, we suggest a more suitable expression to denote "human capital," namely "quality of the workforce." The concept of quality has an intrinsically historical nature because it changes over time according to the needs of different societies. The expression "quality of workers" wants to capture the capacity of workers to produce a "quality output" (the output with some requested characteristics) thanks to a number of skills and personal capabilities specified, formally or informally, by the employer and by the society.

How can we define quality? The word "quality" reminds of a number of attributes that an object or a person has so as to be able to relate to the environment it/(s)he belongs to. In any case, it is a relative concept. Usually, the characteristics needed by workers are specified by a contract or by an informal interview.[7] A more educated and trained worker, however, could not earn a higher wage if the institutional context has a number of formal or informal institutions (collective bargaining, welfare state but also corruption and rent seeking) that cut the link between individual wage and level of education. In other words, the kind of knowledge each society is endowed with varies according to its institutional framework and this induces individuals to develop certain "capabilities" rather than others.[8]

Labor Quality and Active Citizenship

Quality of the workforce (or labor quality) is a more comprehensive definition than human capital as it includes not only education but also all the other capabilities (health, longevity, psychological conditions, psychomotor-based skills, cognitive capabilities and social relationships—David and Foray 2001)[9] that affect the workers' productivity. Labor quality can be considered to be part of the more general notion of "active citizenship," fully explained hereafter (European Commission 2002). According to this view, public education policies should aim at creating not only a productive worker but also a "quality citizen," that is, a citizen who participates actively in social, political and economic life (active citizenship). This view is already present in many policy statements. For instance the European Commission openly declares that: *In a knowledge society education and training rank among the highest political priorities. Acquiring and continuously updating and upgrading a high level of knowledge, skills and competencies is considered a prerequisite for the personal development of all citizens and for participation in all aspects of society from active citizenship through to labor market integration* (European Commission 2002: 4). In other words, as Commons anticipated in 1913, an effective educational system should develop the individual capabilities necessary to be active in all aspects of social life. An individual whose capabilities are well developed will also be economically active and capable of participating in the labor market. However, it is important to recall that this set of capabilities varies across societies according to their formal and informal institutions; not surprisingly we can have institutions that allow individuals to invest in capabilities that can stifle changes and create the conditions for "social necrosis" (see the contribituon of Dewey (1916) who explained the difference between formal and informal education and the importance of the social environment).[10] In other words, the propensity individuals have to be active citizens and so to participate in all dimensions of social life is affected by the institutional context they are in. This implication can be easily tested using econometric analysis where proxies of the quality of the workforce are regressed on measures of institutional quality.

Data Description

There is a lack of empirical research on the quality of the workforce and of institutions.[11] The present study aims at investigating the relationship between lifelong learning (as a proxy of active citizenship) and the quality of institutions.[12] The measurement of "active citizenship" is obviously difficult, but we have chosen the percentage of individuals involved in a lifelong learning program[13] as its proxy. Lifelong learning arrangements are considered also to be an indicator of the government's commitment to the educational and training system, in order to create "active citizenship" as described above. Data on lifelong learning have been sourced from Eurostat (http://epp.eurostat.ec.europa.eu/portal/page/portal/statistics/search_database). The quality of institutions has long been debated in economic theory, but empirical contributions have been insufficient and complex (Kaufmann et al. 2007a). The main difficulty in measuring institutional quality arises from the composite definition of institutions, which have a variety of dimensions.[14] The data on institutional quality are provided by Kaufmann et al. (2007) (http://info.worldbank.org/governance/wgi/sc_country.asp), who also give a detailed explanation on how variables have been constructed.

The data-set is made of eleven countries (Austria, Denmark, Finland, France, Germany, Italy, Netherland, Norway, Spain, Sweden, United Kingdom), observed over the period 1996–2006. Lifelong learning is measured by Eurostat as the "percentage of *persons aged 25 to 64 . . . who received education or training in the four weeks preceding the survey" over "the total population of the same age group."* The worldwide governance dataset by Kaufmann et al. (2007) includes governance indicators for 100 countries over the period 1996–2006. The indicators are constructed by aggregating data on the perception of governance coming from 31 different sources. The indexes vary between −2.5 and 2.5 where larger values refer to better outcomes. The six dimensions measured by Kaufmann et al. (2007) are:

Regulatory quality (RQ) ability of the government to formulate and implement sound policies and regulations that permit and promote private sector development.

Control of corruption (CoC): the extent to which elites and private interests exercise public power for private gain, including both petty and grand forms of corruption, as well as capture of the state.

Rule of law (RoL): the extent to which agents have confidence in and abide by the rules of society and in particular the quality of contract enforcement, the police and the courts, as well as the likelihood of crime and violence.

Political stability and absence of violence (PI): perception of likelihood that the government will be destabilized or overthrown by unconstitutional or violent means, including domestic violence and terrorism.

Voice and accountability (VA): the extent to which a country's citizens are able to participate in selecting their government, as well as freedom of expression and association and free media.

Government effectiveness (GE): the quality of public services, the civil service and the degree of its independence from political pressures, the quality of policy formulation and implementation, and the credibility of the government's commitment to such policies.

The data on lifelong learning are shown in Figure 1, while the Kaufmann indicators for our data-set are plotted in Figures 2–7 (see Appendix 1). For both sets of variables, Italy is the worst performer, whereas Sweden and Denmark are the best ones.

The empirical specification we use is rather straightforward:

$$LL_{it} = \alpha_i + \beta_1 GE_{it-1} + \beta_2 PI_{it-1} + \beta_3 VA_{it-1} + \beta_4 CoC_{it-1} + \beta_5 RoL_{it-1} + \beta_6 RQ_{it-1} + u_{it} \quad (1)$$

Essentially our dependent variable (LL) is regressed on the lagged values of the six indexes of institutional quality. The Kaufmann indexes have been changed in such a way that they are now all positive. We control for endogeneity by introducing the lagged values of the instituional variables. In order to control for time heterogeneity we also add a set of time dummies. To be able to take into account the specific nature of the dependent variable and the fact that there may be unobserved time-invariant characteristics that could be correlated with the explanatory variables, we estimate a fractional response model for panel data. Papke and Wooldridge (2008) show that in the case of a balanced panel data-set (with few time periods), unobserved time-invariant heterogeneity is controlled for by adding the time averages of all explanatory variables to the fractional probit model. All models are estimated with cluster-robust standard errors. To be able to use this estimator, we will have to use the balanced components of the panel data for the years 2002 to 2006.

Results

Table 1 shows the yearly mean of the variables used for the regression, while the marginal effects of Equation (1) are presented in Table 2. The z values have been computed by using cluster robust standard errors. Time dummies have been added to all specifications along with time averages of the independent variables. The estimates from Table 2 give some interesting insights on the relationship between the quality of institutions and the percentage of individuals involved in lifelong learning programs. First of all, we notice that Voice and Accountability, Rule of Law and the index of Political Stability are significant and have the expected positive sign. Unsur-

Table 1

Yearly mean of the main variables

Year	1996	1998	2000	2002	2003	2004	2005	2006
Percentage of individuals involved in lifelong learning programs	9.32	9.40	12.09	11.72	15.42	16.44	17.14	17.26
Regulatory quality	1.13	1.27	1.45	1.51	1.53	1.53	1.43	1.42
Rule of law	1.61	1.59	1.64	1.64	1.61	1.62	1.65	1.70
Political stability	1.00	1.07	1.12	1.10	0.95	0.85	0.83	0.80
Government effectiveness	1.94	1.79	1.81	1.87	1.84	1.75	1.68	1.63
Voice & accountability	1.28	1.39	1.39	1.37	1.38	1.59	1.51	1.48
Control of corruption	1.87	1.90	1.91	1.90	1.90	1.86	1.79	1.80

Sources: Eurostat and Worldbank http://epp.eurostat.ec.europa.eu/portal/page/portal/statistics/search_database; http://info.worldbank. org/governance/wgi/sc_country.asp.

Table 2

Fractional probit model; marginal effects

Independent Variables	Marginl Effect	Z
Political Instability (lagged one period)	0.11	2.66
Government Effectiveness (lagged one period)	−0.016	−0.38
Regulatory Quality (lagged one period)	−0.077	−3.63
Rule of Law (lagged one period)	0.17	1.73
Voice and Accountability (lagged one period)	0.28	3.21
Control of Corruption (lagged one period)	−0.030	−0.52
Constant	0.080	0.56
N	55	

Note: t-ratios computed using cluster robust standard errors. Year dummies and time averages of the independent variables have been added to the specification but estimates are not reported.

prisingly, Political Stability is one of the institutional characteristics most powerfully and permanently correlated to lifelong learning. Countries that are perceived to be more unstable are also the ones where the individuals are less willing to enter lifelong learning because they run the risk of not being able to reap the benefits of the investment in education later on.

The Rule of Law index is significant and positive as well. This indicator measures the extent to which citizens have confidence in and abide by the rules of society. In a sense, this variable indicates a dimension of "social capital," that is, the trust people have in the institutions of the society where they live. If the trust is not sufficiently high, any investment may appear useless to individuals. Equally it is not surprising that the Voice and Accountability index has a positive impact on lifelong learning. Indeed "Voice and Accountability" measures the extent to which the citizens are free to select their government as well as participate in the social and political life. Therefore individuals in a society where citizens can freely express their opinions and associate are also more willing to invest in further education as they know the additional knowledge gained through further education can be of some use to the society.

The Government Effectiveness index has a negative sign but it is not significant. This is not surprising: this index captures the quality of the executive and of the civil service and there is no strong reason to believe that the quality of the institutional architecture can affect the willingness of citizens to invest in further education. Equally, the Quality of the Regulatory Environment has a negative sign (but this time it is a significant variable). In other words, if a government can implement sound regulatory policies that can help the development of the private sector it does not affect the willingness of citizens to get into lifelong learning programs, so suggesting that investing in further education is not necessarily driven by the desire to participate in the labor market.

Interestingly enough, the Control of Corruption index does not seem to have a significant impact on the percentage of individuals getting into lifelong learning, suggesting that at least in European countries individuals' decision of whether or not to investing in human capital is not influenced by the presence of anti-corruption policies (of course, this may not be true in developing countries where it is well-known that accumulation of human capital is influenced by the extent of corruption).

One important policy implication from the empirical analysis is that reforms of the educational system may be useless if the overall institutional context creates perverse incentives that do not support the desired outcome. Indeed, just introducing measures to increase the number of individuals involved in lifelong learning may not necessarily have such an effect if the government is perceived to be so unstable that the investment in education will not produce any personal benefit. Also, if a society is characterized by ceremonial institutions (in Ayres' parlance) it could tend to preserve the existing status quo and the privileges of the existing social groups. In this situation, individuals will be better off by becoming a member of these social groups[15] rather than acquiring additional knowledge.

Conclusions

The primary purpose of this paper is to challenge the traditional idea of "human capital" and propose that it is the quality of the workers that matters, where this is defined as the set of capabilities that allow workers to function in a specific institutional and historical context. The main implication of our results is that individuals may be willing to acquire additional knowledge if they expect that this additional knowldege will help them to contribute to the society where they live. To support this argument we have used insights from both the Institutional and Evolutionary economics and drawn the conclusion that the quality of the workforce is affected by the institutional environment where the workers live and that therefore it can vary across institutional contexts.

We have also shown that this last point is empirically relevant by testing the extent to which the quality of institutions can affect the quality of the workforce proxied by the *country-level percentage of individuals involved in a lifelong learning program.* Indicators of institutional qualities are sourced from the well-known Kaufmann et al. (2007) data-set on governance indicators. Our empirical analysis is conducted on a data-set of 11 European countries observed over 1996–2006. The empirical results confirm our expectations that institutions affect the quality of a country's workforce. Of course the study is not exhaustive and we think additional steps are necessary in two respects: a) first we need to measure "quality of the workforce" and institutional quality more accurately; b) we need also to understand what factors drive the differences in institutional quality across the European countries. Indeed, the available data are far from being complete with respect to the so complex notion of institution that includes a lot of unmeasured dimensions (like informal rules, customs, religion, culture etc.) in addition to the governance indicators.

Notes

1. In his words "commons sense" is: *a complex set of beliefs and propositions about fundamental features of the world which individuals assume in whatever they do in ordinary life* (Lee 2002: 790).

2. The Sixties witnessed an unprecedented growth of papers focusing on the accumulation of "human capital" and its impact on wages (Schultz 1961;

Becker 1964; Kiker 1966). In this context, human capital was defined indirectly as: "expenditures on education, training, medical care, . . . produce human, not physical or financial, capital because you cannot separate a person from his or her knowledge, skills, health, or values the way it is possible to move financial and physical assets while the owner stays put" (Becker 1993: 16). Since factors different from education, training and ability may affect the wage profile the validity of the Becker-Mincer human capital approach has been widely tested.

3. The Old Institutional Economics encompasses mainly the contributions of Veblen, Commons and Mitchell, contributors of the American Institutionalism. The New Institutional Economics—terms coined by Williamson (Chavance 2008: 45)—was borne in opposition to the term Old Institutional Economics. While the first recognized the importance of institutions while mantaining the neoclassical modeling, the second uses the "institutions" to criticise neoclassical orthodoxy (Chavance 2008: 45).

4. Frank Albert Fetter (1863–1949) was an American economist belonging to the Austrian School.

5. Human capital investment implies without any doubt a financial investment. Every financial investment should ensure a financial return, but in the case of investment in human capital, the return is not guaranteed as it depends on the institutional context (including wage bargaining, income distribution etc.). See Bottone G. (2008).

6. For example, in a country where corruption is pervasive, people will tend to use bribes when pursuing their private benefit.

7. In this case, economic theory offers many solutions to the problems of asymmetric information between employer and employee.

8. The idea that "*institutions crystallize both knowledge and ignorance*" (Chavance 2008: 7) was already suggested by authors of the younger "German historical school" and of the American institutionalism (Chavance 2008: 7).

9. An implicit definition of quality of the workforce is given by Gregory Clark (2006) who defines it as the discipline and attitudes toward work shaped by social beliefs and institutions. In other words, historical and cultural patterns are the ground from where formal and informal educational efforts may contribute to the quality of the workforce.

10. It seems useful to quote some important passages from *Democracy and Education* (1916):

> Informal education is important but incidental . . . Formal education allows transmitting from generation to generation all the resources and achievements of a complex society. Hence, one of the weightiest problems with which the philosophy of education has to cope is the method of keeping a proper balance between the informal and the

formal, the incidental and the intentional, modes of education . . . (Chapter 1, par. 3).

When we have the outcome of the process in mind, we speak of education as shaping, forming, moulding activity, that is, a shaping into the standard form of social activity. Just because life signifies not bare passive existence (supposing there is such a thing), but a way of acting, environment or medium signifies what enters into this activity as a sustaining or frustrating condition (Chapter 2, par. 1). A being whose activities are associated with others has a social environment. What he does and what he can do depend upon the expectations, demands, approvals, and condemnations of others . . . (Chapter 2, par. 2)

For it assumed that the aim of education is to enable individuals to continue their education or that the object and reward of learning is continued capacity for growth. Now this idea cannot be applied to all the members of a society except where intercourse of man with man is mutual, and except where there is adequate provision for the reconstruction of social habits and institutions by means of wide stimulation arising from equitably distributed interests. And this means a democratic society . . . . (Chapter 8, par. 1)

11. For estimates of the quality of the workforce in the euro area, see: Schwerdt and Turunen (2006).

12. An implication is that in a country where the quality of institutions is poor, citizens may not be interested in acquiring the educational capabilities needed to participate to the social and economic life of the country.

13. European Commission (2002: 4) will later on define "lifelong learning" as: *the overarching strategy of European co-operation in education and training policies and for the individual. The lifelong learning approach is an essential policy strategy for the development of citizenship, social cohesion, employment and for individual fulfilment.*

14. *The set of formal (rules, laws, constitutions) and informal (norms of behavior, conventions, self-imposed codes of conduct) rules and their enforcement mechanisms, governing and shaping the behavior of individuals and organizations in society* (Straub S. 2000: 6). Synthetically, North (1994) considers institutions to be the incentive structure of a society.

15. Italy is a good example, where several attempts have been made to reform the educational system but these have always been opposed by all the involved parts (students, teachers, trade unions etc.).

References

Ayres, C. (1961). *Toward a Reasonable Society: The Values of Industrial Civilization.* Austin: University of Texas Press.
——. (1962). *The Theory of Economic Progress.* 2nd ed. New York: Schocken Books.
Becker, G. (1964). *Human Capital.* Chicago: University of Chicago Press.
Becker, G. S. (1993). *Human Capital, A Theoretical and Empirical Analysis with Special Reference to Education.* National Bureau of Economic Research. Chicago: University of Chicago Press.
Bottone, G. (2008). "Human Capital: An Institutional Economics Point of View." *ISAE WP* n. 107, available at www.isae.it.
Chavance, B. (2008). *Institutional Economics.* Routledge.
Commons, R. J. (1964). *Labour and Administration.* New York: Sentry Press.
——. (1934). *Institutional Economics. Its Place in Political Economy.* New York: Macmillan.
David, P., and D. Foray. (2001). "An Introduction to the Economy of the Knowledge Society." Department of Economics. *Discussion Paper Series,* n. 84. December. Available at http://www.economics.ox.ac.uk/research/wp/pdf/paper084.pdf
Dewey (1916). *Democracy and Education.* Available at http://www.ilt.columbia.edu/publications/dewey.html.
European Commission. (2002). Directorate-General for Education and Culture. "European Report on Quality Indicators of Lifelong Learning." Report based on the work of the Working Group on Quality Indicators, June. Available at http://www.bologna-berlin2003.de/pdf/Report.pdf.
Fetter, F. A. (1930). "Capital." In *Encyclopaedia of the Social Sciences.* Eds. Edwin R. A. Seligman and Alvindr Johnson. Vol. 3. New York: Macmillan, pp. 187–190.
Gagnon, M.-A. (2007). "Capital Power and Knowledge According to Thorstein Veblen: Reintepreting the Knowledge–Based Economy." *Journal of Economic Issues* 41(2): 593–600.
Gregory, C. (2006). *A Farewell to Alms: A Brief Economic History of the World.* Princeton: Princeton University Press.
Harcourt, G. C. (1982). *Some Cambridge Controversies in the Theory of Capital.* Cambridge: Cambridge University Press.
Hodgson, G. M. (2001). *How Economics Forgot History: The Problem of Historical Specificity in Social Science.* London and New York: Routledge.
Kaufmann, D., A. Kraay, and M. Mastruzzi. (2007). "Governance Matters VI: Aggregate and Individual Governance Indicators 1996–2006." *World Bank WP* n. 4280, July.

———. (2007a). "The Worldwide Governance Indicators Project: Answering the Critics." *World Bank Policy Research Working Paper* n. 4149, March.

Kiker, B. F. (1966). "Historical Roots of the Concept of Human Capital." *Journal of Political Economy* 74(5): 481.

Lee, F. S. (2002). "Theory Creation and the Methodological Foundation of Post Keynesian Economics." *Cambridge Journal of Economics* 26(6): 789–804.

Machiavelli, N. (1513). *Il Principe.* Available at http://www.classicitaliani.it/machiav/critica/Pricipe_traduzione_Bonghi.htm, Chapter VI, paragraph 5.

Mises, L. (1996) (1949). *Human Action: A Treatise on Economics.* 4th Revised Edition. San Francisco: Fox & Wilkes.

Muerga, E. F. (2007). "The Economic Behaviour of Human Beings: The Institutional/Post-Keynesian Model." *Journal of Economic Issues* 42(3): 709–726.

North, D. C. (1994). "Economic Performance Through Time." *American Economic Review* 84(3): 359–368.

OECD (1998). "Human Capital Investment: An International Comparison." OECD.

Papke, L. E., and J. M. Wooldridge. (2008). "Panel Data Methods for Fractional Response Variables with an Application to Test Pass Rates." *Journal of Econometrics* 145(1–2): 121–133.

Robinson, J. (1979). *Collected Economic Papers—Volume Five.* Oxford: Basil Blackwell.

Schultz, T. W. (1961). "Investment in Human Capital." *American Economic Review* 51: 1–17.

Schumpeter, J. A. (1954). *History of Economic Analysis.* Oxford and New York: Oxford University Press.

Schwerdt, G., and J. Turunen. (2006). "Growth in Euro Area Labour Quality." *ECB wp* n. 575, January.

Straub, S. (2000). "Empirical Determinants of Good institutions: Do We Know Anything? *Inter-American Development Bank.* WP 423. Research Department. June.

Veblen, T. B. (1901). "Industrial and Pecuniary Employment." In R. Tilman (Ed.) 1993.

———. (1919). *The Place of Science in Modern Civilization and Other Essays.* New York: Huebsch.

Appendix 1:

Figure 1

Lifelong learning (1996–2006)

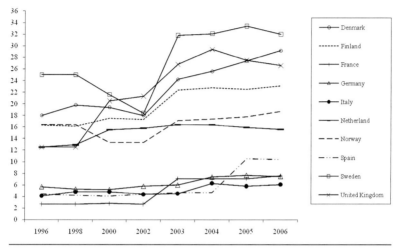

Sources: Eurostat http://epp.eurostat.ec.europa.eu/portal/page/portal/statistics/search_database.

Figure 2

Political stability

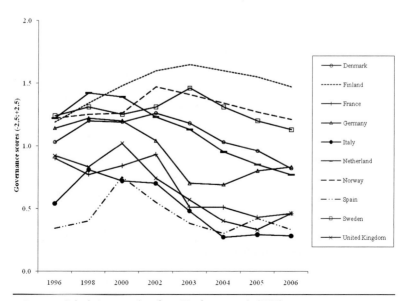

Sources: Calculations on data from Kaufmann et al. (2007).

Figure 3

Government effectiveness

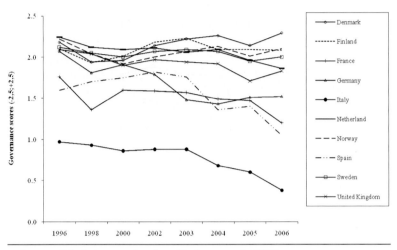

Sources: Calculations on data from Kaufmann et al. (2007).

Figure 4

Control of corruption

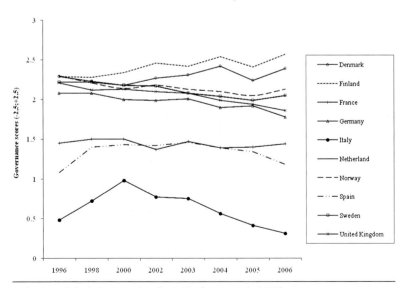

Sources: Calculations on data from Kaufmann et al. (2007).

Figure 5

Rule of law

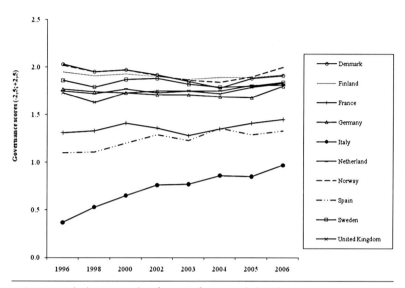

Sources: Calculations on data from Kaufmann et al. (2007).

Figure 6

Regulatory quality

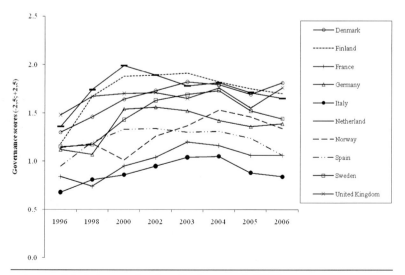

Sources: Calculations on data from Kaufmann et al. (2007).

Figure 7

Voice and accountability

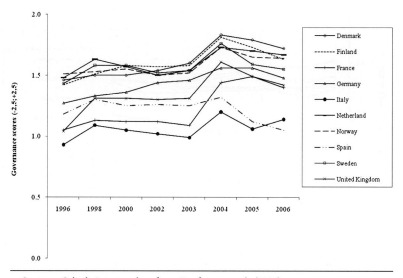

Sources: Calculations on data from Kaufmann et al. (2007).

On Norms: A Typology with Discussion

By Matthew Interis*

Abstract. There is a lack of consensus in the literature, spanning multiple fields, on what exactly a norm is and furthermore on the characteristics differentiating types of norms. This paper provides definitions and a simple typology of norms with a focus on useful, objective distinctions. It is hoped that such a typology will add to the scientific rigor of communication, modeling, and clarity of thought on norms within economics and possibly other disciplines. The viability of "more complete" typologies, which often suffer from a lack of clear criteria for differentiating types of norms, is questioned. Two main properties of a norm are emphasized: (1) whether or not the behavior is simply what *is done* or whether it is what one *should do*, and (2) the source of sanctions for violating a norm, whether oneself, others, both or neither.

Introduction

Even a preliminary investigation into the literature on norms, be it in economics or elsewhere such as psychology or sociology, will reveal some of the vast differences in how authors define a norm, differentiate types of norms, and model norms. The many conceptualizations indicate, perhaps, that there is no standard way of thinking about norms and that approaches to conceptualizing norms are *ad hoc*, and indeed this is true. To a certain extent this must remain the case as norms are important as technical constructs in many academic fields and across many professions, and furthermore the idea of a norm is readily familiar to the common person, making complete consensus all but impossible. Yet, for those of us who deal with norms in a somewhat technical way, I believe a consensus on a few basic concepts pertaining to norms is attainable without much difficulty, and

*Mississippi State University, Department of Agricultural Economics, P.O. Box 5187, Mississippi State, MS 39762. E-mail: interis@agecon.msstate.edu. Phone: (662) 325-4787.
I thank Alan Randall and two anonymous referees for comments on earlier drafts.
American Journal of Economics and Sociology, Vol. 70, No. 2 (April, 2011).

will facilitate understanding both across fields and, of personal importance to me and I hope others, within economics. While a comprehensive overview of the norms literature is beyond the scope of this paper, the present goal is rather to examine sources of confusion within the academic discussion of norms, and to provide a simple typology that does not suffer from the ambiguity of some existing typologies.

What is a Norm?

I begin by discussing the term "norm" itself. As the purpose of this paper is to justify the practicality and validity of the presented typology of norms, it is perhaps best to contrast extant treatments of norms with my own. I define a norm as: a voluntary behavior that is prevalent within a given reference group. There are three main components to the given definition: that a norm is a voluntary behavior, that it must be prevalent, and that it depends on a reference group. I explore each of these in turn.

Arguing that a norm is a behavior may at first seem pointless since most people would agree with the claim. Yet because of the perhaps messy language occurring in the literature, it is possible that this technicality would not be understood.[1] Cialdini et al. (1990) think of a norm as a behavior, emphasizing that a distinction necessary to make when discussing norms is whether a norm is what people generally *do* or whether it is what people *should do*; the norm is the *doing*. Voss (2001), writing from a game-theoretical perspective on norms, defines them as "behavioral regularities in a population of actors," which differs only slightly from my definition given above. While the "population of actors" is akin to the "given reference group," there is a slight difference between a "prevalent behavior" and a "behavioral regularity," the difference being whether the norm is the behavior or the regularity. This difference is trivial, however, since the definition of "regularity" is "something that is regular" (Merriam-Webster's 1994), and what is a behavioral something that is regular other than a regular behavior? In Thibaut and Kelley (1986) a norm is defined as "a behavioral rule that is accepted, at least to some degree, by both members of a dyad" or by a "sizable number" of people in a large group. The word "rule" here could mean something close to "regularity" in the previous example ("As a rule . . .") or could be a more formal rule such as "Stand up when someone enters the room." I would argue still that the norm is technically the doing of the act, and not the rule itself, which specifies the action to be undertaken. Is it more natural to say that "the norm is that people stand up when someone enters the room" or that "the norm is: stand up when someone enters the room"? The difference is subtle, but most would agree that the norm is the "doing" of what the rule says. Coleman (1987) confuses the issue by calling norms "expectations about action . . . which express what action is right and what action is wrong." Rather, his definition would be better phrased as: "a norm is a behavior about which there are expectations as to whether it is right or wrong." Norms are differentiated from beliefs, values, ethics (a system of moral values or beliefs) and the like by the property that norms are behaviors. Beliefs, values, and ethics perhaps *influence* behavior. I place the modifier "voluntary" in the definition simply to differentiate between behaviors over which people make choices and others that are biologically, physically, or otherwise unavoidable such as "people sweat when they feel hot" or "people fall back down when they jump."

Their prevalence (or "regularity" in the sense of Voss (2001)) is the main criterion I use to distinguish norms from other types of behavior. The Merriam-Webster's (1994) dictionary gives three pertinent definitions for a norm: "1. an authoritative standard: model," "2. a principle of right action binding upon members of a group and serving to guide, control, or regulate proper and acceptable behavior," and "3c. a widespread or usual practice, procedure or custom." The second definition, using the phrase "right action," hints at a behavior that is obligatory since what is "right" behavior, either by individual or social standards, is often obligatory. The third definition simply states that the behavior is widespread. The word "authoritative" in the first definition could either refer to an authority on what is done, or on what should be done. Asking two questions would help to clarify the matter since casual observation suggests that when people hear the word "norm" there is indeed a mix of impressions about a behavior being both prevalent and injunctive (both or either of which may distinguish a norm from other types of behavior) as in the Cialdini et al. (1990) distinction: is a behavior that is prevalent but not obligatory considered a "norm"? and, is a behavior that is obligatory but not prevalent (or even practiced at all) considered a "norm"? To answer these questions, I examine stylized cases.

Consider, for example, the choice of Americans to drive a personal vehicle to work each day. Although prevalent, it hardly seems obligatory, in the sense that if I do not need to drive to work there is no reason I should feel obligated to do so barring concerns of practicality. Is driving to work a "norm" then? Alternatively, when I take the bus to work, I typically follow a "board the bus in the order in which you arrived at the bus stop" rule, or "first come, first served." In the past, I have admonished my wife for being rude by boarding the bus before others who have been waiting at the bus stop longer. She promptly responds that no one follows that rule. After observation I discovered that she is likely correct, at least generally speaking. There are other rules that could lead to similar behavior such as the "be considerate" rule (get on the bus, but don't be pushy about it), or the "ladies/others first" rule, but I have no reason to believe that anyone else follows the "first come, first served" rule as rigorously as I do.[2] Often, boarding the bus is a mad scramble between self-interested bus-riders to get on first (especially when it is raining). So is boarding the bus in the order in which you arrived at the stop a "norm"?

By introspection, the reader will presumably feel as though the first instance, that of driving to work, is a norm, whereas the second, boarding the bus in the order in which you arrived at the stop, is not (recall that language is a matter of convention). Although I feel obliged to follow the first come, first served rule at the bus stop (how do I know? Because I get an uncomfortable feeling when my wife gets on the bus "out of line."), yet I do not feel that it is a "norm."

A norm is therefore a behavior more characterized by its being prevalent than being obligatory; an obligatory behavior, without being prevalent, is not a "norm" according to the given definition. What exactly it *is* I leave to someone else to determine. Of course I hope this conclusion I have drawn is not dependent upon the specificity of my examples, but again, it is ultimately a matter of agreement. So when Cialdini et al. (1990) refer to a norm in the sense of a behavior that people are obliged to engage in, by the above conclusion I claim that there is an implication that the behavior is prevalent (to whatever extent) within some reference group in order to justify the use of the term "norm." Of course, *how* prevalent a behavior must be to be considered a norm is up for debate (see Jones 2005). As a final remark on this point, the word "norm" is derived from the Latin "norma" meaning a carpenter's square (Merriam-Webster's 1994), which is used to make the same angle (right angle) repeatedly, so there was originally no injunctive sense of the word.

The third component of the definition is that the norm depends on a given reference group. I think of tipping 15 percent at restaurants as a norm (perhaps I am cheap because others tip 20 percent standard), but someone from Central America would not consider it so, since tipping so high or at all is not customary there. Regarding the above examples, it should be asked whether driving to work is a norm within the reference group "Americans" and whether boarding the bus in order of arrival at the stop is a norm amongst bus-riders in Columbus, Ohio, for example.

Descriptive Versus Injunctive Norms

Norms are often used to *explain* various decisions that seem inexplicable based on traditional economic analysis (see Becker 1996 for an enlightening discussion). Alternatively, they can be viewed as behaviors *resulting from* signaling equilibria, as in E. Posner (2000) or Bernheim (1994). This distinction is similar to the one made by Cialdini et al. (1990) who call norms that are simply what people do "descriptive" norms, and norms that are what people *should* do "injunctive" norms. The former have no effect on behavior and simply describe a regularity of behavior. The latter do affect behavior, the word "injunctive" implying a requirement "to do or to refrain from doing a specified act" (Merriam-Webster's 1994). R. Posner (1997) clarifies that a norm is a behavior that is regularly complied with (the descriptive norm sense); however, it is not necessary that people have preferences over the norm as Becker (1996) requires (in which case the norm would have an effect on behavior, the injunctive sense).

The sense of "should" referred to by Cialdini et al. (1990) is "rules or beliefs about what constitutes morally approved and disapproved conduct." The use of the word "morally" indicates that not only are there incentives to follow a norm, but that the incentives specifically relate to moral standards of "right and wrong" as judged by some subjective, but commonly held, standard. I use the phrase "injunctive norm" in a more general sense (without reference to morals specifically) to refer to any norm that one is obliged to follow due to the threat of sanctioning for its violation. Without specifically asking someone, it is not possible to tell whether they engage in a behavior because of moral reasoning (I give money to a homeless person because I think it is the "right" thing to do) or prudential reasoning (I give money to a homeless person because I think he will harm me otherwise) or other reasoning. I do not include under injunctive norms those that are enforced through what Posner and Rasmusen (1999) call "automatic sanctions," whereby violation of a norm results in negative consequences due to coordination failure among agents, such as when one drives on the incorrect side of the road. Rather, because norms are psychological and sociological phenomena, I am referring to sanctions originating from oneself or others, which are inflicted voluntarily. Jones (2007) makes a similar distinction between what he calls "conditioning" (rewards and punishments) from one's "fellow creatures" or from the "natural world," for example (Jones'), shivering due to failure to wear a shirt.

The Role of Sanctioning

There seems to be agreement, specifically in the economics literature, that norms involve sanctioning (for example, Grasmick et al. 1991; Holländer 1990; Posner and Rasmusen 1999; and Voss 2001 all emphasize sanctions).[3] Horne (2001) incorporates sanctions into her definition, stating that norms are "rules, about which there is at least some consensus, that are enforced through social sanctions."

The source of sanctioning has implications for the modeling of how injunctive norms affect behavior. For example, suppose an individual has utility that depends on an action taken and any sanctioning resulting from that action being taken:

$$U = u(x, s(x, m))$$

where x is the action taken, m is the injunctive norm action, and s is sanctioning that occurs, which is a function both of the action taken and the norm. For a self-sanctioned norm (sanctioning for violating the norm is self-imposed), the function s could be independent of one's action being observed by others. Sanctioning could perhaps be a function of the deviation of behavior from the norm, $s(x-m)$, or take on another functional form. An example of such a self-sanctioned norm could be giving an offering when attending church. One who gives nothing to the offering plate may not be sanctioned by others, but yet may self-sanction, for example, in the form of guilt.

For an externally-sanctioned norm, sanctioning stems from external sources and so depends on observation. It may look something like:

$$s = s(x, m, p)$$

where p is, for example, the proportion of the population that observes the action, or perhaps a probability density function of being observed. An example of an externally-sanctioned norm as defined here could be "picking one's nose." Perhaps one picks his nose and feels no worse off so long as no one sees him. But because the behavior is not well accepted in our society, he might be ridiculed (incur external sanctioning) if he were caught picking.[4]

A key point to remember is that norms are social phenomena. As Voss (2001) notes, "norms exist, in a sense, independently from the consciousness of individuals." The source of sanctioning (the term "injunctive" also) indicates a generalization over the reference group to which the norm applies. For example, the norm "holding the door open for someone behind you" is primarily sanctioned externally; one is more likely to regret not doing so as a result of scorn from the person in whose face the door was shut, rather than self-imposed guilt. Similarly, the norm of making an offering in church is primarily sanctioned by oneself. These are generalizations over the entire population of potential norm adherents. Any given individual, however, may experience sanctioning externally or internally. Perhaps more commonly, one experiences both self and external sanctions for violating a norm. For example, perhaps if one lies to someone he feels bad because he believes it is wrong to lie, but if the other person finds out, he will feel even worse (especially, perhaps, if the other person finds out before he has had the chance to confess). An obvious starting point in modeling this case is a linear combination of the two modeling suggestions above. From an experimental point of view, however, one cannot control for self-sanctioning anyway; only external sanctioning can be limited. For modeling purposes, assumptions about sanctioning should be clearly stated.

Summary

A diagrammatic summary is presented in Figure 1, and it adopts the labels used in Cialdini et al. (1990) to indicate presence of sanctioning.[5] According to Voss (2001), norms can be thought of as part of a subset of the class of conventions, distinguished from conventions in general by the necessity of sanctioning (similar to Lindbeck 1997). Voss' definition of "convention" is similar to the definition of a descriptive norm. As an example of this classification system, consider Kolstad's (2007) definition of a social norm from the evolutionary game theory literature: "(1) a behavioral regularity; (2) that is based on a socially shared belief of how one ought to behave; (3) which triggers the enforcement of the prescribed behavior by informal social sanctions."

Figure 1

A Typology of Norms

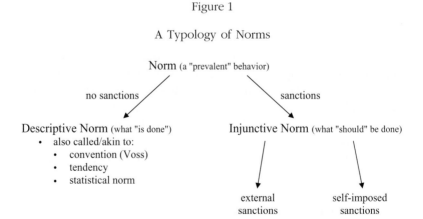

From point (1) we determine that the behavior is a norm, point (2) indicates it is injunctive, and point (3) indicates it is externally sanctioned; it is an externally-sanctioned (injunctive) norm by the classification system in the figure. Bernheim (1994) clarifies terms further by calling a norm that is persistent and widely followed a "custom" and a norm that is transitory and confined to a small group a "fad." As a final note, how behaviors transition from being sanctioned externally to being sanctioned internally (self-sanctioning) is an interesting but young vein of research within economics (see, for example, Rodriguez-Sickert et al. 2008; Bisin and Verdier 2001), although Sherif (1966) gives an early effort in the social psychology literature.

Comments

I have no objection to modifiers of the word "norm" that provide context, such as "conversational," "smoking," or "outgroup" norms, which generally might describe the situation or group to which the norm applies. With the exception of these context modifiers (which make no claims about the inherent nature of a norm), I question, however, the usefulness of distinctions that go beyond (1) whether or not there are sanctions for violating a norm, and (2) whether the sanctions originate externally or internally, as presented here.

Gibbs (1965) provides a typology of norms that at first glance appears to be one of the most comprehensive. It accounts for nineteen different classes of norms, which are distinguished from each other by: whether or not there is a collective evaluation of the behavior (whether or not it "ought" to be done), whether or not there is a collective expectation about the behavior (whether or not it will be done), whether there is a high or low probability of incurring sanctioning, whether the sanctioner has a particular status, and whether the sanctions include the use of force or not. The last two criteria seem to lack interest to the general discussion on norms as they are somewhat specific. The first two are similar to the distinction between a descriptive norm and an injunctive norm given here. However, even Gibbs admits that there are conceptual problems with his typology, the main one being that there is no meaningful criterion that can be applied to a collective evaluation, collective expectation, and probability of sanctioning. Indeed, there is no clear way to determine whether the probability of sanctions is high or low. Because this is the case, there seems to be no meaningful way in which to apply this criterion. I think the reason it is also difficult for him to set a criterion for collective evaluation and collective expectation is because he fails to integrate these concepts with sanctioning. In the typology presented above, if there is the possibility of sanctioning, then this is a signal that there is a collective evaluation of behavior. If a behavior is a descriptive norm, people will likely have a collective expectation about the behavior (that it will be undertaken).

Bernheim's (1994) definitions of "custom" and "fad" also suffer from this same problem. Exactly how persistent (in terms of time) and how widely followed must a norm be to be considered a custom? How transient must a norm be to be a fad?[6] There is no obvious answer to these questions. At least the terms "custom" and "fad" are common enough in everyday speech that most people will have the understanding that indeed the former is persistent over time and relatively widely followed, and that the latter passes in and out of fashion relatively quickly. While fads, customs, and conventions might fit under the umbrella of "norms" in common speech, it is difficult to see how to differentiate these ideas, except through arbitrary distinctions of time and prevalence, for example.

Morris (1956) proposes a typology based on the salience of norms, that is, how prominent they are across a spectrum of properties (for example, number of adopters, number of different groups to which the norm applies). Each property is measured along a continuum, for example, few adopters to many adopters. Again, while discussion of such properties might be useful, for purposes of rigorous communication, there is no objective way of determining what constitutes "many" or "few" adopters. While Morris does not make the error of creating an extensive but arguably ineffective classification of norms (because of the subjective nature of the distinctions) as Gibbs does, he does call a norm that is adopted by everyone, everywhere, and that is heavily sanctioned an "absolute" norm, and one with limited application and weak enforcement a "conditional" norm. But how strongly sanctioned and widely adopted must a conditional norm be before it becomes absolute?

Lack of clear criteria to differentiate norms is one problem in the literature, and another is the lack of distinction between terms in the first place. In particular, the phrase "social norm" is used often in the literature without having any clear distinction from "norm." Authors often use the two interchangeably (Ostrom 2000; Cialdini et al. 1990; Posner and Rasmusen 1999, to name a few) and this might be forgivable since it is potentially cumbersome to write and read "social norm" repeatedly if simply "norm" will suit the purpose of communication. But the problem is that using "norm" in place of "social norm" is acceptable only if it is understood by the reader what a "social norm" is, and too often it occurs that there is no distinction made between a "social norm" and a "norm." According to the definition of a norm presented above, a norm already implies a reference group to which the behavior applies, so it is by nature "social." I mean here that the modifier "social" is often used, if implicitly so, to indicate the norm takes place in some "society," but this is so for any norm, however large or small the society happens to be. I would therefore argue that using the term "social" is redundant in this sense and generally adds little to one's understanding of the characteristics of the norm being addressed. Relating the terms "social" and "moral" to the source of sanctioning (external and internal, respectively), as proposed by Nyborg (2003), might be a convenience, but particularly the word "moral" is too closely associated with other meanings. There is no reason to believe self-sanctioning necessarily results from moral deliberation. Fehr and Fischbacher (2004) state that social norms are enforced by informal social sanctioning, but it is unclear whether this serves as a distinction from whatever "non-social" norms might be.

Conclusion

Psychological phenomena, norms are nonetheless commonly incorporated into economic theory and modeling. Yet there is a lack of consensus in the language of norms, not necessarily unique to economics. I adopt the following conceptualization of norms.

A norm is a voluntary behavior that is prevalent, to some degree, within some reference group. In general, a given behavior is not prevalent everywhere, and just how prevalent it must be is up for discussion. Norms can further be classified along two dimensions. The first is whether or not violation of the norm results in sanctioning, which I define as punishment or reward voluntarily inflicted by someone on the norm violator. If violation of a norm does result in sanctioning, it is called an "injunctive" norm. If no more can be said about a prevalent behavior other than that it is what people generally *do*, it is simply a "descriptive" norm.

The second characteristic is whether or not sanctioning for violating an injunctive norm originates from oneself (for example, guilt, loss of self-respect) or from others (for example, looks of scorn, shame, physical harm). As economists we are concerned with incentives, so distinguishing the source of sanctioning is useful since therefrom spring the incentives to follow the norm. The external sanctioning of a norm implies the necessity of observation of one's behavior. Furthermore, external sanctioning and internal sanctioning are likely to differ in terms of their nature, intensity, and other characteristics.

Besides a general lack of consensus in the literature about the important dimensions along which to classify norms, there are at least two other concerns. The first is that of unnecessary distinctions or distinctions that cannot be isolated conceptually or empirically. For example, using the probability of sanctioning as a distinguishing characteristic of norms is not useful because there is no clear delineation between a "high" and a "low" probability of sanctioning. Similarly, there is no clear criterion for how long a norm must exist to become a custom. The second problem is lack of defining terms in the first place, a main offense being the use of the phrase "social norm" when there is no clear distinction between it and a "norm."

When making these distinctions it is important to remember that norms are social phenomena and that therefore, whether or not there are sanctions for deviating from a norm, and if so, their source, is a generalization over the population of potential norm adherents. A given individual might experience self-sanctioning, external-sanctioning, both, or neither.

As one reviewer pointed out, it is difficult to judge whether simple or more expansive typologies are more useful for the researcher. My opinion is that it largely depends upon the purpose at hand. While the aim of fuller typologies is to increase clarity of communication further than simple ones, they often suffer from the problem that the distinctions lack clear, objective criteria. This actually may be acceptable in some instances when the general gist of the meaning is all that is required; the common person has a fairly standard understanding of what a fad is and what a custom is, for example. When, however, the meaning is more critical for communication, the effectiveness of more complete typologies diminishes. This might be the case in modeling that involves norms, where, for example, it makes a difference whether or not a person will receive external sanctions if caught violating an injunctive norm. A further disadvantage of more expansive typologies is that they often come with an equally expansive set of terminology that has the potential to become cumbersome. Here I have tried to make the reader aware of discrepancies in the norm literature and present an objective and useful tool that will aid communication on the topic of norms.

Notes

1. I say "perhaps messy" because it is of course possible that some authors would in fact disagree with the claim that a norm is a behavior.

2. As a matter of probability and unless I am completely crazy, others are bound to follow this rule as well, but my point is that I have no reason to say this behavior is prevalent.

3. Morris (1956) goes so far as to say that norms *always* include sanctions, in contrast to values, which never do (1956: 610).

4. Most of the literature on why people might *sanction others* for violating norms has been based on the premise that it is in the interest of those sanctioning for the norm to perpetuate. Willer et al. (2009) argue that people sometimes sanction others for violating norms in the absence of which the sanctioners themselves would be better off.

5. Sanctioning/no sanctioning and external sanctioning/self-sanctioning provide clear distinctions. The only aspect of this typology that is somewhat arbitrary is the "prevalence" of the behavior in the first place, and this is due to the conventional aspect of language. More scientifically rigorous standards often relate to the distribution of behavior around the mean.

6. Bikhchandani et al. (1992) develop a theory on the fragility of norms based on informational cascades.

References

Becker, G. (1996). *Accounting for Tastes*. Cambridge, MA: Harvard University Press.

Bernheim, B. D. (1994). "A Theory of Conformity." *Journal of Political Economy* 102(5): 841–877.

Bikhchandani, S., D. Hirshleifer, and I. Welch. (1992). "A Theory of Fads, Fashion, Custom, and Cultural Change as Informational Cascades." *Journal of Political Economy* 100(5): 992–1026.

Bisin, A., and T. Verdier. (2001). "The Economics of Cultural Transmission and the Dynamics of Preferences." *Journal of Economic Theory* 97(2): 298–319.

Cialdini, R. B., R. R. Reno, and C. A. Kallgren. (1990). "A Focus Theory of Normative Conduct: Recycling the Concept of Norms to Reduce Littering in Public Places." *Journal of Personality and Social Psychology* 58(6): 1015–1026.

Coleman, J. S. (1987). "Norms as Social Capital." In *Economic Imperialism: The Economic Method Applied Outside the Field of Economics*. Eds. Radnitzky, G. and P. Bernholz, pp. 133–153. New York: Paragon House.

Fehr, E., and U. Fischbacher. (2004). "Third-Party Punishment and Social Norms." *Evolution and Human Behavior* 5(2): 63–87.

Gibbs, J. P. (1965). "Norms: The Problem of Definition and Classification." *American Journal of Sociology* 70(5): 586–594.

Grasmick, H., R. Bursik Jr., and K. Kinsey. (1991). "Shame and Embarrassment as Deterrents to Non-Compliance with the Law: The Case of an Anti-Littering Campaign." *Environment and Behaviors* 23(2): 233–251.

Holländer, H. (1990). "A Social Exchange Approach to Voluntary Cooperation." *American Economic Review* 80(5): 1157–1167.

Horne, C. (2001). "Sociological Perspectives on the Emergence of Social Norms." In *Social Norms*. Eds. Hechter, M. and K. Opp, pp. 3–34. New York: Russell Sage Foundation.

Jones, T. (2007). "What's Done Here—Explaining Behavior in Terms of Customs and Norms." *Southern Journal of Philosophy* 45(3): 363–393.

—— (2005). "How Many New Yorkers Need to Like Bagels Before You Can Say 'New Yorkers Like Bagels?' Understanding Collective Ascription." *Philosophical Forum* 36(3): 279–306.

Kolstad, I. (2007). "The Evolution of Social Norms: With Managerial Implications." *Journal of Socio-Economics* 36(1): 58–72.

Lindbeck, A. (1997). "Incentives and Social Norms in Household Behavior." *American Economic Review* 87(2): 370–377.

Merriam-Webster's Collegiate Dictionary, 10th ed. (1994). Springfield, MA: Merriam-Webster, Inc.

Morris, R. (1956). "A Typology of Norms." *American Sociological Review* 21(5): 610–613.

Nyborg, K. (2003). "The Impact of Public Policy on Social and Moral Norms: Some Examples." *Journal of Consumer Policy* 26(3): 259–277.

Ostrom, E. (2000). "Collective Action and Evolution of Social Norms." *Journal of Economic Perspectives* 29(5): 747–765.

Posner, E. A., Ed. (2000). *Law and Social Norms*. Cambridge and London: Harvard University Press.

Posner, R. (1997). "Social Norms and the Law: an Economic Approach." *American Economic Review* 87(2): 365–369.

Posner, R. A., and E. B. Rasmusen. (1999). "Creating and Enforcing Norms, with Special Reference to Sanctions." *International Review of Law and Economics* 19(4): 369–382.

Rodriguez-Sickert, C., R. A. Guzman, and J. C. Cárdenas. (2008). "Institutions Influence Preferences: Evidence from a Common Pool Resource Experiment." *Journal of Economic Behavior and Organization* 67(1): 215–227.

Sherif, M. (1966). *The Psychology of Social Norms*. New York: Harper and Row.

Thibaut, J. W., and H. H. Kelley. (1986). *The Social Psychology of Groups*. New Brunswick, NJ: Transaction, Inc.

Voss, T. (2001). "Game-Theoretical Perspectives on the Emergence of Social Norms." In *Social Norms*. Eds. Hechter, M. and K. Opp, pp. 105–136. New York: Russell Sage Foundation.

Willer, R., K. Ko, and M. Macy. (2009). "The False Enforcement of Unpopular Norms." *American Journal of Sociology* 115(2): 451–490.

The Battle of Methods in Economics

The Classical Methodenstreit—Menger vs. Schmoller

By Marek Louzek*

Should an economic theory be built abstractly, deductively and hypothetically, regardless of empirical reality; or is economics condemned to be restricted to the dry collection of empirical facts and their compilation into dull statistics? Does exact knowledge mean getting rid of all empirical evidence, or conversely, making a radical move towards empiricism? Is methodological individualism, as opposed to methodological collectivism, indispensable for economics or vice versa?

The above questions are not at all new in economic theory; they have appeared as early as the end of the 19th century in what is referred to as *Methodenstreit* between Carl Menger and Gustav Schmoller. It is useful to take a look at this dispute in greater detail because it is regarded as one of the most significant methodological disputes in the history of economics. In some sense, it had anticipated the methodological disputes in contemporary economics.

As early as the last third of the 19th century, German economists argued that Austrian economic theories were unfounded because they were non-empirical, non-realistic and hence unusable, while Austrians criticized the Germans stating that their historical method only covered a mere description of the existing phenomena and failed to seek generally valid economic laws and relations. Who was more accurate?

*The author is an Associate Professor of Economics at Charles University Prague, Faculty of Philosophy and Arts, and Prague's University of Economics. Direct correspondence to: Marek Louzek, Center for Economics and Politics, Opletalova 37, 110 00 Prague 1, Czech Republic; e-mail: louzek@post.cz.

American Journal of Economics and Sociology, Vol. 70, No. 2 (April, 2011).

Concept of the First Battle of Methods

In the English language literature, the *Methodenstreit* is usually described as a dispute between the abstract-deductive method represented by Menger on one side and the empirical-inductive method represented by Schmoller on the other side. This description is supported, in various versions, by Schumpeter (1972: 814), Seligman (1962: 274), Lekachman (1959: 249), Newman (1952: 195), Landreth (1976: 275), Ingram (1967: 235) and Haney (1949: 550). The first person who brought this concept to the Western literature was Böhm-Bawerk (1890: 244–271). John Neville Keynes (1891), the father of the famous John Maynard Keynes, also played an important role in the dissemination of the standard Anglo-Saxon interpretation. The seeds of the future terminology had already been present with one of the participants of the dispute, Schmoller. He primarily understood his dispute with Menger as the struggle between induction and deduction (Schmoller 1883).

Although the definition of the first battle of methods as a dispute between the abstract-deductive method and the empirical-inductive method is attractive and quite widespread, one can also find some faults in it. These faults lead some authors—especially German and Austrian writers—to arrive at the idea that the traditional concept of *Methodenstreit* is too reductive and needs to be broadened—Kerschagl (1948: 29–33), Ritzel (1950: 118–124), Albert (1962: 142). The related arguments are as follows.

Firstly, *Methodenstreit* cannot be reduced to a dispute between the abstract-deductive and empirical-inductive method because the key polemic between Gustav Schmoller and Carl Menger also included some other points of controversy, including the issue of the justifiability of exact economic laws. This issue is related to the first dispute to a certain degree, but not completely. Furthermore, the third important aspect of the *Methodenstreit* is relatively separate—it is known as the dispute over methodological individualism versus collectivism in economics and social sciences.

Secondly, the *Methodenstreit* cannot be reduced to a dispute between an abstract-deductive and empiric-inductive method for the reason that this terminology itself is an interpretation. This interpretation is very close to the terminology of one of the participants of the dispute, Schmoller; however, Menger never used his terminology. Instead, he spoke about the exact and empirical-realistic orientation of scientific research (*die exakte und die realistisch-empirische Richtung der Forschung*).

Thirdly, the *Methodenstreit* can hardly be reduced to a personal dispute between Menger and Schmoller. The polemic of Menger and Schmoller just touches the surfaceof a dispute that is far deeper and more fundamental. Some authors expressed the opinion that Schmoller did not enrich the discussion with anything original and that the truly dignified opponent of Menger in the *Methodenstreit* had been Wilhelm Roscher, a representative of the older German historical school (Milford 1995).

In this article, we will explain the classic *Methodenstreit* or the first battle of methods as a methodological dispute that took place in the 19th century between the Austrian school of economics led by Menger and the German historical school led by Roscher originally and later by Schmoller. This article will distinguish three main issues of discussion: 1) a dispute about the justifiability of deductive or inductive methods in economics, 2) a dispute over the existence of exact laws in economics, 3) a dispute over methodological individualism versus collectivism in social sciences.

Academic Background

During the first battle of methods in Germany, in the 19th century, economics was not wholly established as a completely autonomous sovereign discipline, equally self-assured as, for example, history, philosophy or natural sciences (Häuser 1988). Universities did not have an economics department; national economy issues were usually included in history, and economic statistics were the only focus that was taught. Even in England and Scotland during the 19th century, political economics was becoming a discipline of its own very slowly. Long after Adam Smith, economists continued to work in a variety of departments (most commonly in the departments of history or moral sciences). The first provable economic professorship in England came into being at East Indian College in Haileybury in 1805. It was called a Chair for History and Economics and its holder was Thomas R. Malthus (Moore 1999).

At European universities, there were only classical sciences such as theology, law, philosophy and, later on, medicine and natural sciences. The new economists were emerging from virtually all these disciplines, perhaps with the exception of medicine and partly theology (however, Galiani, Turgot and Marshall studied theology and Thomas R. Malthus worked as a pastor before taking up the professorship of economics and history).

Economics was most strongly influenced by *philosophy, jurisprudence* as well as *natural sciences.* The English branch of economics became increasingly autonomous primarily according to the example set by natural sciences, while in Germany, economics split off from mainly history and law. The *Methodenstreit* can be compared to a labor pain accompanying the birth of separate economic theories, which were distinguished from history in Germany (Hodgson 2001).

The three disciplines that stood at the birth of economics were far more strictly separated at the German universities than at the English universities. Similarly regarding the division of scientific disciplines, there was virtually no difference between Austrian science and German science but there was quite a substantial chasm between the continental universities and the English schools. According to Häuser (1988), the different organizational structure of the universities was the main reason why no similar dispute, in comparison with the *Methodenstreit* in the German cultural area, broke out in England.

As opposed to students at universities of the continental type, English students were concurrently studying various disciplines; interdisciplinarity was much more developed in Great Britain than in Central Europe. For example, Adam Smith studied mathematics, classical philology and philosophy in Glasgow and Oxford. Malthus was educated in mathematics, natural sciences and linguistics. Keynes, in addition to economics, also studied history, politics, mathematics and arts.

As opposed to this, the German and Austrian universities separated the individual disciplines into isolated *faculties* and students only had a limited possibility of obtaining broader education and having contact with other disciplines. This institutional separation resulted in more competition among the discipline-specific departments and the drive for prestige more often tempted each department to highlight its own merits and, conversely, to question the merits of others.

Thus, separation of theoretical economics from its maternal sciences—philosophy and law—was significantly more painful in Germany and Austria and was accompanied by harder clashes than in England. When the German economists succeeded in winning their new department, they soon after closed themselves in their offices and the contact with their colleagues remained minimal. It was not only economics but also natural sciences that took a very long time before they were emancipated from their powerful predecessor disciplines.

With its philosophical roots, German economics is, of course, not exceptional: names such as Locke, Hume, Smith or Mill prove that English economics also had significant philosophical predecessors. The law-related roots of economics can also be traced very clearly in France and Italy. Names such as Montesquieu, Bodin, Verri and Beccaria symbolize not only famous law authorities but also the seeds of the new economic science in France and Italy.

In spite of this, the law tradition remains typical of Germany and its influence can hardly be compared with other states. Cameralistics was essentially a German-Austrian version of mercantilism. The two basic features of Cameralism, which German economics retained in the form of the historical school throughout the 19th century, is the close interrelation with law and the immediate relation to political power.

In the last third of the 19th century, the Austrian school started to split off from this traditional German trend. Austrians tried to get beyond the shadow of the historical method and wanted to create a real theory. Germans interpreted this departure from the fixed line of historicism and law as a betrayal. The first battle of methods, one of the most significant methodological disputes in the history of economics, broke out.

Carl Menger and Investigations into the Method of Social Sciences

The most significant theoretical economic work of Menger is deemed to be the *Principles of Economics* ([1871] 1981). At the time of publication of the *Principles*, the school known as the younger historical school dominated in German economics. The scholars belonging to this group were usually oriented towards practical political issues. They demanded a historical-descriptive method for economics and, in their opinion, scientific knowledge was to be postulated in such a way so that it could be quickly used in economic and social policy (Oakley 1997).

Therefore, Menger's exact and individualist methodology had a low chance of success in the German community of economists. However, the object of mistrust on the part of German historians was not the theory of subjective value, as it is sometimes claimed. The theory of subjective value had a long-standing tradition in Germany, supported by such names as Hufeland, Roscher, Knies, Rau and Hildebrand (Streissler 1990: 31–68).

It was Menger's explicit requirement for methodological individualism that prompted ferocious resistance among German historians. Methodological individualism requires that social science should base the explanations of social phenomena on individual preferences. Methodological individualism, along with the theory of subjective value, was last presented by Hufeland and Menger continued exactly in this line of thought. Virtually all German economists after Hufeland advocated the principle of methodological collectivism and that was the main reason why they disagreed with Menger (Milford 1990).

Although Menger was passionately convinced of the accuracy of his theory, he started to slightly revise his work as early as 1873, that is, merely two years after the first publication of *Principles*. He left his economic theory unchanged; however, he decided to support the economic teachings with more accurate philosophical, gnoseological and methodological reflections. The methodological investigations, which had only been included in the preface in the first edition of *Principles*, were to permeate and accompany the whole work in the second edition (Alter 1982).

Since he was unable to reconcile himself with the fact that his economic theory had not been met with a proper response in Germany, he energetically settled his score with German national economics in an article titled "The Split of German National Economists" in 1873. However, the culmination of his theoretical break-up from German economics takes place in his key methodological work *Investigations into the Method of the Social Sciences, with Special Reference to Economics* ([1883] 1985).

Menger (1985) tries to define economics as a theoretical science. The key problem he deals with is distinguishing between historical and theoretical sciences dealing with society and the economy. Menger holds the opinion that the distinguishing criterion is that historical sciences are concerned with the analysis of specific, *individual* phenomena, while theoretical sciences analyze that which is *general* and common to the phenomena (or certain groups of phenomena).

Purchase, sale, supply, demand, price, capital or interest rates are typical phenomenal forms of economy. Regular decrease of price resulting from increase of supply, decrease of interest rates resulting from increase of savings are typical relations or correlations between the phenomena that we can see in the national economy. The task of economics as a theoretical science is to analyze the general essence of these phenomena and the general relations among them (Hutchison 1992).

Thus, distinguishing *economics as a theoretical science* from history does not, of course, mean to say that historians should not be concerned with the national economy. In Menger's opinion, *the same phenomenon* can be explained both in a historical way and a theoretical way. An increase in revenues from land or a decrease in interest on capital can be explained historically as a result of specific individual circumstances. However, these phenomena can also be interpreted (no less valuably) in a theoretical way—as a consequence of exact economic laws. Both approaches are justified.

> Theoretical economics can consist only in the exposition of the general nature and the general connection of the laws of economic phenomena, but by no means, for instance, in the exposition of the nature and connection of individual phenomena of economy, such as in historical presentations, or in practical rules for the economic activity of people. The theory of economy must in no case be confused with the historical sciences of economy, or with the practical ones. (Menger (1985: 51)

In Menger's opinion, theoretical research can take two different paths:

1) A scientist tries to grasp the full empirical reality, the totality of phenomena in their entire complexity, and then sorts the sum of the real phenomena into certain phenomenal forms and subsequently presents patterns or coexistences of these phenomena and phenomenal forms as he experienced them in practice. This method of work led to the establishment of what is known as a *realistic-empirical orientation of theoretical research.*

2) A scientist focuses on a certain specific aspect of phenomena or phenomenal forms, while assuming that all the other aspects and circumstances are constant. Thus, he/she examines the general relations of the subsequence and coexistence of phenomena (or certain aspects of phenomena), while assuming that the other components of the empirical reality are constant. This method led to establishment of what is known as *exact orientation of theoretical research.*

Both the exact and the realistic orientation of theoretical research are therefore justified. Both are means for understanding, predicting, and controlling economic phenomena, and to these aims each of them contributes in its own way. Anybody who denies the justification and usefulness of the exact or the realistic orientation is comparable to a natural scientist who one-sidedly values physiology highly, perhaps under the pretext that chemistry and physics are based on abstractions, and would deny the justification of the latter or their justification as means for the understanding of organic structures. Otherwise, he/she resembles a physicist or chemist who would deny to physiology the character of a science because its laws are for the most part only "empirical" (Menger 1985: 64–65).

In order to specifically show the fundamental difference between exact and empirical analyses, Menger uses the law of demand as an example. If a layman were to formulate the law of demand, he would probably say that if the need for a commodity increases, then the demand will increase and consequently the market price will increase. However, such a formulation is in fact insufficient. The law of demand can be formulated in two different manners: *exactly* and *empirically*.

The exact law of demand says: *If the need for a commodity increases, then <u>under otherwise identical conditions</u> its market price will always increase.*

As opposed to that, *the empirical law of demand* states: *If the need for a commodity increases, then its market price will <u>usually</u> increase.*

The key difference between these two formulations lies with the fact that while the empirical law of demand is based on experience, the exact law is based on the empirical framework, but at the same time also adds other non-empirical (ideal) assumptions. Of these model assumptions, the most important one is the thesis that other conditions of the examined relation are unchanged (the *ceteris paribus* condition).

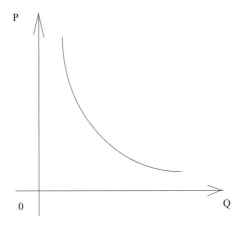

However, these assumptions have an important consequence: while the empirical law of demand is valid only *in relative terms*, for example, "normally," "usually," according to the observed information, the exact law is valid *in absolute terms* and does not permit any exceptions. This difference between the exact and empirical laws is absolutely fundamental and also has a key importance for theoretical economics. While the empirical law of demand is only valid in some cases, the exact law of demand is valid—under the defined assumptions—absolutely and inevitably, and it cannot be refuted by pointing out an empirical fact that is in conflict with it.

> The law that the increased need for an item results in an increase of prices, and indeed that a definite measure of the increase of need also results in an increase in prices determined according to its measure, is not true—is

unempirical, when tested by reality in its full complexity. What else does this say, that the results of exact research do not find their criterion in experience? (Menger 1985: 71–72)

The goal of exact theoretical science is to find the simplest elements of social or natural phenomena and then, by putting together their mutual relations, correlations and interplays, to explain more complicated phenomena. In Menger's opinion, this approach is also justified in a situation where the simplest elements, at which the exact analysis arrived, are of non-empirical nature. In Menger's opinion, this means that the social sciences have a great advantage over the natural sciences.

> The ultimate elements to which the exact theoretical interpretation of natural phenomena must be reduced are "atoms" and "forces". Neither is of empirical nature. One cannot imagine "atoms" at all, and natural forces only by a representation, and by these we merely understand unknown causes of real motions. From this there arise ultimately quite extraordinary difficulties for the exact interpretation of natural phenomena. It is otherwise in exact social sciences. Here the human *individuals* and their *efforts*, the final elements of our analysis, are of empirical nature, and thus exact theoretical social sciences have a great advantage over the exact natural sciences. (Menger 1985: 142)

In Menger's opinion, the exact method of theoretical research in the field of the organic world does not deny the unity of natural organisms at all. Rather it searches for the origin and functions of these individual formations and tries to explain how the real units function. According to Menger, for this purpose, it is always necessary to use the methodological individualism (as opposed to the empirical-realistic method of scientific research). Menger demonstrates an exact analysis on the origin and emergence of money and a number of other social institutions (Zuidema 1988).

Gustav Schmoller

It is with Gustav Schmoller that the *Methodenstreit* is most frequently associated (in addition to Carl Menger). Schmoller wrote a review of Menger's book in a journal called *Jahrbuch für Gesetzgebung, Verwaltung und Volkswirtschaft* (Schmoller [1883], 1888) in 1883 and the review was not very commending. As a contrast, Schmoller used

Dilthey's work "Introduction to Human Sciences," which he, conversely, praised highly (Dilthey 1883). The passionate discussion that broke out in response to this review is labeled as the first battle of methods (Hutchison 1988).

Schmoller's review is important in several respects. Firstly: Schmoller was the first one who interpreted Menger's exact and empirical orientation of scientific research in the terms of abstract-deductive and empirical-inductive method. "The two paths, which Menger sees in economics, are called realistic-empirical and exact by him. By this, he means that which is usually referred to as inductive and deductive procedures" (Schmoller 1888: 280).[1]

The new label was gradually accepted in economics and has persisted in standard interpretations of the *Methodenstreit* until today. More importantly, Schmoller's not quite self-evident opinion that the difference between an abstract-deductive method and an empirical-inductive method is not fundamental because both methods are integral parts of economic analysis was also accepted.

> The division into two orientations of scientific research, on which Menger bases his reflections, undoubtedly has certain justification . . . but this contract must be understood as a chasm that can be overcome. The individualist science or—a descriptive science provides the material for the general theory. This material gets more complete as all the important aspects, transformations, causes and effects are better described. (Schmoller 1888: 278)

In Schmoller's opinion, the deductive and inductive methods are not in conflict with each other; rather, they supplement each other. Every consistent descriptive work that involves collecting empirical or historical data is then a prerequisite for obtaining general pieces of knowledge. First, we must gather rich empirical material, and only then can we build a general theory. If we create complex deductive theories regardless of the reality, they become mere daydreams.

> When a presumption of the pursuit of one's own interest had been used as a seeming constant for price examinations at one time, it was done to explain the simplest market processes. But it is a mistake to make this a rule for future research or examination of more complex national economic processes. In any case, one must always be aware, if one uses this

procedure, that science based on hypotheses will always only provide hypothetical forecasts. However, such forecasts are only seemingly exact. (Schmoller 1888: 281)

Schmoller criticizes Menger for restricting theoretical economics merely to a discipline dealing with value, price and the essence of money. Menger does not need to examine other aspects of social and economic life. However, in Schmoller's opinion, the undesired result is a questionable theory that is sheer speculation and is suspended in mid-air (Peukert 2001).

Schmoller stated in a ridiculing manner, "Menger says that who wants laws must abstract. We answer that in the end, all our thinking and cognition is based on abstraction. However, the point is to abstract in the correct manner so that our abstractions result in scientific truths and not schematic phantoms or visionary escapades as is, regrettably, often the case" (Schmoller 1888: 283). Schmoller admits that Menger's criticism of the German historical schools was valid in certain specific cases. Nevertheless, he emphasizes that it is not possible to draw broad conclusions about an entire scientific discipline from a few isolated blunders.

> The conclusions contained in the second book of *Investigations* are correct in many respects. One could also partly agree with the list of sins of the historical school, but does this completely cancel the justifiability and merits of the entire scientific discipline? Menger is absolutely incapable of understanding the fundamental causes and merits of the historical school because he lacks the authority to do so. The historical school represents a return to the scientific grasp of reality instead of vague abstractions lacking the desired connection to reality. (Schmoller 1888: 287)

To Schmoller's harsh criticism, Menger responded by the pamphlet "Errors of Historicism in German Economics" (Menger [1884] 1970: 1–99). However, this polemic treatise was not a very strong one because the substantive essence of the dispute got lost among the caustic attacks against Schmoller, and key arguments were also missing. Of course, such arguments did exist, but Menger simply did not have enough time for them (Schumpeter 1972: 814).

The standard of argumentation of the founder of the Austrian school of economics is indicated by a sharp quote. "I would like to point out all the possible and impossible distortions of my words by Schmoller.

There is no doubt that Schmoller has achieved a true mastery in his personal and vulgar style. Yes, after all, it is the only mastery that can be attributed to this man with a brilliant knowledge of the German language" (Menger 1970: 16).

In the "Errors of Historicism," Menger does not present any new arguments; he only more or less repeats the ideas that had already been expressed in the *Investigations*. He insists that it is useful to distinguish between exact and realistic-empirical methods of scientific research; he insists on a strict separation of history from theoretical social science, and criticizes the methodological collectivism of Schmoller.

Menger even provoked Schmoller by sending him his pamphlet for review directly to *Jahrbuch für Gesetzgebung, Verwaltung und Volkswirtschaft*. Schmoller flared up and immediately sent the pamphlet back to Menger with an insulting cover letter, the text of which he published in the *Jahrbuch* at the same time: "It is impossible not only to read but even to review something so outrageous" (Bloch 1940: 432).

Interpretations of the First Battle of Methods

Why did such a sharp controversy take place between Menger and Schmoller? Why did both participants of the dispute insult each other in spite of the fact that both of them were openly building on the work of Wilhelm Roscher? Was their dispute only an unfortunate misunderstanding resulting from the need for scientific prestige or was it really inevitable? Was the *Methodenstreit* only a methodological dispute or were different philosophical roots also reflected in it?

There are a number of interpretations of the *Methodenstreit* in literature. The standard economic interpretations are presented by Eugen von Böhm-Bawerk (1890: 244–271), J. N. Keynes (1891: 5–31) and J. Schumpeter (1972: 814–815). These authors claim that the first battle of methods had been overdone and unnecessary. The standard interpretations express that there are no large programmatic differences between Menger and Schmoller that would justify such an enormous intensity of the dispute.

Neo-Austrian interpretations, presented by Ludwig von Mises (1933: 68) and/or F. A. von Hayek (1930: 393–420) usually emphasize the deep meaning of *Methodenstreit* and tend to take sides with Menger. The specific feature of Neo-Austrians is that instead of methodological pluralism officially advocated by both Menger and Schmoller, they demand methodological monism. Thus, the situation that prevailed in the middle of the 19th century has been reversed to a considerable degree.

Consensualist interpretations are close to the standard economic interpretations in the sense that they seek compromise between the clear-cut Austrian and German positions. However, unlike standard interpretations, they recognize the noetic value of the dispute. Karel Engliš, a Czech economist (1992), sees the *Methodenstreit* through the eyes of his teleological method (explaining social phenomena through their purpose); Gerhard Ritzel (1950: 89–129), a Neo-Historian, tends to be more of a fan of Schmoller but also recognizes Menger's merits.

Philosophical interpretations are focused on the broader intellectual context of the dispute or they try to address some of the deeper epistemological issues. The most significant philosophical interpretations of the *Methodenstreit* include S. Bostaph (1978), R. Hansen (1968) and U. Mäki (1990). Most authors emphasize the Aristotle tradition, on which Menger's background was based, and the Neo-Kant tradition, with which Schmoller was raised.

The standard economic interpretations are right in saying that the *Methodenstreit* was a dispute that was overdone to a certain degree. The statement that the dispute was unnecessary is somewhat less acceptable. The *Methodenstreit* ultimately revealed certain hidden assumptions on both sides and compelled both camps to clearly formulate their stances. The *Methodenstreit* cleared the air significantly, and it is highly unlikely that the first battle of methods could have been avoided.

The analysis of the philosophical context shows that the dispute reached far deeper than just pure methodology. In the *Methodenstreit*, two different philosophical traditions—*the Austrian and the German*—were also reflected. Carl Menger, as the founder of the Austrian school of economics, was firmly tied to the philosophical tradition of Austria connected with such names as Bolzano, F. Brentano, the Brentano School, Meinong, Ehrenfels, and later on with early Witgenstein, Neurath and Popper. It is a tradition that is strongly essentialist, focused on logics and, in this sense, it is neo-Aristotelian, rationalistic and probably even pre-Kantian. The deeply rooted Catholicism, which was able to retain its scholastic-Aristotelian values more easily, undoubtedly contributed to the persistence of Neo-Aristotelianism in Austria.

A conspicuous trust in the ability of words and language to objectively portray reality existing independently of people (which, after all, was accepted by the Viennese Circle) is characteristic of Menger's methodology of the economic science. Menger constantly tried to search for the essence (*wesen*) of economic goods. This is necessarily connected with methodological essentialism, which can already be found with Aristotle.

Gustav Schmoller, as the leading figure of what is known as the younger phase of the German historical school, is rooted in a completely different national tradition. Since the times of Kant, German philosophy has had a strongly idealistic orientation (Kant, Fichte, Schelling, Hegel). It is true that in the 19th century, there was a "reversal" of objective idealism into an opposite position, for example, into materialism (Feuerbach, Marx), but there emerged a compromise in the form of what is referred to as German Neo-Kantianism.

Marburg's Neo-Kantianism, which was closest to Schmoller, rehabilitated Kant and, in the times of the general prime of natural sciences, it did not forget to emphasize the strong empirical component. This has connection with Schmoller's deliberate empiricism and inductivism. The intellectual climate of Germany of the 19th century had a strong historicist and organicist orientation. This was also manifested in Schmoller's historicism and methodological collectivism.

Menger spoke out against Schmoller at the moment when he felt that Schmoller was putting the methodology itself—the inductive procedures, the historical empiricism and methodological collectivism—in absolute terms and was making them the only justified approach in social sciences in general. This criticism was justified in relation to the "factual" Schmoller, not to the "ideological" one (Backhaus 1989: 31–54). The ideological Schmoller, when attacked, of course, insisted on the principle of methodological pluralism.

Menger created an original economic theory, which built on the traditional subjectivism of German economics, but he replaced its methodological collectivism by methodological individualism. In Menger's view, there are two types of economic theory—a theory built in an exact, essentialist, and deductive manner, and a theory based on empiricism, realism, and induction. His *Principles* represent a bold attempt to demonstrate the sustainability of the exact approach.

In *Investigations*, Menger shows that he does not build monist theory in the sense that he would claim that his exact and methodological-individualist theory represents the only justified approach in economics, or in social sciences in general. Quite the opposite, he tries to justify the exact approach as such. He attempts to prove that induction, historicism, and methodological collectivism do not represent the only permitted method, which seemed to be advocated by the statements and practice of some German historians.

Schmoller interpreted the *Investigations* as an open attack against himself and a threat to the academic positions of the German historical school. In his review, he sneered at Menger and called him a creator of daydreams. Menger responded by writing an even sharper treatise entitled "Errors of Historicism." The sharpness of the controversy is surprising due to the fact that both of them, in principle, agreed with the validity of both alternative methods (Hodgson 2001).

Even the direct successors of Menger in the camp of the Austrian school remain methodological pluralists. Both Wieser ([1911] 1929) and Böhm-Bawerk (1890) defended the opinion that various methods are admissible in economics. However, they believed that due to the long-term neglect of economic theory in the German cultural area of the 19th century, it was more meaningful to develop a pure economic theory.

It was not until the "Neo-Austrian" revolution of Ludwig von Mises and F. A. von Hayek that the methodological stances became radicalized and the situation that had prevailed in the middle of the 19th century was in a way reversed. Both authors support categorical methodological monism, which takes on the form of individualist-composite method with Hayek and the form of praxeology as *a priori* economics with Mises.

The *Methodenstreit* really appears to be a turning-point dispute. A dispute where a gradual intellectual transformation takes place in the field of theoretical economics towards a more exact, deductive, and composite approach. The personal quarrel between Menger and Schmoller is just a single spark in this deep and fundamental transformation of economic methodology.

Discussion

Regarding the evaluation of the dispute between Menger and Schmoller, we should advise against hasty conclusions. It is too simplistic to believe, like for example, Nardinelli and Meiners (1988), that there is a sort of insurmountable conflict between theory, abstraction, and deduction on one side and history, realism, and induction on the other side, which became evident in the *Methodenstreit* and continues until today. This opinion mixes several things together.

The dispute between the abstract-deductive and empirical-inductive methods cannot be conflated with the dispute between theory and history because the abstract-deductive and empirical-inductive methods are two different methods used *within* economics and they do not draw any dividing line between economics and history. Pure history can hardly be classified as an empirical-inductive discipline because history only collects facts but does not draw any general conclusions from them (the principle of induction).

Dispute Between Induction and Deduction

If we take a close look at economic theory, we will find out that abstract-deductive as well as empirical-inductive methods are both applied in it. An example of pure abstract-deductive theory is virtually the entire core of *neoclassical economics*. It builds its model on the fundamental assumption of *homo economicus* and other assumptions, and the conclusions drawn from it can neither be verified nor refuted by everyday experience.

Another example of an abstract-deductive theory is the *public choice theory*. This is based on the assumption that politicians behave in such a way so as to maximize their chances of re-election. This assumption is not so much based on empirical observation but it is more a specific application of the general neo-classical model of *homo economicus*.

The well-known *Phillips theory* on the relation of unemployment and inflation rates can be presented as an example of an empirical-inductive theory. A. W. Phillips carefully studied the statistics on unemployment and nominal wages in the United Kingdom over a period of more than one hundred years and arrived at the conclusion that there is an inverse relation between unemployment and the change in nominal wages. We are not concerned with examining whether Phillips' theory is true now; the point, however, is that Phillips originally used the classic empirical-inductive method: he simply collected empirical-statistical data and then drew a general conclusion from them (induction).

If economists forbid themselves to use the empirical-inductive method for dogmatic reasons, they would deprive themselves of a significant theory, which undoubtedly enriched the economic literature with an original contribution. Incidentally, monetarists in their criticism of Neo-Keynesian economics used nothing other than an empirical-inductive method. M. Friedman and A. Schwartz examined the inflation rate and money supply statistics in the United States and arrived at the conclusion that the inflation rate increases in direct proportion to the amount of money in the economy.

Thus, in principle, both methods—the abstract-deductive as well as the empirical-inductive—are used in economics. However, this does not mean that they can be freely substituted and combined with one another. Each method understandably plays its own role and has its advantages and drawbacks. Some are trying to use a combination of the two methods, which is referred to as "retroduction" (Lawson 1997; Bhaskar 1998).

The basic property of the abstract-deductive method is that its conclusions cannot be verified or falsified by experience. This stems from the fact that this method is based on certain assumptions, which are set beforehand and that often need not correspond to experience. As we have seen with Menger, the exact law of demand is valid absolutely and inevitably and it cannot be simply refuted by pointing to a certain empirical fact that seemingly contradicts it.

The empirical-inductive method works differently: it is based on empiricism but its conclusions do not acquire absolute and inevitable validity. It can easily happen that a fact that contradicts the postulated general law will appear in the future. In that case, the theory in question is refuted and should be replaced with a new, more credible theory. This is in accordance with the falsification doctrine of R. K. Popper and Imre Lakatos (Blaug 1994).

Exact Laws and Empirical Laws

As we have seen, the result of the abstract-deductive method is economic laws, which may be absolute, *exact* and eternally valid, but they are hovering somewhere in mid-air and the meaningfulness of such a theory can be questioned. The empirical-inductive method may provide realistic *empirical* laws but they can easily be refuted. Which is better?

It seems that this dichotomy cannot be resolved satisfactorily. It is more a matter of choice of the specific author and a matter of what he/she prefers: whether he/she prefers a perfect, mathematically formalized, abstract-deductive system or whether he/she instead prefers a less ambitious, realistic but more easily refutable, empirical-inductive model. The difference between the two laws follows from the type of formalization.

Empirical laws originate from the generalization of observed relations between empirical magnitudes. For example, when Phillips observed the statistics on nominal wages and unemployment in the United Kingdom, covering the period of one hundred years, and he expressed the opinion that the same relation would continue to exist, he formulated an empirical (statistical) law. This law has the property that it can be refuted (and was refuted).

Exact laws originate from modeling artificial assumptions and from drawing conclusions from these assumptions and axioms. Logically, no experience can then refute them. An exact law of demand works absolutely generally and inevitably, provided that the assumptions are met, especially the *ceteris paribus* condition and the assumption of *homo economicus* maximizing profit. In principle, this law cannot be refuted.

However, the chasm between exact and empirical laws can be overcome. An empirical law can be re-formulated into an exact form and vice versa. For example, the empirical law of demand (an increase of price *is usually* followed by a decrease of the demand for the commodity concerned) can be rewritten as follows: an increase of price, under otherwise identical conditions, will *always* result in a decrease of the demand for the commodity concerned, provided that the given assumptions are met.

It is exactly the non-empirical nature of the assumptions of the exact (abstract-deductive) theory that can explain why economists are willing to admit simultaneously the validity of more theories that provide different forecasts. For example, if we convert the Neo-Keynesian and monetarist model of aggregate supply and demand into a formalized form, we will find out that both theories can be regarded as valid although they provide opposite recommendations for economic policy.

Methodological Individualism Versus Collectivism

A serious issue that has continually been raised in economics and social sciences is the dispute over methodological individualism versus methodological collectivism. Regrettably, several things are often confused in this debate. First, ontological individualism is not distinguished from the methodological one. Second, at other times, the difference between methodological and political individualism is neglected.

Ontological individualism does not necessarily have to imply *methodological* individualism and vice versa (Goldstein 1958). For example, a number of sociologists will sign, with a clean conscience, the thesis that there are in fact no higher social aggregates and entities, and yet they will insist that in sociological research, it is expedient to base the research on broader collectives, whose members are people, because it is expedient from the point of view of the issue under examination (methodological collectivism).

An ontological collectivist, if we could find someone like this today, could work as an economist on a scientific project that uses method-ological individualism as a method (a tool or instrument). Methodological individualism is necessary in all those cases where we want to deduce a certain balanced structure of a spontaneous order from individual preferences.

The *Methodenstreit* can also be understood in an original way and can be described as the dispute in which two methodological approaches and paradigms were split, which we today call economics and sociology. Menger's individualist theory symbolizes economics and Schmoller's methodological collectivism and historicism tends to focus on sociology.

However, this description is not meant in any absolute terms. Since there are a number of topics on the border between economics and sociology, it would be unfortunate to forego a method that can cast an interesting light on a certain problem or at least show it in a new context. Not only the German historical school, but also, in the 20th century, French structuralism resembles sociology.

There is also no logical connection between *political* and *methodological* individualism (Schumpeter 1922: 88–98). It is certainly possible to imagine an economist who uses methodological individualism in his scientific work, but inclines to left-wing parties in politics. There is no contradiction in this because economics, as a value-neutral science, does not directly verge to any ideological position.

Even methodological collectivism does not necessarily imply left-wing tendencies. It is very well possible to imagine a sociologist who, in his office, searches for empirical correlations among statistical macro-aggregates and, at the same time, votes for a classical liberal party in elections. Methodological collectivism (or individualism) only uses scientific aids and methods and certainly does not pre-determine ideological convictions (Hodgson 2007).

Some would object that although there is no *logical* relation between a political and methodological position, there is at least a certain *psychological* relation: it seems to be an empirical fact that most economists tend to have more (classical) liberal political opinions and most sociologists conversely have strong social or corporatist orientation. That is true.

This psychological relation can most easily be explained as follows: a standard economist raised in a neoclassical paradigm, provided that in his/her science he takes the standpoint of individuals as the starting point and examines their influence on the spontaneous market equilibrium, progresses in his economic analysis sort "from the bottom" and has a natural tendency to assume the freedom of the examined individuals. Since he/she understands market equilibrium as something positive, he/she develops a psychological tendency to promote individualism in politics.

A sociologist who always sees the behavior of individuals in the context of the development of certain social entities and collectives does not see an individual primarily as a free being but as a person considerably determined by his/her surroundings and social environment. Naturally, the sociologist will then reject those political doctrines that are based on the concept of a free individual, and will be inclined to support those ideologies that want to approach society "from above."

Educated scientists should avoid making one-sided statements. Scientific humbleness remains the message of the *Methodenstreit*.

Summary

The classic methodological disputes in economics include the first battle of methods. It took place between Carl Menger, the founder of the Austrian school, and Gustav Schmoller, a member of the young German historical school. In a sense, it has continued until today. The first battle of methods was manifested in three topics: induction versus deduction; exact laws versus empirical laws; and the dispute about methodological individualism versus collectivism.

Although the two adversaries took irreconcilable positions, in fact both methods are a part of economics: the deductive one as well as the inductive one. Exact laws obtained by means of the abstract-deductive method are created by the neoclassics. Some macroeconomic and also microeconomic theories are examples of empirical theories. Today, a theoretical economist commonly creates models, which are empirically tested at the next stage.

The first battle of methods was one of the most important events in the history of economic thought. For Menger, economics was no longer concerned with the study of economic systems but it was a discipline focused on the economic aspects of human behavior. It initiated the process in which economics was transformed from the science of economy to the science of choice.

Note

1. This and all other translations are made by the author.

References

Albert, H. (1962). "Der moderne Methodenstreit und die Grenzen des Methodenpluralismus." *Jahrbuch für Sozialwissenschaft* 13: 142–169.
Alter, M. (1982). "Carl Menger and Homo Oeconomicus. Some Thoughts on Austrian Theory and Methodology." *Journal of Economic Issues* 16(1): 149–160.
Backhaus, J. (Ed.) (1989). *Gustav Schmollers Lebenswerk.* Düsseldorf: Verlag Wirtschaft und Finanzen GmbH.
Bhaskar, R. (1998). *The Possibility of Naturalism.* London: Routledge.
Blaug, M. (1994). *Methodology of Economics, or How Economists Explain.* Cambridge: Cambridge University Press.
Bloch, H. S. (1940). "Carl Menger. The Founder of the Austrian School." *Journal of Political Economy* 48(3): 428–433.
Böhm-Bawerk, E. von. (1890). "The Historical vs. the Deductive Method in Political Economy." *Annals of the American Academy of Political and Social Science* 1: 244–271.
Bostaph, S. (1978). "The Methodological Debate Between Carl Menger and the German Historicists." *Atlantic Economic Journal* 1978(3): 3–16.
Dilthey, W. (1883). *Einleitung in die Geisteswissenschaften.* Leipzig: Duncker & Humblot.
Engliš, K. (1992). *Economics—A Purpose Oriented Approach.* New York: Columbia University Press.
Goldstein, L. J. (1958). "The Two Theses of Methodological Individualism." *British Journal for the Philosophy of Science* 9(33): 1–11.
Haney, L. (1949). *History of Economic Thought.* New York: Macmillan.
Hansen, R. (1968). "Methodenstreit in den Sozialwissenschaften zwischen Gustav Schmoller und Karl Menger." In *Beiträge zur Entwicklung der Wissenschaftstheorie im 19. Jahrhundert.* Ed. Alwin Diemer. Meisenheim am Glan: 137–173.
Häuser, K. (1988). "Historical School and Methodenstreit." *Journal of Institutional and Theoretical Economics* 144: 532–542.
Hayek, F. A. (1930). "Carl Menger." *Economica, New Series* 1(4): 393–420.
Hodgson, G. M. (2001). *How Economics Forgot History.* London: Routledge.

———. (2007). "Meanings of Methodological Individualism." *Journal of Economic Methodology* 14(2): 211–226.

Hutchison, T. W. (1988). "Gustav Schmoller and the Problems of Today." *Journal of Institutional and Theoretical Economics* 144(3): 527–531.

———. (1992). "Carl Menger on Philosophy and Method." In *The Politics and Philosophy of Economics*. Ed. Terence W. Hutchison. Aldershot: Gregg Revivals: 176–202.

Ingram, J. K. (1967). *A History of Political Economy*. New York: Augustus M. Kelley.

Kerschagl, R. (1948). *Einführung in die Methodenlehre der Nationalökonomie*. Wien: Hölder-Pichler-Tempsky.

Keynes, J. N. (1891). *The Scope and Method of Political Economy*. London and New York: Macmillan.

Landreth, H. (1976). *History of Economic Theory*. Boston: Houghton Mifflin.

Lawson, T. (1997). *Economics and Reality*. London, Routledge.

Lekachman, R. (1959). *A History of Economic Ideas*. New York: McGraw-Hill.

Mäki, U. (1990). "Mengerian Economics in Realist Perspective." *History of Political Economy, Annual Supplement* 22: 289–310.

Menger, C. ([1884] 1970). "Irrthümer des Historismus in der deutschen Nationalökonomie." Wien 1884. In *Gesammelte Werke III*. Ed. C. Menger. Tübingen: J.C.B. Mohr: 1–99.

———. ([1889] 1970). "Grundzüge einer Klassifikation der Wirtschaftswissenschaften." Gustav Fischer 1889: Jena. In *Gesammelte Werke III*. Ed. C. Menger. Tübingen: J.C.B. Mohr: 185–218.

———. ([1871] 1981). *Principles of Economics*. New York, London: New York University Press.

———. ([1883] 1985). *Investigations into the Method of the Social Sciences*. New York, London: New York University Press.

Milford, K. (1990). "Menger's Methodology." *History of Political Economy* 22: 215–230.

———. (1995). "Roscher's Epistemological and Methodological Position. Its Importance for the Methodenstreit." *Journal of Economic Issues* 22: 26–53.

Mises, L. von. (1933). *Grundprobleme der Nationalökonomie*. Jena: Gustav Fischer.

Moore, G. C. (1999). "John Kells Ingram, the Comtean Movement, and the English Methodenstreit." *History of Political Economy* 31(1): 53–79.

Nardinelli, C., and Meiners, R. E. (1988). "Schmoller, the Methodenstreit, and the Development of Economic History." *Journal of Institutional and Theoretical Economics* 144: 543–551.

Nau, H. H., and Steiner, P. (2002). "Schmoller, Durkheim, and Old European Institutionalist Economics." *Journal of Economic Issues* 36(4): 1005–1025.

Newman, P. Ch. (1952). *The Development of Economic Thought*. New York: Prentice-Hall.

Oakley, A. (1997). *The Foundations of Austrian Economics from Menger to Mises*. Cheltenham: Edward Elgar.

Peukert, H. (2001). "The Schmoller Renaissance." *History of Political Economy* 33(1): 71–117.

Ritzel, G. (1950). *Schmoller versus Menger. Eine Analyse des Methodenstreites im Hinblick auf den Historismus in der Nationalökonomie*. Frankfurt am Main.

Schmoller, G. ([1883] 1888). "Zur Methodologie der Staats- und Sozialwissenschaften." *Jahrbuch für Gesetzgebung, Verwaltung und Volkswirtschaft*, 8 (1883). In *Zur Literaturgeschichte der Staats- und Sozialwissenschaften*. Ed. Gustav Schmoller. Leipzig: Duncker & Humblot: 275–304.

Schumpeter, J. (1922). *Das Wesen und der Hauptinhalt der theoretischen Nationalökonomie*. Berlin: Duncker & Humblot.

———. (1972). *A History of Economic Analysis*. London: Allen and Unwin.

Seligman, B. (1962). *Main Currents in Modern Economics*. New York: Free Press of Glencoe.

Streissler, E. (1990). "The Influence of German Economics on the Work of Menger and Marshall." *History of Political Economy, Supplement* 22: 31–68.

Wieser, F. ([1911] 1929). "Das Wesen und der Hauptinhalt der Theoretischen Nationalökonomie." *Jahrbuch für Gesetzgebung, Verwaltung und Volkswirtschaft im Deutschen Reich*, 2 (1911). In *Gesammelte Abhandlungen*. Ed. F. Wieser. Tübingen: J.C.B. Mohr: 10–34.

Zuidema, J. R. (1988). "Carl Menger, Author of a Research Programme." *Journal of Economic Issues* 15(3–4): 13–36.

Emily Greene Balch, Political Economist

By Robert W. Dimand[1]

ABSTRACT. The first female economist to win a Nobel Prize was Emily Greene Balch, who shared the Nobel Peace Prize in 1946 for the same anti-war activism for which she lost her Wellesley professorship of economics and sociology in 1918. Balch, an outspoken pacifist, social reformer, and defender of ethnically-diverse immigration, has largely been forgotten in the history of economic thought and of sociology. Her contributions and her remarkable career warrant attention.

Introduction

In 2009, the political scientist Elinor Ostrom became the first woman to win the Royal Bank of Sweden Prize for Economic Science in Memory of Alfred Nobel (jointly with Oliver Williamson). But a female economist won a Nobel Prize more than six decades earlier: Emily Greene Balch shared the Nobel Peace Prize in 1946 for the same pacifist activism for which she lost her Wellesley professorship of economics and sociology in 1918 (see Balch 1972; Randall 1964).

The social reformer Emily Greene Balch was a very political economist, striving to relieve poverty, opposing the spread of war, and defending the economic, social, and cultural benefits of an open immigration policy. Within the literature on pacifism, Mercedes Randall (1964) and Kristen Gwinn (2010) have written lively biographies of Balch, and Randall edited an invaluable anthology of Balch's writings, *Beyond Nationalism* (Balch 1972). Randall's contributions and histories of the American women's peace movement aside, Balch has received little attention, apart from short entries in Fred Lee's *History of Heterodox Economics* (2009: 234) and in reference works such as *Notable American Women* (Solomon 1980), *American National Biography* (Opdycke 1999), and *A Biographical Dictionary of Women Economists* (R. Dimand in Dimand, Dimand, and Forget 2000), so that she has escaped the collective memory of the economics profession and, apart from Deegan (1983, 1991), sociology. Balch

American Journal of Economics and Sociology, Vol. 70, No. 2 (April, 2011).

is known to historians of the American women's peace movement, but in that literature Harriet Hyman Alonso (1995: 6) stresses that Balch "was and still is virtually unknown in the land of her birth" and Judy Whipps (2006: 123) reports that "today she remains virtually unknown even to feminist thinkers." The *Encyclopaedia Britannica* allots two paragraphs to Balch, listing the years she taught at Wellesley without saying anything about her departure from the college (Wood 1968). Balch's name was absent from commentaries on Ostrom's and Yunus's prizes. Even Agnar Sandmo (2007), discussing economists and the Nobel Peace Prize (in the context of the economist and micro-credit pioneer Mohammed Yunus winning the Peace Prize, and of Walras's much earlier unsuccessful candidacy for the prize), overlooked her, Joseph Dorfman mentioned her only once in his monumental, five-volume *The Economic Mind in American Civilization* (1946–1959: III, 243), and then only to quote Balch (1899) as stating that the "most important contemporary work in economic theory is that based largely . . . on the conception of marginal utility." Dorfman did not mention that, after more than two decades of successful and innovative teaching at Wellesley College, Balch was not reappointed to her professorship in 1918 for the same anti-war and social reform activism for which she shared the 1946 Nobel Peace Prize.[2] She remains the only woman economist to win a Nobel Prize (as distinct from the Royal Bank of Sweden Prize) and the only American economist to win the Peace Prize. Balch was the second American woman to win the Nobel Peace Prize, preceded by her close friend Jane Addams. The issues she raised, immigration, eradication of poverty, prevention of war, and the economic role of women, remain live issues.

The Education of a Political Economist

Emily Greene Balch was born in Jamaica Plain, Massachusetts, in 1867, the second of six surviving children of a former school-teacher and of a lawyer who, on the eve of the Civil War, had been secretary to the abolitionist Senator Charles Sumner. She entered Bryn Mawr College in 1886, earning her A. B. with Bryn Mawr's first graduating class in 1889. At Bryn Mawr, Balch studied with the sociologist Franklin

Giddings and with an assistant professor of history and government who was a founding member of the council of the American Economic Association in 1885 and later president of the American Political Science Association, the American Historical Association, Princeton University, and the United States of America—Woodrow Wilson. As the first winner of the Bryn Mawr Fellowship for European Study, Balch spent 1890–1891 at the Sorbonne, researching and writing her monograph on *Public Assistance of the Poor in France*, which was published by the American Economic Association in 1893 as a double issue of its first series of publications (her former teacher Franklin Giddings was chair of the AEA Publications Committee). A turning point in her life was meeting Jane Addams of Hull House and the economic historian Katharine Coman of Wellesley College while attending in 1892 the Summer School of Applied Ethics convened at Plymouth, Massachusetts, by Felix Adler, founder of the Ethical Culture Society. Regretting that in France she had studied the poor without meeting them, Emily Balch became active in social work. In December 1892, she joined in founding Denison House, a Boston settlement house patterned on Chicago's Hull House, and served as Headworker for a year until her Bryn Mawr classmate Helena Dudley was available for the post. In 1894, she attended the national convention of the American Federation of Labor as a delegate of Boston's Central Labor Union.

Emily Balch studied economics for a semester at the Harvard Annex (later Radcliffe) in 1893, under the intellectual influence of the historical economist William Ashley, and spent a quarter taking courses in economic theory and sociology at the University of Chicago in 1895. Together with another of Ashley's graduate students, Mary Kingsbury (later Simkhovitch), Balch spent 1895–1896 at the University of Berlin, attending the seminars of the public finance specialist Adolf Wagner and of Gustav Schmoller, founder of the "Younger Historical School." Balch recalled that "As [the University] was not regularly open to women students I got permission from the Reich Cultus Minister, the Rector of the University, and separately from each professor with whom I was to study. My friend, Mary Kingsbury and I were curiosities" although they found several German and Polish women among the graduate students in economics. Balch and Kingsbury attended the

International Socialist Workers and Trade Union Congress in London in July 1896 (Balch 1972: 40–47).

Balch hoped to complete a PhD at the Massachusetts Institute of Technology, but at that time MIT's degree requirements included chemistry, which she had not studied. However, she returned from Germany in 1896 on the same ship as Katharine Coman, who was then teaching economics single-handedly at Wellesley and later the author of the lead article in the first issue of the *American Economic Review* (see Coman 1891, 1911a, 1911b; Balch 1915; Vaughn 2004; Robin Bartlett on Coman in Dimand, Dimand, and Forget 2000). Coman invited Balch to join Wellesley, initially grading student papers, but teaching economics courses from the second semester. Balch was at Wellesley from 1896 to 1918. From 1900, she taught sociology as well as economics (see Deegan 1983), the first person to teach sociology at Wellesley. Emily Balch taught innovative courses on the history of socialism, labor problems, social pathology, immigration, consumption, and the economic role of women, as well as introductory economics (taking a marginalist approach based on the writings of Böhm-Bawerk), sociology, statistics, and economic history. The English Fabian H. G. Wells, writing about his visit to Wellesley in 1906, expressed surprise that Marx's *Capital* (Volume I, the only volume then translated into English) was still used as a textbook for the course in socialism, to which Balch responded by pointing out that her course was on the history of socialism (Randall 1964: 103). Her courses on the economic role of women and on consumption led to articles on "The Education and Efficiency of Women" (1910b) and on "The Economic Role of the Housewife" (1914).

Scholar and Reformer

Balch chose to live solely on her earnings, giving away her unearned income from her father's estate. In 1899 she lent $200 to a striking shoe-makers union in Marlboro, Massachusetts, and was later "told by President Caroline Hazard[3] of Wellesley that this loan was the reason that she had been kept on as a mere assistant without normal promotion" (Randall 1964: 109). Balch helped found the Women's Trade Union League in 1903, and later served as president of its

Boston branch. She served on the Massachusetts Factory Inspection Commission (1908–1909) and Boston's City Planning Board (1914–1917), and chaired the Massachusetts Minimum Wage Commission (established 1913), which drafted the country's first minimum wage law. Like Coman, she was active in the Consumers League. Promoted to associate professor in 1903, Balch declared herself a socialist in 1906 and accepted reappointment at Wellesley only on condition of Wellesley president Ellen Pendleton knowing that. Together with her Wellesley colleague Vida Scudder, Balch organized a three-day conference on "Socialism as a World Movement" in Boston in 1909.

Influenced by Fabians such as H. G. Wells, Christian Socialists such as Charles Kingsley, and the "socialism of the chair" of her professors in Berlin, Balch was a socialist but "never a follower of Marx . . . I never accepted the theory or practice of the class struggle, which I rejected both on scientific and ethical grounds. But the existing competitive system seemed to me so bad that I hated to appear to acquiesce in it. A system in which production was shaped not with the purpose of making what was needed and of making it beautiful and good of its kind, but with the purpose of making a profit appeared to me a basic topsy-turvyism which had widespread vicious results. To make the fundamental relation of men in the whole economic field competitive self-seeking, instead of cooperation or mutual benefit, appeared to me the negation of Christianity or any other decent ethical system" (Balch 1972: 49).

Among economists, Emily Greene Balch was the outstanding opponent of the Immigration Restriction League, in which such economists as John R. Commons and Irving Fisher were prominent (see Commons 1907). The proponents of immigration restriction, alarmed by new waves of immigration to the United States from Central, Eastern, and Southern Europe rather than the British Isles, eventually achieved in the early 1920s legislation limiting annual immigration from any country to 2 percent of the number of Americans of that national origin recorded in the 1890 census (before the main sources of immigration changed). Emily Balch spent 1904–1905 on sabbatical in Austria-Hungary, visiting the sources of Slavic immigration to the United States (becoming a close friend of Tomas and Charlotte Garrigue Masaryk[4] in Prague) and 1905–1906 on unpaid leave, visiting centers of Slavic immigration in the United States. Balch lived with a Czech worker's family in New York City for several months, to learn Czech before her travels in Austria-Hungary (Balch 1910a: v, 1972: xxiii–xiv). Her *magnum opus* of 536 pages, *Our Slavic Fellow Citizens* (1910a), was a scholarly but passionate defense of the social, cultural, and economic benefits of free immigration from diverse sources, described by the *Encyclopaedia Britannica* as "the most sympathetic and thoroughgoing study of Slavic immigration ever made" (Wood 1968). She upheld this cause in many venues, including the annual meeting of the American Economic Association, in a discussion published in the *Papers and Proceedings* Supplement to the second volume of the *American Economic Review* (Balch et al. 1912a, 1912b). Balch welcomed diverse immigration to build "themselves and us alike into a greater and wiser culture," embracing "Catholic and Jew, Italian and Pole, Slovak and Yankee and Chinaman" (Balch 1972: 32). Upon the outbreak of the Second World War, Balch again defended this view in her 1939 Women's International League for Peace and Freedom leaflet on *Refugees as Assets* (revised in 1940 and reprinted in Balch 1972: 60–62), presenting economic and cultural as well as humanitarian arguments for welcoming refugees from Nazi Germany, and opposing "what seemed to me the narrowminded and pusillanimous policy of the American State Department" (Balch 1972: 60).

Given Balch's monumental defense of Slavic immigration against anti-immigrant sentiment, it is surprising that the only recent mention of Balch by an economist known to me is a paragraph by Nancy Folbre (1994: 185–86) stating that "Miss Emily Balch of Wellesley College expressed views more in keeping with Commons" and that "the perceptions of national and racial interest promoted by Balch, Ross, Commons, and Walker testify to the complex grid of opposition that reformers faced." Since no further identification of Balch is provided (apart from repeating the title "Miss"), readers are not alerted to how startling this view of Balch is in light of the anti-racist stand on immigration that was then the focus of Balch's efforts and the long commitment to internationalism for which she eventually shared the Nobel Peace Prize. Folbre cites only a brief comment by Balch (1907) on an article by E. A. Ross, with no mention of *Our Slavic Fellow Citizens* (Balch 1910a), a full-scale treatise diametrically opposed to

Commons's *Races and Immigrants in America* (1907) and to the earlier writings of Francis Amasa Walker, the founding president of the American Economic Association.

Folbre (1994: 186) quotes a startling sentence that shows Balch in 1907 as influenced at least fleetingly by the eugenic arguments of her opponents. Criticizing Sidney Webb for proposing "the social endowment of motherhood" (family allowances), Balch wrote that "if you want simply to have more people, to have any kind of people, depraved people quite as well as any other class, measures like this, like feeding school children, are a good thing; but if you believe it is important to have not only more people, but most particularly to have more of the right kind of people, than any measure of encouragement should be most carefully selective in character" (Balch 1907: 625). Such criticism of even school lunches as promoting indiscriminate population growth is anomalous for a writer whose career began with a sympathetic account of public assistance to the poor in France, who campaigned for (and helped administer) Massachusetts's minimum-wage law, and whose straightforward diagnosis of the problem of poverty was that "What the Poor Need is Income" (Balch 1913). Whether her brief comment on Ross was a passing aberration or a misjudged attempt to argue on her opponent's home ground, it was wholly unrepresentative of Balch's life's work. At the very least, the comment discovered by Folbre strikingly demonstrates the pervasiveness of eugenic arguments among American economists early in this century, affecting even so steadfast a pro-immigration internationalist as Emily Greene Balch.

Working for Peace in Time of War

In 1913, Balch received a five-year contract as full professor and as head of Wellesley's Department of Economics and Sociology, succeeding her long-time friend Katharine Coman. Although dying of cancer, Coman left for Europe to survey systems of social insurance for the American Association for Labor Legislation. A pacifist since the Spanish-American War, Balch joined Jane Addams among the forty American delegates to the International Congress of Women at The Hague in 1915, urging a conference of neutral countries to offer mediation to resolve World War I (Addams, Balch, and Hamilton 1915). In support of this plan, Balch visited Scandinavia and Russia, and lobbied President Woodrow Wilson, who had been one of her teachers at Bryn Mawr, and British Cabinet ministers Sir Edward Grey and Lord Crewe. Balch visited Wilson six times from July to December 1915 (Alonso 1995: 12). She spent several months with the International Committee on Mediation in Stockholm in 1916. Wilson studied the proposals of the International Conference of Women until his copy was dog-eared, and stated that "I consider them by far the best formulation which up to the moment has been put out by any body" (Balch 1972: xxv–xxvi). However, as Balch later reflected, "In spite of real interest in the plan in some responsible quarters, it was wrecked by President Wilson's refusing to take it up. He doubtless felt that he could act better alone when the time came, but when it came he was no longer a neutral but completely involved in the power politics of the Allies" (1972: xxvi).

Balch wrote for *The Nation* in New York City during a sabbatical (1916–1917) and unpaid leave (1917–1918), opposing conscription and defending civil liberties, including those of conscientious objectors and the foreign-born. Combining scholarship with advocacy, she also published academic articles on "The Effect of War and Militarism on the Status of Women" (1916) and "War in Its Relation to Democracy and World Order" (1917b) and a book on how to end the war, *Approaches to the Great Settlement* (1918). Balch wrote a deliberately tactless letter to be read into the *Congressional Record* on April 5, 1917, on "Tabulation of motives behind votes of Congressmen on eve of War Declaration" (1917a), but, displaying empathy for her former teacher Wilson, spoke of a "war urged by the President on a reluctant Congress upon the grounds of the most disinterested idealism." Balch was in the gallery the next morning at 3:00 a.m. when Congress voted for war (Whipps 2006: 125). She acted as liaison among such groups as the Women's Peace Party, the Emergency Peace Federation, and the American Union Against Militarism (predecessor of the American Civil Liberties Union), and was prominent in demonstrations. Her Wellesley contract expired in 1918. The following year, the board of trustees narrowly refused to reappoint her, nominally for her lengthy absence from the college, despite vehement protests by Wellesley College president Ellen Pendleton, alumnae trustees, and Balch's department (Randall 1964; Corcoran 1970). In claiming that extension of Balch's leave of absence was the issue, the Wellesley trustees were less forthright than President Nicholas Murray Butler of Columbia University, who announced in a 1917 Commencement Day address the suspension of academic freedom for the duration of the war and then proceeded to purge a junior instructor[5] who, before the war, had been indiscreet enough to work for the pacifist Association for International Conciliation at the invitation of the Association's then-head—Nicholas Murray Butler (Metzger 1955: 225, 227). At the age of fifty-two, twenty-three years after joining Wellesley, Emily Greene Balch lost her academic position for the same anti-war activism for which, after another world war, she was to share the Nobel Peace Prize. In her heavily ironic words, Balch "overstrained the habitual liberality" of Wellesley College (quoted by Randall 1964: 246). President Pendleton invited Balch to give the Armistice Day address in 1935, and a later Wellesley president, Mildred McAfee Horton, supported efforts to put Balch forward for the Nobel Peace Prize. Balch was always polite about Wellesley College, having deliberately risked her job to follow her deeply-held beliefs in opposing the war. "No word of censure or recrimination ever passed her lips" (Randall 164: 257) but, although she lived in Wellesley, Massachusetts, until her ninetieth year, she left her papers to Swarthmore College.

In January 1919, Archibald Stevenson, a New York lawyer working for the Military Intelligence Division of the War Department, gave a Senate subcommittee a list of sixty-two "dangerous, destructive and anarchistic" individuals including Jane Addams and Emily Greene Balch. New York State's Lusk Commission singled out Addams and Balch in its 1920 report on "Revolutionary Radicalism," and devoted a chapter to emphasizing that the People's Council of America for Democracy and Terms of Peace had advocated a negotiated end to World War I because its activists were "crafty" agents of Imperial Germany and Bolshevik Russia trying to overthrow the US Government. The Daughters of the American Revolution expelled Addams because as International President of the Women's International League for Peace and Freedom, she was part of a "world revolutionary movement . . . to destroy civilization and Christianity . . . and the government of the United States." The US War Department's "Spider Web Chart" in 1923 included Addams and Balch among people linked to organizations tinted red to violet, with the WILPF in red as subversive (Alonso 1995: 14–15). But by the later 1920s the Red Scare had abated, and US Government support for the Briand-Kellogg Pact outlawing war (ratified by Congress in 1928, and named in part for US Secretary of State Frank Kellogg) made the peace movement respectable again. Balch gave a series of lectures in England urging ratification of the Briand-Kellogg Pact (Jahn 1946: 3) and Addams also campaigned in support of the treaty. President Herbert Hoover sent Jane Addams flowers when she won the Nobel Peace Prize in 1931. In contrast, when Balch won the Peace Prize in the early days of the Cold War, neither President Harry Truman nor any other US official congratulated her, and a *New York Times* editorial regretted that she had won the prize instead of the international leaders who had founded the United Nations (Alonso 1995: 16, 19).

Raised a Unitarian, Balch joined the London branch of Society of Friends (the Quakers) in 1921. At about the same time, she rejected socialism, as having become too closely identified with Marxism rather than with pacifism. Both as a pacifist and as an intensely spiritual person (see Faver 1991), Balch emphatically preferred the methods and goals of Gandhi to those of Lenin. Active in the International Congress of Women in Zurich in May 1919, Balch was the founding international secretary-treasurer (until 1922 and again in 1934–1935) of the Women's International League for Peace and Freedom (WILPF), the Geneva-based permanent organization established by the congress. Balch traveled Central Europe and the Balkans urging women to attend the WILPF congress that she organized in Vienna in 1921, and taught peace education in WILPF summer schools. She succeeded Jane Addams as president of the American section in 1931 (the year Addams won the Nobel Peace Prize) and as honorary international president in 1937. With five other Americans (including two African-American women and her fellow Quaker, the University of Chicago economist Paul H. Douglas of the Cobb-Douglas production function), Balch investigated conditions in Haiti in 1926, and urged the removal of the US Marines who had occupied Haiti since 1915 (Balch 1927, edited and largely written by Balch). As an economist, she addressed

WILPF congresses in Washington, DC, on "Economic Aspects of a New International Order" in 1924 (Balch 1972: 110–115) and in Dublin on "Economic Imperialism with Special Reference to the U. S." in 1926 (Balch 1926, 1972: 140–44). Since these addresses were published in the proceedings of those congresses (the 1926 paper also in the pacifist journal *Pax International*), and perhaps also because of their subject matter, they escaped the notice of most mainstream economists. Appalled by Nazi Germany's threat to dominate Europe and persecution of the Jews, and in view of the Pearl Harbor attack, Balch supported the US war effort in World War II as the lesser evil (as did her fellow-Quaker Paul Douglas, who joined the Marines at the age of fifty), but remained in the WILPF and urged its members to aid the interned Japanese-Americans. She defended the rights of conscientious objectors and opposed the Allied demand for unconditional surrender. In 1946, she shared the Nobel Peace Prize with John R. Mott of the Student Christian Movement. In contrast to this post-war recognition of an anti-war activist, at the end of World War I, the 1919 Peace Prize was awarded to Balch's former teacher, President Woodrow Wilson (and the 1945 prize went to Cordell Hull, recently retired as US Secretary of State). After World War II, Balch's writings emphasized internationalization of waterways, air routes, polar regions, and strategic bases, and an international reconstruction corps (Balch 1972: Part V). In January 1961, Balch died in Cambridge, Massachusetts, at the age of ninety-four, after four years in a nursing home.

Conclusion: A Pioneer to Remember

The history of economics has been written largely as the history of economic theory. Emily Balch did not contribute to pure economic theory, any more than did her teachers, the historical economists William Ashley at Harvard and Gustav Schmoller in Berlin and the sociologists Albion Small in Chicago and Franklin Giddings at Bryn Mawr. She was, however, an important figure in the broader arena of political economy, writing, teaching, and agitating on the alleviation of poverty, on the economic role of women, and on the economic, social, and cultural benefits of the "new immigration" from Central and

Eastern Europe. She particularly stressed the desirability of ethnic and cultural diversity. Her pacifist activism went beyond the boundaries of economics, but it included an acerbic critique of what she saw as the economic imperialism of her own country. She did more noteworthy things than just remark about the use of marginal utility in economic theory in the 1890s. Emily Greene Balch has largely been forgotten by the economics discipline, although Mercedes M. Randall of the WILPF succeeded in bringing her to the attention of the Nobel Peace Prize committee and, through Randall's subsequent biography of Balch and edition of Balch's selected writings, a different audience of readers interested in pacifism. Balch's political economy cannot be adequately or fairly summarized as promotion of "national and racial interest." On the contrary, she defended ethnically-diverse immigration and embraced internationalism and pacifism.

Emily Greene Balch deliberately decided to put her academic position as department head and full professor at risk to struggle for a mediated end to the First World War. She lost her chair, but stood by her beliefs, and, in the wake of another world war, shared the Nobel Peace Prize. Her use of economic arguments to combat racially-motivated proposals to restrict immigration and her emphasis on the social and cultural benefits of ethnic diversity provide a notable contrast to the views of such leading American economists as Commons, Fisher, and Walker. However, the 1907 comment reported by Folbre (1994) reveals an anomalous eugenic argument against indiscriminately aiding the poor, out of line with Balch's major writings. Balch's story should be of particular interest to women economists as the first female economist to win a Nobel Prize, to social economists as an economist who was also a pioneering sociologist, to members of Economists for Peace and Security (EPS) as a Nobel Prize-winning pacifist economist, and more generally to anyone interested in academic freedom and in the moral responsibility of academics as public intellectuals to move beyond their immediate academic role to strive for world peace and social reform and against racism. It is one among many fascinating, hitherto-neglected stories forming the rich heritage of women's participation in the disciplines of economics (see Dimand 1995, 1999; Dimand, Dimand, and Forget 2000) and of sociology (see Deegan 1988, 1991; Blasi 2005). Emily Greene Balch was an active and useful political economist, and deserves a place in a history of political economy that extends beyond the history of economic theory.

Notes

1. Department of Economics, Brock University, St. Catharines, ON L2S 3A1, Canada, dimand@brocku.ca. I wish to dedicate this paper to the memory of Laurence Moss, who encouraged me to write about Balch.

2. Furthermore, Dorfman's association of Balch with marginal utility is misleading: while she discussed Böhm-Bawerk's subjective theory of value in her course on economic theory just as she discussed Marx in her course on the history of socialism, her own research and her own overall approach to economics were shaped far more by attending the lectures of the non-neoclassical historical economists William J. Ashley at the Harvard Annex and Gustav Schmoller in Berlin. Balch's intellectual formation as an economist in the 1890s was just a few years too early for Thorstein Veblen to be a major influence on her thought.

3. Caroline Hazard, an heir to the Allied Chemical fortune, was the sister-in-law of the economist Irving Fisher.

4. The philosopher Tomas Masaryk, from 1919 the first president of Czechoslovakia, married Charlotte Garrigue, a music student from New York, and adopted her last name as his middle name.

5. The dismissal did not entirely ruin the career of the instructor in politics, Dr. Leon Fraser, since he eventually became a director of the Bank for International Settlements and President of the National City Bank, now Citigroup (Balch 1972: 103). Nicholas Murray Butler shared the Nobel Peace Prize with Jane Addams in 1931.

References

Addams, J., E. G. Balch, and A. Hamilton. (1915). *Women at The Hague.* New York: Macmillan, 1915; reprinted in Volume 2, pp. 7–148, of *Jane Addams's Writings on Peace*, Eds. J. Whipps and M. Fischer, Bristol: Thoemmes Press, 2003.

Alonso, H. H. (1995). "Nobel Peace Laureates, Jane Addams and Emily Greene Balch: Two Women of the Women's International League for Peace and Freedom." *Journal of Women's History* 7(2): 6–26.

Balch, E. G. (1893). "Public Assistance of the Poor in France." *Publications of the American Economic Association* First Series 8(4–5): 1–180.

——. (1899). *An Outline of Economics.* Cambridge, MA: Co-operative Press.

——. (1907). "Comment: Western Civilization and the Birth-Rate." *American Journal of Sociology* 12(5): 623–626.

——. (1910a). *Our Slavic Fellow Citizens.* New York: N. Y. Charities Publication Committee.

——. (1910b). "The Education and Efficiency of Women." In *The Economic Position of Women.* Ed. Helen Marot. New York: Columbia University Press (*Proceedings of the Academy of Political Science in the City of New York*), 61–71.

Balch, E. G. (1913). "What the Poor Need is Income." *Survey* (American Association for Labor Legislation), 30 (September): 755–756.

——. (1914). "The Economic Role of the Housewife." *Home Progress* 4 (September): 620–624.

——. (1915). "Katharine Coman: A Biographical Sketch." *Wellesley College News* 23 (April): 20–25.

——. (1916). "The Effect of War and Militarism on the Status of Women." *American Sociological Society Publications* 10: 39–55.

——. (1917a). "Letter: Tabulation of Motives Behind Votes of Congressmen on Eve of War Declaration." *Congressional Record,* 65th Congress, April 5, 55: 338.

——. (1917b). "War in Its Relation to Democracy and World Order." *Annals of the American Academy of Political and Social Science* 72 (July): 28–31.

——. (1918). *Approaches to the Great Settlement,* with introduction by Norman Angell. New York: B. W. Heubsch.

——. (1926). "Economic Imperialism with Special Reference to the United States." *Pax International* 2(1), reprinted in Balch (1972), 140–144.

——. ed. (1927). *Occupied Haiti, Being the Report of a Committee of Six Disinterested Americans Representing Organizations Exclusively American, Who, Having Personally Studied Conditions in Haiti in 1926, Favour the Restoration of the Independence of the Negro Republic.* New York: The Writers Publishing Company; reprinted New York: Garland Publishing, 1972.

——. (1939). *Refugees as Assets,* Women's International League for Peace and Freedom, revised 1940, reprinted in Balch (1972), 60–62.

——. (1972). *Beyond Nationalism: The Social Thought of Emily Greene Balch.* Ed. Mercedes M. Randall. New York: Twayne Publishers, 1972.

Balch, E. G., H. S. Person, W. Kent, C. W. Mixter, W. E. Hotchkiss, R. Seubert, and F. L. Hutchins. (1912a). "Industrial Efficiency and the Interest of Labor: Round Table Discussion." *American Economic Review* Supplement 2: 117–130.

Balch, E. G., W. F. Wilcox, J. W. Jenks, and M. J. Kohler. (1912b). "Restriction of Immigration: Discussion." *American Economic Review* Supplement 2:63–78.

Blasi, A. J, Ed. (2005). *Diverse Histories of American Sociology.* Leiden: Brill.

Coman, K. (1891). "The Tailoring Trade and the Sweating System." *Publications of the American Economic Association*, First Series, 6 (January/March): 144–147.

———. (1911a). "Some Unsettled Problems of Irrigation." *American Economic Review* 1(1): 1–19.

———. (1911b). "Government Factories: An Attempt to Control Competition in the Fur Trade." *American Economic Review* Supplement 1(2): 368–388.

Commons, J. R. (1907). *Races and Immigrants in America.* New York: Macmillan.

Corcoran, T. (1970). "Vita Dutton Scudder: The Impact of World War I on the Radical Woman Professor." *Anglican Theological Review* April, 164–181.

Deegan, M. J. (1983). "Sociology at Wellesley College: 1900–1919." *Journal of the History of Sociology* 5 (Spring): 91–117.

———. (1988). *Jane Addams and the Men of the Chicago School, 1892–1918.* New Brunswick, NJ: Transaction Books.

———. ed. (1991). *Women in Sociology: A Bio-Bibliographical Sourcebook.* New York: Greenwood Press.

Dimand, R. W. (1995). "The Neglect of Women's Contributions to Economics." In *Women of Value: Feminist Essays in the History of Economics.* Eds. M. A. Dimand, R. W. Dimand, and E. L. Forget. Cheltenham, UK, and Brookfield, VT: Edward Elgar Publishing.

———. (1999). "Women in the Canon of Economics." In *Reflecting on the Classical Canon in Economics: Essays in Honour of Samuel Hollander.* Eds. E. L. Forget and S. J. Peart. London and New York: Routledge.

Dimand, R. W., M. A. Dimand, and E. L. Forget, Eds. (2000). *A Biographical Dictionary of Women Economists.* Cheltenham, UK: Edward Elgar Publishing.

Dorfman, J. (1946–1959). *The Economic Mind in American Civilization, 1606–1933,* 5 vols. New York: Viking.

Faver, C. A. (1991). " 'Creative Apostle of Reconciliation': The Spirituality and Social Philosophy of Emily Greene Balch." *Women's Studies* 18: 335–351.

Folbre, N. (1994). *Who Pays for the Kids? Gender and the Structures of Constraint.* London and New York: Routledge.

Gwinn, K. E. (2010). *Emily Greene Balch: The Long Road to Internationalism.* Urbana, IL: University of Illinois Press.

Jahn, G. (1946). "The Nobel Peace Prize 1946: Presentation Speech by Gunnar Jahn, Chairman of the Nobel Committee." http://nobelprize.org/nobel_prize/peace/laureates/1946.

Lee, F. S. (2009). *A History of Heterodox Economics.* London and New York: Routledge.

Metzger, W. P. (1955). *Academic Freedom in the Age of the University.* New York: Columbia University Press.

Opdycke, S. (1999). "Balch, Emily Greene." In *American National Biography.* Eds. J. A. Garraty and M. C. Carnes. New York and London: Oxford University Press, 2: 39–40.

Randall, M. M. (1964). *Improper Bostonian: Emily Greene Balch, Nobel Peace Laureate, 1946.* New York: Twayne Publishers.

Sandmo, A. (2007). "Retrospectives: Léon Walras and the Nobel Peace Prize." *Journal of Economic Perspectives* 21(4): 217–228.

Solomon, B. M. (1980). "Balch, Emily Greene, Jan. 8, 1867–Jan. 9, 1961. Peace Advocate, Social Reformer, Economist." In *Notable American Women: The Modern Period.* Eds. B. Sicherman and C. H. Green. Cambridge, MA: Belknap Press of Harvard University Press: 41–45.

Vaughn, G. F. (2004). "Katharine Coman: America's First Woman Institutional Economist and a Champion of Education for Citizenship." *Journal of Economic Issues* 38(4): 989–1002.

Whipps, J. D. (2006). "The Feminist Pacifism of Emily Greene Balch, Nobel Peace Laureate." *NWSA Journal* 18(3): 122–132.

Wood, A. E. (1968). "Balch, Emily Greene." *Encyclopaedia Britannica* 2: 1068.

Who Do Heterodox Economists Think They Are?[1]

By Andrew Mearman*†

Abstract. This paper attempts to engage with the established debate on the nature of heterodox economics. However, it starts from the position that previous attempts to classify and identify heterodox economics have been biased towards *a priori* definition. The paper aims to inform the discussion of the nature of heterodoxy with some empirical analysis. The paper examines survey data collected from a small/medium-sized sample of AHE members on the core concepts in economics. The paper applies factor analysis to the data. It also applies principles of biological taxonomy, and thence cluster analysis to the problem. The paper finds that within the self-identified community of self-identified heterodox economists there is little agreement as to whether members are pluralist, or what their attitude is to the mainstream. Indeed, there is little agreement on any core concepts or principles. The paper argues that there is little structure to heterodox economics beyond that provided by pre-existing (or constituent) schools of thought. Based on this study, heterodox economics appears a complex web of interacting individuals and as a group is a fuzzy set. These results would lead us to question further strict distinctions between heterodox, mainstream and pluralist economists.

Introduction

What is heterodox economics? The term is now established in the literature, arguably more firmly than at any other time. It was used

*Andrew Mearman's research interests include economic methodology, economic pedagogy, and the economics of the environment. He has published articles on these topics in journals such as *Oxford Economic Papers*, *Cambridge Journal of Economics* and *Metroeconomica*.

†Bristol Business School, University of the West of England, BS16 1QY, UK, E-mail: Andrew.Mearman@uwe.ac.uk

American Journal of Economics and Sociology, Vol. 70, No. 2 (April, 2011).

originally in the 1930s and 1940s (Ayres 1936; Commons 1932, 1936; Gruchy 1947, 1948) but has gained popularity mainly in the 1990s and beyond (see Lee 2009 for a full historical treatment). The term is even being used by mainstream economists (heterodox approaches have their own JEL classification, B5). Projects are being funded to investigate how heterodox economics might enhance economics teaching and to develop resources to do this (for example, in the UK via the Economics Network). The Association for Heterodox Economists has now held 11 successful annual conferences plus numerous other events, including postgraduate training workshops and seminars. All of this suggests that the heterodox economics community is vibrant; and thus by extension, heterodox economics is strong.

At the same time though, there is considerable debate as to what exactly heterodox economics is. In the next section of the paper it will be briefly argued that there is no agreed concept of heterodox economics, only competing definitions based usually on totalizing dualistic distinctions between orthodox (or mainstream) and heterodox. These definitions often lack a clear evidential base and many are *a priori* in nature. This paper tries to move away from this *a priori* approach and attempts to contribute to the debate by investigating the nature of heterodox economics empirically.[2] In that respect this paper draws on modern biological taxonomic literature. This treatment takes seriously the notion that heterodox economists know who they are and what heterodox economics is by asking them about their core beliefs in economics. A range of statistical techniques is then applied to the data. The principal methods of statistical analysis used are factor analysis and cluster analysis. Factor analysis explores relations between variables but, in contrast to regression analysis, does not assume they are independent. Cluster analysis examines the extent of similarity between *cases* (individuals); it is used extensively in biological analysis of breeding populations of animals. The results from the analyses suggest that heterodox economics is difficult to define, and that the heterodox community is a diverse complex of individuals, groups and ideas. Strict distinctions between heterodox and other approaches to economics seem unwarranted. However, more research is needed.

Heterodox Economics

This section offers a very brief meta-analysis of definitions of heterodox economics. A longer treatment of the conceptual issues underpinning this paper can be found in Mearman (2010). There it is argued that existing treatments of heterodox economics often treat it as simply being "not orthodox economics"; heterodox and mainstream economics are often treated as being strictly distinct; the meaning of heterodox economics is often fixed; the nature of the category of heterodox economics does not match the nature of heterodox economics as it is held to be. Further, there exists a multitude of competing definitions of heterodox economics, some of which are what Dequech (2007–2008) calls "intellectual" (based on core concepts), and some which are "sociological" (based on memberships of groups). The former tend to ignore social aspects, and the latter tend to be very complex and produce anomalous results. From a third, "biological" perspective, existing treatments are often *a priori* (not based on evidence), or based on a weak or unspecified evidence base; and they tend to have opaque logic of inference from the evidence to a definition of heterodox economics.

The literal meaning of heterodox is "not orthodox." This could mean simply different from the orthodox, but often it means opposed to the orthodox. Sometimes these distinctions are strict. Dequech (2007–2008) offers a helpful analysis of existing definitions of heterodox and finds that it is difficult to arrive at one that adequately describes the current heterodox community other than "not orthodox." This is rather unsatisfactory in several ways. First, the grounds for establishing strict distinctions of that type are themselves very strict and may not hold (Dow 1990). Second, a definition of "not orthodox" implies a clear definition of "orthodox," which is itself contentious (see Colander, Holt, and Rosser 2004).[3] Third, defining heterodox as not orthodox appears to undersell heterodox economics, which in its traditional composite elements, such as Marxism and Keynesianism, would appear to be more than merely critique. Both Marxism and Keynesianism, for example, contain constructive programs of economic theory (albeit in an interdisciplinary way), economic method, logic, ontology, politics, ethics, etc. that differ from those espoused by the orthodoxy. Consequently, perhaps aware of the agenda of not appearing merely critical, several economists have offered explicit or implicit definitions of heterodox economics.

Thus we have a range of definitions. Some of these definitions are intellectual (based on ideas), others are sociological (based on group memberships), some are both. Lee (2010) defines heterodox economics as a community based around a set of ideas, but identifies it principally as being based on the notion of an analysis of the provisioning process as being necessarily social, whereas mainstream economics views the provisioning process in asocial (individualistic) terms. Lawson (2006) adopts a different level of analysis to define mainstream economics in terms of the insistence on the use of mathematical modeling in economics and that heterodox economics entails the rejection of this approach. The composition of the Association for Heterodox Economists defines heterodoxy in terms of specific pre-existing schools of non-mainstream thought. Yet, the contents of George (2008) suggest heterodoxy as being newer challenges to the mainstream, such as new approaches to axiomatization, evolutionary economics, experimental methods and new growth theory. Others attempt to define the mainstream (and by implication, heterodoxy). Arnsperger and Varoufakis (2009) define neo-classical economics in terms of methodological individualism, methodological instrumentalism and methodological equilibriation. By implication, heterodox economics does not meet these critieria. Davis (2009) echoes these treatments somewhat by arguing that heterodoxy has a shared vision of the embedded individual interacting with and affecting structures in historical time.

A consequence of the tension between sociological definitions of heterodox economics and the intellectual definitions is that we now face a range of definitions of heterodox economics that do not appear to describe it very well. There are two layers to this problem. First, the category heterodox economics does not tend to be of a similar nature to the object. Treatments of heterodox economics, as already argued, tend to treat it as mutually exclusive from orthodox economics, and treat both as crisp, well defined sets of objects. They tend to arrive at either a(n Aristotelian) single essential definition of heterodox or at least a definition of clear (Wittgensteinian) "family resemblance" between disparate groups. Lawson's (2006) treatment can be seen as an example of the former. Many other treatments tend to define heterodox economics in terms of factors common to a number of schools of thought. However, these simple definitions belie the widely acknowledged complexity of heterodox economics (see Mearman 2010).

Second, the definitions lead to unsatisfactory descriptions of current heterodox communities. It could be argued that Lawson's definition succeeds, because it is arguable that none of the current heterodox communities insist on the use of mathematics. It is also strongly arguable that the mainstream does insist on mathematical modeling; it is also true that such a movement is a powerful force in economics. Thus, Lawson's definition has some utility. However, in other ways it is rather unsatisfactory, perhaps because it appears rather narrow. Further it fails to capture the extent to which some economists who would otherwise be classified as heterodox—such as Sraffian or neo-Ricardian economists, some Post Keynesian economists (for example, Mark Setterfield) and indeed many ecological economists (for example, Victor 2008)—make extensive use of mathematics, modeling and simulation. The definition itself—although Lawson would acknowledge the wider nature of heterodoxy—also does not capture the notion identified by Lee (2010) as heterodox economics as a concatenation of ideas.

However, if we try to apply many of the other definitions, such as Lee's (2010), Davis' (2009) and Arnsperger and Varoufakis' (2009), different problems are encountered. We arrive at main categories that create large groups of "others", i.e., those who do not fit well into any of them. The most obvious anomaly is Austrian economists. Sociologically, because Austrian economists tend to participate less in heterodox events and societies than, say, Post Keynesians, they might not be considered heterodox. However, intellectually, it is easier to argue they are heterodox. For example, they do not believe in individual rationality in the mainstream sense, see markets as non-equilibrium systems, note the importance of time, history and change, and emphasize uncertainty. They certainly do not fit into Davis' (or Arnsperger and Varoufakis') description of mainstream economics. However, neither do they accord with many aspects of heterodox groups: for instance, they neglect power, they tend to be politically different from other heterodox groups, and they view markets as essentially likely to be effective. So, on policy they are closer to the mainstream than to heterodox economics. Further, they are also methodologically individualist (albeit differently from mainstream economists). Thus they do not fit into Lee's category of heterodox economics either.

Similar arguments could be made about many heterodox schools. It is easy to see why Dequech (2007–2008) might have reached his conclusion that apart from in their opposition to the mainstream, there is no way to define heterodox economics. It would seem that any adequate definition of heterodox economics must capture its nature as a concatenation; but it must also be able to capture the current diversity of the heterodox community. These two requirements are in many ways contradictory: one suggests coherence, the other does not.

A biological perspective suggests further criticisms of existing treatments of heterodox economics. One criticism of the above approaches is that they are *a prioristic* and analytical. They are not based on evidence, their evidential base is unclear, or the logic of inference used to move from evidence to a definition of heterodox economics is unclear. These concerns inform the approach adopted in this paper. It is possible to define heterodox economics in terms of concepts; but equally it can be defined in terms of populations of self-defined heterodox economists. That way, one can identify heterodox economic ideas but also the make-up of a self-identified heterodox economist. Indeed, this is the approach taken in recent developments in zoological taxonomy: there has been a move away from thinking in terms of types to thinking in terms of populations of breeding creatures (see Mayr 1969). This may generate an image unpleasant to some, of economists breeding. And of course, in some ways it is an inappropriate metaphor. In other ways, though, it might capture quite well the activities of economists exchanging ideas, acting in communities, borrowing on the genetics of the groups they are in, sharing common ancestors. Such an approach would require an historical account of individual economists, which is beyond the scope of this paper.[4] However, one key idea present in the new zoological taxonomy is adopted here: that of gathering together a "breeding population"[5]—viz. self-identified heterodox economists—and then building up descriptions of heterodoxy from statements made by those economists about the fundamentals of economics. Such is the approach of this paper.

Data Collection

Data was collected via a questionnaire. The questionnaire was received in three ways: first, questionnaires were distributed at the conference of the Association for Heterodox Economists (AHE) conference in Cambridge, UK in July 2008. An announcement was made by the author at the conference for questionnaires to be completed. In order to capture people who did not complete the questionnaire at the time, and also to capture people who are self-identified heterodox economists by virtue of being AHE members, two further appeals were made to attract respondents via the AHE listserv. Respondents were able to either post or e-mail their responses to the author. It should be noted that in terms of data reliability this may raise concerns because of order effects (see, for example, Macauley et al. 1971). However, soliciting responses from the listserv also reduces possible bias in the conference attendees.

The questionnaire can be viewed in the Appendix. It was headed "What are the core economic precepts?" in order to deflect respondents from its main purpose; namely to ascertain a definition of heterodox economics. The heading also had the benefit of being usable in wider groups of economists. The questionnaire asks respondents to offer their degree of agreement with a series of statements. Respondents could agree completely (with a score of 10), disagree completely (score of 0) or offer partial agreement/disagreement or hedge their answers by choosing intermediate points on the scale.[6] Thus the questions were a form of semantic differential rating scale. As an innovation, respondents answered on a sliding scale that had no numbers to guide them. This was done because it was felt that respondents might be drawn to choose given numbers, as anchor points. It was feared that such anchor effects would generate clustering of responses. This might reduce variation in the data and affect our ability to analyze it.[7,8]

The questions were derived from the literature on heterodoxy and from schools regarded as traditionally heterodox. Principally two main criteria were used for selection: 1) mainstream concepts, in order to assess the extent to which heterodox economics is merely a rejection of the mainstream; and 2) concepts from the literature associated with heterodox economics. In order to reflect the literature, a mixture of methodological and meta-theoretical points was included. Inevitably there will be concepts potentially includable that have been omitted. The most obvious candidate is any explicit reference to institutions; i.e., the concept of institutions was not used explicitly, although things that may be considered as institutions (e.g., money) were included. However, many of the concepts included (e.g., history and power) are of relevance to institutionalist economists. The intention in the balance of questions was to address key elements of mainstream economics plus other elements from other constituent schools of heterodox economics. Thus, the inclusion of class should score highly amongst Marxist and Post Keynesian economists, money should score highly with Post Keynesians, uncertainty with Post Keynesian and Austrians, power with Marxists and institutionalists, gender with feminists and perhaps institutionalists and Marxists, etc. However, it may also be true that many self-identified heterodox economists retain beliefs or use concepts held by the mainstream. This explains further the relevance of placing responses on a sliding scale rather than on a yes/no basis.

Four issues with the data should be noted. First, responses were measured off the page manually. This may generate some measurement and rounding error.[9] Second, it may be argued that respondents' feelings may not be accurately measured by this scale. This is unavoidable in such survey situations. In a pilot draft of the questionnaire respondents were asked a supplementary question for each main question: "how confident are you in your answer?" However, this led to what was judged to be an unreasonable level of detail and was removed. Third, some people may be serial high responders. This could bias the scores overall in favor of those people. It is possible to recalibrate these scores but it was decided that they should remain as recorded, because the strength of feeling expressed may well be reflected in the strength of feeling within the organization. So, if specific groups of people tended to hold strong views, this would influence the tenor of debate within the larger group. This could be a finding *per se*. For this reason, as well as wanting to preserve the original data as much as possible, raw data scores were kept.[10] Fourth, it could be argued that the questions address different types of thing. As in Dow (2004), we can imagine schools of thought as layered; the layers may be things such as ontology, methodology, methods, theories, and policy. In some sense, the lower levels might be said to be causes of the higher levels (ontology clearly might affect methods). Further, some concepts might bridge across schools of thought, and even outside heterodox economics. For example, pluralism might be one such concept. If one took a pluralist position, this would imply a range of methods being used, and it might imply that an economist holds both that gender and class are important foundations for theory. So, the economist's attitude to pluralism would be to a degree a cause of their response to the questions on class and gender. In a regression analysis, for example, it would be an error to specify heterodox as defined by pluralism and defined by gender because pluralism partly defines gender. However, in cluster analysis this is unproblematic. In taxonomy, cluster analysis is used to group objects on the basis of similarity in terms of characteristics (such as size, color) in order to then assess the identity (in terms of genetic data) of the objects. However, "characteristics" can be of different types, such as diet, mating behavior, location, prey, and color, which are as varied as between pluralism and gender (for example). So there is license to include variates of different types in a cluster analysis. On the other hand, for our research question, including too wide a variety of variates, encompassing theory, etc., would make it less likely that clusters are identified. Consequently, we have chosen variates that are all broadly methodological, so that clusters are more likely; it also allows the number of variates to be reduced.

Data Analysis

The data has been analyzed in a range of ways. Descriptive statistics, as ever, can aid the narrative considerably. These are followed by a discussion of factor analysis and cluster analysis that were applied to the data.

Descriptive Statistics

Forty-three responses were received. Based on an AHE membership of roughly 250,[11] this is a response rate of 17 percent. This is somewhat disappointing although within the normal range for online surveys. One might conventionally interpret the rate and the low n as making the data poor and the results also. There are two main issues here. One is that the small sample makes inference difficult. All inferences to populations from samples should be done carefully and in this case the need is stronger. However, if we take the results as totally sample specific, then references to superpopulations and statistical significance become irrelevant. For our purposes, the sample *is* the population. Second, the small sample affects the efficacy of the techniques used. The results from the analysis should be viewed even more cautiously than usual. As a final point, we should note that some of the questionnaires were not completed, with one or two questions unanswered. These missing values were filled by imputing values using an iterative expectation-maximization method in SPSS.

Descriptive statistics are shown in Table 1. A list of variates and abbreviations is found at the end of the paper. The descriptive statistics show some predictable and some more surprising results. The variation in responses is quite pronounced, although it differs between questions. There is a strong willingness to recognize oneself as heterodox (unsurprisingly in this context), and (to a lesser extent) as pluralist, perhaps reflecting that pluralism was the theme of a succession of AHE conferences. The score for mainstream is not high, yet clearly non-zero, suggesting that the heterodox group still recognizes some mainstream label. That suggests that the strict distinction often made between mainstream and heterodox is not supported by this data. There may be some key issues that cause disagreement in the heterodox community. E.g., labor and scarcity have large standard deviations. However, there were also high scores for history and power, which are traditional heterodox concerns. The scores for uncertain and fallibility are also high, although for both (echoing the

Table 1a

Descriptive statistics of survey data

	N	Mode	Mean	SD
Mm	43	0.00	0.1341	0.17317
He	43	1.00	0.8221	0.19436
Pl	43	1.00	0.7105	0.29207
Ra	43	0.00, 0.10	0.2186	0.21906
Eq	43	0.00	0.1773	0.22206
Cl	43	1.00	0.6701	0.26847
Po	43	0.00	0.2047	0.24344
Na	43	0.90	0.7166	0.24807
Un	43	0.90	0.7291	0.25053
Fa	43	0.90	0.7093	0.31496
Pw	43	0.90	0.8047	0.25816
La	43	1.00	0.6839	0.32363
Sc	43	0.00	0.3651	0.30910
Ge	43	0.50	0.5558	0.30437
Ma	43	0.20	0.3488	0.28316
In	43	0.20	0.2139	0.23055
Mk	43	0.20	0.3058	0.25523
Mo	43	0.50	0.5416	0.29516
Hi	43	0.90	0.9081	0.12580
Sex	43		0.19	

Table 1b

Age statistics

	n	min	max	mean
Total	42	27	77	49.83
Age up to 44	17			
Age 45–59	13			
Age 60 or over	12			

statistics for pluralist) variation of response is also quite high. On the basis of these data, both mainstream and heterodox economics are more like fuzzy sets than strictly distinct.

Table 2 shows statistically significant correlations between variates. The first thing to note is that there is a strong negative correlation ($r = -0.438$) between heterodox and mainstream. This statistic supports the thesis that heterodox economics is analytically defined (at least partly) as a rejection of mainstream economics. However, in an association such as the AHE, such an oppositional stance will inevitably also reflect sociological factors. Also possibly significant is that the opening questions were in terms of how the respondent sees themselves, rather than in judging concepts. If we then look at the correlation between heterodox and mainstream *concepts*, the picture is less clear. Correlations between heterodox and concepts such as positive, rational, equilibrium, markets, maths and even scarcity are negative but small. There is stronger evidence of rejection of mainstream economic concepts in the stronger correlations between those concepts and specific traditionally heterodox concepts: for example, class is strongly negatively correlated with several mainstream concepts. History is strongly negatively correlated with equilibrium (echoing Robinson 1974 perhaps), individuals and scarcity. Power has consistent negative correlation with mainstream concepts. Further, mainstream concepts are correlated with each other, as are several groups of traditionally heterodox concepts: for example, class is strongly positively correlated with power, labor, gender and negatively with individuals (not surprisingly), positive and markets. Uncertain is strongly correlated with fallibilism, (negatively with) maths and, perhaps reflecting feminist thought, with gender.

Factor Analysis

The correlations suggest (together with the practical benefit of reducing the data) factor analysis might be appropriate.[12] Significantly, Table 2 suggests significant groups of concepts that are correlated with each other. These associations can be readily assessed by factor analysis, the results of which are shown in Table 3, which displays factors derived by principal components analysis after a varimax rotation.[13]

Table 2

Correlations between variates

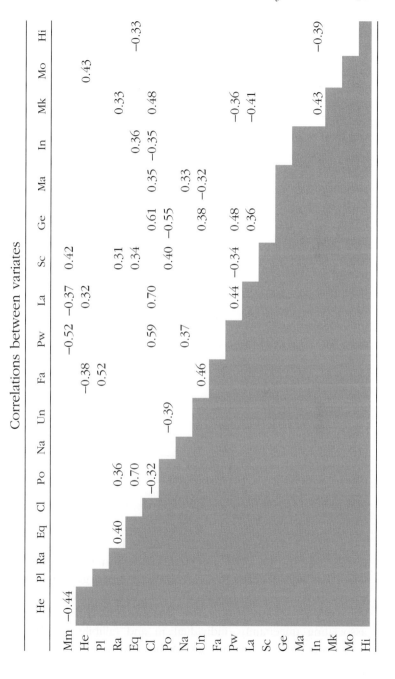

	He	Pl	Ra	Eq	Cl	Po	Na	Un	Fa	Pw	La	Sc	Ge	Ma	In	Mk	Mo	Hi
Mm	−0.44																	
He									−0.38	−0.52	−0.37	0.42					0.43	
Pl									0.52		0.32							
Ra				0.40		0.36						0.31				0.33		
Eq						0.70						0.34			0.36			
Cl						−0.32				0.59	0.70		0.61		−0.35	0.48		−0.33
Po								−0.39				0.40	−0.55					
Na										0.37				0.33				
Un									0.46				0.38	−0.32				
Fa																		
Pw											0.44	−0.34	0.48			−0.36		
La													0.36			−0.41		
Sc																		
Ge																		
Ma																		
In																0.43		
Mk																		
Mo																		−0.39
Hi																		

Table 3

Factor analysis results

	Factor				
	1	2	3	4	5
positive	**0.859**				
equilibrium	**0.853**				
scarcity	**0.564**				
rational	**0.515**				
class		**0.871**			
labor		**0.866**			
power		**0.652**			
markets		**−0.626**			
gender		**0.551**			
fallibilism			**0.775**		
uncertain			**0.773**		
individuals			**0.616**		
natural				**0.830**	
maths				**0.666**	
money					**0.835**
history					**0.650**
Cronbach's alpha	0.723	0.542	0.614	0.488	0.353
eigenvalues	4.219	2.284	1.992	1.436	1.297
% variance explained	26.370	14.277	12.448	8.977	8.104

Extraction Method: Principal Component Analysis.
Rotation Method: Varimax with Kaiser Normalization.
Kaiser-Meyer-Olkin Measure of Sampling Adequacy: 0.640
Bartlett's Test of Sphericity: Approx. Chi-Square 269.198 (p = 0.000)

The results shown in Table 3 are intuitively sensible and reflect the results from the bivariate correlations shown in Table 2. The second factor has high loadings on class, power, labor, gender and (negatively) markets. Factor 2 might thus be called a "radical" (or perhaps Marxist-feminist) grouping. Factor 3 might be an "Austrian" grouping, associating uncertainty, individualism and fallibilism.[14] Factor 4 is perhaps a "Post Keynesian" group that stresses money and history.

Factor 5 suggests an "ecological economics" group that stresses natural systems, but also the use of mathematics.

Factor 1 might be called a mainstream factor. Significantly, this factor groups rational, equilibrium and scarcity. This may reflect a bias within heterodox economics as to what constitutes the mainstream: i.e., if heterodox economists associate scarcity, equilibrium and rationality with the mainstream, they may reject them more easily. The finding also partly supports Davis' (2009) definition of the mainstream in terms of equilibrium, rationality and individualism. However, the adoption of individualism by Austrian economists means that the adoption of individualism alone cannot be a definition of the mainstream; it also complicates the division between mainstream and heterodox. Further, the mean scores for "mainstream concepts," although consistently lower than heterodox concepts, are consistently non-zero. Also, although there was a significant negative correlation between mainstream and heterodox, the correlation coefficient was only |0.438|, meaning that many respondents regard themselves mainly as clearly defined heterodox economists—yet with an important element of mainstream economics thrown in. Heterodox economists are a mixture of concepts and influences. An alternative interpretation is that heterodox and mainstream are overlapping categories. This would be significant given that treatments of mainstream and heterodox often treat them as strictly distinct. The other clear finding for this group is that in terms of concepts, heterodox economics remains a concatenation of ideas (echoing Lee's (2010) term) *and* groupings of individuals.

Factor analysis assesses relationships of interdependence between variates. However, it is arguable that this method looks at the data inappropriately. For example, Byrne (2009) argues that variable-based analysis reifies variables as existing independently of individuals. An alternative is to examine cases. This is apt because one of the things we are interested in is whether anything called heterodox economics coheres around individuals. This approach reflects the argument that heterodox economists are able to self-select and that by examining them we can divine what heterodox economics is. Here we might draw on the literature on taxonomy. In that discipline a move has occurred from typological descriptions of objects to one based on genetics (see, for example, Mayr 1969). In new approaches, objects are grouped into phena (i.e., some similarities) and then genetic connections are sought. The latter approach therefore takes certain characteristics (such as size or color) as ways of grouping objects (cases). In the literature this is described as *numerical taxonomy* (Goto 1982). Such an approach would examine relationships between numerical measures of characteristics of each case. This stage of analysis would then lead to explanations of genetic relationships; which here would mean historical studies of people's education and influences. The principal goal of this section of the paper is to identify groupings of cases that occur. For this purpose, *cluster analysis* shall be used. Cluster analysis involves the examination of relations between cases rather than between variates. Indeed, at this point, the paper shifts its focus from variates and very much onto cases.

Cluster Analysis

Cluster analysis has several advantages.[15] Its main advantage is that it allows the data to speak—"the classification of data as suggested by natural groupings of the data themselves" (Hair et al. 2006: 559). Cluster analysis allows a variety of research goals to be pursued, and is particularly useful for basic description of complex data sets. Like factor analysis it can be a useful means of data reduction.[16] This flexibility has allowed it to be used in a range of settings, and not just in zoology and related areas. However, there are some disadvantages of cluster analysis. Cluster analysis is not capable of inference, which *to some* limits it usefulness. The technique itself will always generate clusters, perhaps giving the impression that more structure is present than is actually the case. The principal disadvantage of the method is that each clustering identified is highly dependent on the cluster variates specified by the researcher. Thus, the extent to which the data speak for themselves is restricted. Cluster analysis therefore does not avoid the problem of *a priori* classification; although it could be said to mitigate it somewhat.

　　Clusters are formed on the basis of either similarity or dissimilarity. Either way, some measure of (dis)similarity is necessary. There are two main schools of thought on this question: to use distance mea-

Table 4

Correlations between cases: Summary

No. of large correlations	No. of cases	Case numbers
0–10 ("marginal")	8	4, 12, 16, 18, 21, 31, 35, 40
11–20	6	2, 19, 27, 30, 37, 38
21–30	17	1, 5, 7, 8, 9, 11, 15, 20,23, 24, 25, 26, 28, 33, 36, 41, 43
31+ ("core")	12	3, 6, 10, 13, 14, 17, 22, 29, 32, 34, 39, 42

sures or correlational measures. The correlational approach suggests that we simply correlate between cases rather than variables. This may allow us to find groupings based on association. Often this is done to identify what might be described as outliers. In this paper these correlations constitute a significant piece of analysis because they allow us to examine the existence and nature of groups.

Table 4 summarizes the set of bivariate correlations between cases across responses to all questions. A strong correlation is one that is greater than $|0.5|$.[17] It shows that 29 of the 43 cases are strongly correlated with at least 21 other cases. Twelve cases have strong correlations with at least 31 others. That suggests that there is a core set of cases that have a degree of disagreement across issues of concern. However, although many of the correlations of these cases with others were with other core members, not all were. Take case 3 as an example. It had the (joint) highest number of strong correlations with other cases, 33. Of these 33, 10 were with other "core" cases; but one was with a "marginal" case (with 10 or fewer strong correlations) and many more (22) were with cases in the middle. Meanwhile there are also peripheral members who are correlated with few other cases. In some instances these peripheral members are connected to core members, in other cases, they are only connected to the main group via other peripheral members. On this basis, the community of heterodox economics then looks like a complex system of interconnections.

Correlational methods look at patterns in the cases but not the distances between them, so they are perhaps less able to identify (dis)similarity. The distance method allows us to begin forming clusters on the basis of (dis)similarity in terms of distance. In hierarchical cluster methods, this occurs iteratively, as the most similar (least dissimilar) observations are progressively grouped together.[18] Ultimately, one cluster may form (unless we choose to specify the number of clusters that will form). In this sense, cluster analysis is usually agglomerative.[19] Also, though, because it is iterative, we arrive at hierarchical clusters in which the early clusters have closer relationships between cases than the later ones do.

Several options are available when distance measures are used, but perhaps the most popular is the Squared Euclidean distance (SqED). It has a number of advantages (see Hair et al. 2006: 575). Then one must choose a clustering algorithm. There are several options available, all with advantages and disadvantages, mainly in terms of their ability to form clusters. All hierarchical methods do have problems, for instance, of the persistence of early clusters and the influence of outliers. Hair et al. (2006: 591) recommend that some trial and error is used, to test whether the structures identified would change if outliers are excluded. Here it was decided, as an exploratory move, to use Ward's method. Ward's method is susceptible to outliers but is more likely to construct clusters of roughly equal sizes.

Once measure and clustering algorithm have been selected, one must choose grouping variates. In zoology, for instance, some (set of) characteristics has to be chosen as the basis for grouping cases. These might be in terms of size or color. Some *a priori* choice must be made as to how to group the cases. The debate between typology (species as ideal types) and species as empirically breeding populations is thus undercut. The judgment of the investigator is thus crucial.

Cluster analysis requires that the variates used are independent of each other (without altering the fact that cluster analysis is an interdependence technique). There is some debate about the merits of using factors extracted from the data (as above) (see Hair et al. 2006: 582); their chief benefit being that they ensure independence of variates. An alternative method is to take variates from each of the factors as the clustering characteristics. In small samples, multicollinearity problems may make the clusters generated very sensitive to the data. That caveat applies here and adds another degree of caution to our analysis. However, in data analysis, a correlation between variates of r > |0.7| is often used as a rough indicator of multicollinearity; in our sample no correlations are that high. That suggests multicollinearity may not be serious. In this instance, all the variates were left in the grouping algorithm.[20]

When cluster analysis is performed, a dendrogram is produced, which gives a visual sketch of relations between cases. The dendrogram is shown in Figure 1. In the dendrogram, cases that are most similar are located next to each other. The tree-like diagram shows the connection between the cases. The lines show groupings. The closeness of cases is shown by the position of the vertical line. The further to the right is that line, the less similar the cases are. So, for example, case 26 is closely related to case 36; it may be said to be in the same group as case 29 or even case 30, but is further away from them than from case 26. The furthermost vertical line indicates that eventually the hierarchical cluster method always generates a single cluster.

At this point the judgment of the investigator is crucial in deciding how many clusters there are in the data. Effectively a cut must be made at what is considered an appropriate point. In Figure 1 this cut would appear at a distance of roughly eight. That indicates that there are four clusters in the data: from cases 26 to 24, then 5 to 11, then 19 to 23, and finally 9 to 35. These clusters have membership sizes twenty, four, eleven and eight respectively, which bears similarity to the correlational data above. Further, we can see that cases 16, 18, 21, 31 and 35 are all part of the bottom cluster, which appears highly distinct from the other three.[21] The existence of these clusters having been shown, they can be investigated further.

Table 5 shows mean scores for all variables for each cluster. Obviously there are difficulties of comparing samples of different sizes. Nonetheless, a few key points can be made. Cluster A, the largest, is characterized by a rejection of the label "mainstream" and to some extent of mainstream concepts (apart from individuals and markets). The second feature of cluster A is an acceptance of the label as heterodox and pluralist and a matching acceptance of general heterodox concepts such as class, uncertainty, fallibilism, power, money and history. It could be argued that this cluster exemplifies the recently

Figure 1

Dendrogram; Ward's method; cluster variates: all variates

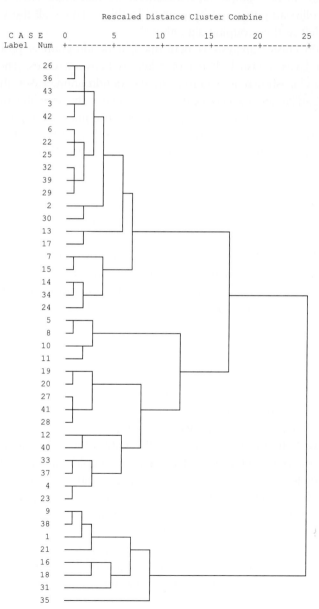

Table 5

Variable means by cluster

	Cluster A (n = 20)	Cluster B (n = 4)	Cluster C (n = 11)	Cluster D (n = 8)
mainstream	0.0708	0.0000	0.2136	0.2500
heterodox	0.8750	0.8625	0.8045	0.6938
pluralist	0.7425	0.4250	0.7909	0.6625
rational	0.1625	0.1250	0.2455	0.3688
equilibrium	0.1086	0.0250	0.3182	0.2313
class	0.7482	1.0000	0.6818	0.2938
positive	0.1075	0.0000	0.3864	0.3000
natural	0.7350	0.7500	0.6922	0.6875
uncertain	0.9050	0.4875	0.5045	0.7188
fallibility	0.8825	0.1375	0.7091	0.5625
power	0.9050	0.9750	0.8091	0.4625
labor	0.7675	1.0000	0.7736	0.1938
scarcity	0.2200	0.0875	0.6364	0.4938
gender	0.6550	0.8000	0.5000	0.2625
maths	0.2850	0.5750	0.5545	0.1125
individuals	0.2425	0.0250	0.1680	0.3000
markets	0.3575	0.0250	0.2091	0.4500
money	0.6523	0.5875	0.4175	0.4125
history	0.9450	0.9375	0.9091	0.8000
age	48.75	54.50	47.40	53.25
sex	0.35	0.0000	0.09	0.00

developing picture of heterodoxy as being non-mainstream but pluralist, with a concern for methodological issues. Almost all of the female respondents to the survey are in this group, although it is far from clear why this would occur. Cluster B is different, exhibiting much stronger rejection of the mainstream and its concepts, maximum scores for class and labor and much lower scores than the other clusters for uncertainty and fallibilism. Methodologically this group scored much higher than cluster A on the need for maths in economics. Cluster B seems like a Marxist group and indeed its cluster members are self-identified radicals.

Cluster C is different from clusters A and B in that it does not reject the label of being mainstream, whilst accepting the labels of heterodox and pluralist. This cluster is similar to cluster A but more pluralist. The members of this cluster reject the strict distinctions between the three categories. Further, although this cluster accepts many of the traditional heterodox concepts such as power, labor and class, it also accepts mainstream notions such as rational, equilibrium, positive, maths and crucially, scarcity. Above, when factor analysis was conducted, a factor was extracted that was labeled "mainstream" whereas the view of cluster C suggests instead this use of mainstream concepts alongside heterodox ones is another exhibition of pluralism. Unfortunately these individuals are difficult to identify from the information gleaned so it is difficult to draw too many conclusions. It should also be noted that in the dendrogram, arguably cluster C might have been split into two, so perhaps not too much coherence should be expected. Cluster D is in some ways the most interesting cluster because it contains most of the cases identified as peripheral. The cluster score for mainstream is similar to cluster C, but the score for heterodox is lower. Accordingly, scores for core heterodox concepts such as class, power, gender and particularly labor are clearly lower than for the other clusters. As a corollary, cluster D's scores for individuals, markets and rational are much higher than for the other clusters. Looking at the cases who are members of this cluster, they appear to be members of underrepresented elements of heterodox thought, such as behavioral economics, Austrian economics and American institutionalism.

Conclusions

The data examined here suggests that the group that calls itself heterodox economics is a complex object. Some key factors can be identified: a belief that history, natural systems, uncertainty and power are all important to understanding economics. There is some rejection of the mainstream label and associated concepts although the data suggests that heterodox economics is not merely a rejection of the mainstream. However, even surrounding these general conclusions, there was considerable diversity and little evidence of structure. Overall, it seems that heterodox economics is not a monolith. Heterodox economics may be better conceived of as a fuzzy set or as an open, complex system.

Clearly there are reasons to be cautious about these findings, not least because of the size of the data set, and that there is only one drawing from the group. Further, the data only reveal patterns in nominal data—at best we have identified only nominal essences. More work must be done to establish the natures of these groups. Drawing on biological literature, a next step is to establish the genealogy of the cases and groups of cases and draw on existing literature in the history of economic thought, plus conduct deeper analysis on individual cases. This work would try to ascertain with whom these economists are "breeding" (their ideas) and who their (intellectual) ancestors and descendants were. Clearly the analysis here needs to be complemented by historical and social analyses found in, for example, Lee (2009). Future research might apply the same method to a group of mainstream economists.

In addition, the criticism should be borne in mind that the responses to the questions do not exhaust the nature of heterodox economists. Many readers may object to the analytical approach taken in the paper and may argue that, instead, a superior treatment that reflected more clearly social categories such as power relations was warranted. As such, heterodox economists are defined in terms of who they know, which conferences they attend, by whom their graduate work was supervised, for instance. Their membership in groups and their political and work environments (i.e., whether they are disadvantaged when searching for employment) will also matter. Another simple definition of heterodox might be those economists excluded from the mainstream. This has some utility, in that it captures the treatment of groups of economists according to power structures and individual labels. However, analytically it begs as many questions as it raises, for instance, about the nature of the mainstream, which in effect leads us little further than where we started. Thus, the present study should be viewed bearing in mind its limitations and acknowledging that a fuller treatment of the nature of heterodoxy would require sociological enquiry.

It is clear that the interpretation of the results in the study is contestable and that final conclusions depend on the approach of the investigator. One element of this judgment is whether the investigator tends towards regarding the groups within the heterodox population, or indeed heterodox and mainstream, as separate. In the taxonomy literature, a distinction is often made between "lumpers" and "splitters"—those whose instinct is to, respectively, lump together similar but different cases, or emphasize the differences and split them up. Whenever a category is made, there is a dynamic between the desire to analyze and the desire to lump. The desire to analyze is reinforced by a desire to split. The difference between lumpers and splitters is defined by their emphasis of similarity or of difference. The empirical evidence here supports either urge: it suggests considerable heterogeneity in that little structure can be found within the community of self-identified heterodox economists. However, in other ways, there are reasons to lump: there is a shared dislike of the mainstream; and concepts such as history are almost universally held. It would seem that there has been a tendency in the methodological literature discussed at the start of the paper to split. Splitting is something humans like to do; whether this act is helpful or not is debatable. Given the apparent fuzziness of the categories involved, it seems that splitting ought to be done cautiously, provisionally and be open to revision.

Notes

1. This paper has benefited from comments received at a session of the Association for Heterodox Economics conference at Kingston University, July 2009. Thanks go to the discussant at that session, Ioana Negru, and to Lynne Chester, Paul Downward and Don Webber for other comments. Finally, the editor and two anonymous referees have led the paper to be improved greatly. The usual disclaimer applies.

2. De Benedictis and Di Maio (2010) investigate empirically the effect of schools of thought on beliefs about the economy in Italian economists, but they define heterodox *a priori* and examine its effects on attitudes. This paper attempts to define heterodox based on attitudes.

3. Those authors note that there is also debate about whether to use orthodox and mainstream synonymously. They argue that to do so would be a mistake.

4. The scale of this task is illustrated by works that might be said to aim to do the same thing: histories of schools of thought (King 2002); or works that link past economists to newer ideas, such as Critical Realism (see, for example, Fleetwood 1996), or general equilibrium theory (Hollander 1981).

5. A breeding *population* comprises the people who are breeding. This is not the same as a breeding *program*, i.e., PhD schemes.

6. For the purpose of analysis, the numbers were converted to values between 0 and 1.

7. One possible method for analyzing the data was Qualitative Comparative Analysis (see Ragin and Rihoux 2008), which is significantly disrupted by responses at or around 0.5.

8. See Weng (2004) and the references therein for a discussion of how anchoring might affect reliability of measurement.

9. A fifth concern might be that question 10 may be read as a double question, capturing attitudes towards fallibilism and pluralism. However, it should be stated that although respondents often commented on elements of the questionnaire they objected to, none objected to question 10. Also, an analysis of the responses to questions 10 and 3 (on pluralism) show considerable variety. The pattern of responses to those two questions suggest some respondents were monist (low scores on both questions), epistemological pluralist (high scores on both), pluralist for non-epistemological reasons (high score on question 3, low on question 10) or though being fallibilist objected to the label pluralist (high on question 10, low on question 3), perhaps because of an oppositional mindset (those respondents having a much stronger negative correlation between mainstream and heterodox than other respondents). Finally, the data was re-estimated without data from question 10 and this only created minor changes in the outcomes. Where these differences were important they are noted below.

10. In results not shown here, descriptive statistics for each case were generated. Particular attention was paid to the mean and mode scores for each case, as well as standard deviation. Cases with means lower than 0.4 and higher than 0.6, SD higher than 0.4, and mode at either 0 or 1 were examined further. Although some tentative patterns may be found, such as that self-confessed Marxists often answered 0 or 1, and 0 for concepts such as rational and 1 for labor, power and class, no clear overall pattern emerged.

11. No precise figure was available for AHE membership in 2008. The number was 167 in 2006, and 258 in 2007. Each year there are new members but also some memberships lapse. The figure of 250 is a rough estimate.

12. It should be noted that OLS regression analysis was also applied to the data, with "heterodox" as the dependent variate. However, when the inde-

pendent variates were individual variates, and then factors, in both cases the results were unconvincing. The estimations were subject to problems of small coefficients, low explanatory power and non-normality of residuals.

13. The results of this analysis must be treated with care, given the low sample size. There are 16 variates shown here and only 43 cases. The ratio of cases to variates is thus lower than 3:1, whereas most treatments of factor analysis usually recommend a ratio of 5:1 or even 10:1 (Hair et al. 2006: 122).

14. When the data was re-estimated omitting question 10, markets moved from the radical factor into the Austrian factor. This is also intuitively reasonable.

15. Hair et al. (2006: ch. 8) discuss the key concepts in cluster analysis. Much of this discussion draws on that source. Interested readers should consult Hair et al.

16. As with factor analysis, small data sets may reduce the power of cluster analysis; however, as Hair et al. (2006: 571, 581) make clear, requisite size of data set is determined by its ability to represent the population. The requisite size is therefore an *ex post* empirical issue. Given that our results are plausible, we can set aside this concern.

17. This figure may be considered arbitrary—and indeed it is somewhat— but in this case the figure filters out even correlations that are statistically significant at the 5 percent level so is quite strict. Further the findings from this technique are compared with others, so any loss from arbitrariness is mitigated.

18. It is also possible to have non-hierarchical cluster methods such as *k-means* methods that pre-determine a number of clusters (see Hair et al. 2006: 581, 585).

19. As Hair et al. (2006: 584) note, cluster formation can be divisive, it begins with all cases in a single cluster and then breaks that down into smaller groups of cases. Most computer packages appear to be agglomerative: SPSS takes that approach.

20. As insurance against these problems, clusters were also estimated with factors as grouping variates, and with different combinations of factors and raw variates. Comparing these solutions, there was a degree of commonality: 24 cases seemed to remain in the same cluster whatever the grouping variates. However, this small number did not allow much further exploration. Further, it could be argued that by selecting raw variates (from different factors) the problem of multicollinearity is addressed but the problem of *a priori* definition of the groups is reintroduced. If the clusters derived from selected variates are thus rejected, we are left to choose between using all the variates and just the factors. However, the latter course resulted in even less structure (six clusters from 43 cases). Thus, it was decided to explore further the original solution using all the variates.

21. However, there are anomalies, such as cases 1 and 9, both of which had many strong correlations with other cases. In support of the clusters, though, a second cluster analysis using average linkage method largely confirms the original clusters: cluster D is split into two, cluster A loses one member (case 17, who goes to B, which otherwise remains intact) and cluster C loses two members (cases 12 and 40).

References

Arnsperger, C., and Y. Varoufakis. (2009). "Neoclassical Economics—Three Identifying Features." In *Pluralist Economics*. Ed. E. Fullbrook. London: Zed books.

Ayres, C. (1936). "Fifty Years' Development in Ideas of Human Nature and Motivation." *American Economic Review* 26(1): 224–236.

Byrne, D. (2009). "Case-Based Methods; What They Are; Why We Need Them; How to Do Them." In *The Sage Handbook of Case-Based Methods*. Eds. D. Byrne and C. Ragin. London: Sage.

Colander, D., R. Holt, and B. Rosser. (2004). "The Changing Face of Mainstream Economics." *Review of Political Economy* 16(4): 485–499.

Commons, J. (1932). "Institutional Economics: Comment." *American Economic Review* 22(2): 264–268.

——. (1936). "Institutional Economics." *American Economic Review* 26(1): 237–249.

Davis, J. (2009). "The Nature of Heterodox Economics." In *Ontology and Economics: Tony Lawson and His Critics*. Ed. E. Fullbrook. London: Routledge.

De Benedictis, L., and M. Di Maio. (2010). "Within and Between Disagreement Across Schools of Thought in Economics: Evidence from Italian Economists." mimeo.

Dequech, D. (2007–2008). "Neoclassical, Orthodox, Mainstream, and Heterodox Economics." *Journal of Post Keynesian Economics* 30(2): 137–160.

Dow, S. C. (1990). "Beyond Dualism." *Cambridge Journal of Economics* 14: 143–157.

——. (2004). "Structured Pluralism." *Journal of Economic Methodology* 11(3): 275–290.

Fleetwood, S. (1996). *Hayek's Political Economy: The Socio-Economics of Order*. London: Routledge.

George, D. (2008). *Issues in Heterodox Economics*. New York: Wiley.

Goto, H. (1982). *Animal Taxonomy*. London: Edward Arnold.

Gruchy, A. (1947). *Modern Economic Thought: The American Contribution*. New York: Prentice-Hall, Inc.

——. (1948). "The Philosophical Basis of the New Keynesian Economics." *Ethics* 58(4): 235–244.

Hair, J., W. Black, B. Babin, R. Anderson, and R. Tatham. (2006). *Multivariate Data Analysis.* New Jersey: Pearson.

Hollander, S. (1981). "Marxian Economics as General-Equilibrium Theory." *History of Political Economy* XIII: 121–154.

King, J. (2002). *A History of Post Keynesian Economics Since 1936.* Cheltenham: Elgar.

Lawson, T. (2006). "The Nature of Heterodox Economics." *Cambridge Journal of Economics* 30(4): 483–505.

Lee, F. (2009). *Challenging the Mainstream: Essays on the History of Heterodox Economics in the 21st Century.* London: Routledge.

———. (2010). "The Pluralism Debate in Heterodox Economics." *Review of Radical Political Economics,* forthcoming.

Macauley, C., N. Kogan, and A. Teger. (1971). "Order Effects in Answering Risk Dilemmas for Self and Others." *Journal of Personality and Social Psychology* 20(3): 423–424.

Mayr, E. (1969). *Principles of Systematic Zoology.* New York: McGraw-Hill.

Mearman, A. (2010). "What is this Thing Called 'Heterodox Economics'?" UWE Bristol, Economics Discussion Paper series 10/06.

Ragin, C., and B. Rihoux. (2008). *Configurational Comparative Methods: Qualitative Comparative Analysis (QCA) and Related Techniques.* New York: Sage.

Robinson, J. (1974). "History Versus Equilibrium." *Thames Papers in Political Economy.*

Victor, P. (2008). *Managing Without Growth: Slower by Design, Not Disaster.* Cheltenham: Elgar.

Weng, L.-J. (2004). "Impact of the Number Response Categories and Anchor Labels on Coefficient Alpha and Test-Retest Reliability." *Educational and Psychological Measurement* 64(6): 956–972.

List of variates and abbreviations

Variate abbreviation and corresponding survey question	How variate is referred to in the text
Mm: I consider myself a 'mainstream' economist	Mainstream
He: I consider myself a 'heterodox' economist	Heterodox
Pl: I consider myself a 'pluralist' economist	Pluralist
Ra: Economic agents are rational (usually maximisers)	Rational
Eq: Economic systems tend towards equilibrium	Equilibrium
Cl: Class is an essential factor in understanding economic outcomes	Class
Po: Economics is a positive science	Positive
Na: Economics should explicitly take into account natural systems	Natural
Un: Economic outcomes are inherently (non-probabilistically) uncertain	Uncertain
Fa: All economic theories, methods and approaches are fallible: a variety is needed	Fallibilism
Pw: Power is an essential factor in understanding economic outcomes	Power
La: Labour inputs are an essential determinant of the value of a product	Labour
Sc: Economics is the study of scarcity and choice	Scarcity
Ge: Gender is an essential factor in understanding economic outcomes	Gender
Ma: Economic enquiry requires the use of mathematical methods	Mathematics
In: Economics is primarily concerned with individuals	Individuals
Mk: Markets are generally the best way to ensure that wants and needs are met efficiently	Markets
Mo: Money is a determinant of real economic activity	Money
Hi: In understanding economics, history and time are of crucial importance	History

Appendix: Questionnaire Tool

WHAT ARE THE CORE ECONOMIC PRECEPTS?

This survey is being conducted by Andrew Mearman (Bristol Business School, UWE). It is an investigation into the concepts and methods which economists regard as core. **Please indicate on the sliding scale between 0 and 10 the extent to which you agree with the statement (0 = completely disagree, 10 = agree completely).** All responses will be treated anonymously. The questionnaire should not take more than 5 minutes to complete. **Thank you for your time.**

	Disagree	Agree
Example: Elephants are grey	0_____x_10	
1. I consider myself a 'mainstream' economist	0_____10	
2. I consider myself a 'heterodox' economist	0_____10	
3. I consider myself a 'pluralist' economist	0_____10	
4. Economic agents are rational (usually maximisers)	0_____10	
5. Economic systems tend towards equilibrium	0_____10	
6. Class is an essential factor in understanding economic outcomes	0_____10	
7. Economics is a positive science	0_____10	
8. Economics should explicitly take into account natural systems	0_____10	
9. Economic outcomes are inherently (non-probabilistically) uncertain	0_____10	
10. All economic theories, methods and approaches are fallible: a variety is needed	0_____10	
11. Power is an essential factor in understanding economic outcomes	0_____10	
12. Labour inputs are an essential determinant of the value of a product	0_____10	
13. Economics is the study of scarcity and choice	0_____10	

14. Gender is an essential factor in
understanding economic outcomes

0_____10

15. Economic enquiry requires the use of
mathematical methods

0_____10

16. Economics is primarily concerned with
individuals

0_____10

17. Markets are generally the best way to
ensure that wants and needs are met
efficiently

0_____10

18. Money is a determinant of real
economic activity

0_____10

19. In understanding economics, history
and time are of crucial importance

0_____10

20. Which journal would you consider the 'best' in which you could
attempt to publish? (please state) _____

21. What is your age? _____

22. What is your sex? _____

23. What is your institution? _____

All responses will be treated anonymously.

Thank you for taking your time to complete this questionnaire.

Microeconomics After Keynes: Post Keynesian Economics and Public Policy

By STEVEN PRESSMAN*

ABSTRACT. Post Keynesian economics has mainly focused on macro-economic issues and ignored microeconomic policy issues. This paper begins to remedy this gap. It outlines the main principles of the Post Keynesian approach, distinguishes them from neoclassical economics, explains how these principles can be applied to microeconomic issues, and then draws out some policy implications that differ mark-edly from neoclassical theory on the issues of health care and pro-ductivity growth.

Introduction

Post Keynesian economics is mainly a school of macroeconomic thought (see Davidson 2005; Holt and Pressman 2001; Lavoie 2006). It has focused on issues such as financial instability, exchange rate regimes, unemployment, trade deficits, and inflation, and it has made significant contributions to the policy debates in these areas. Unfortunately, Post Keynesians have virtually ignored microeconomic policy issues such as immigration, crime, and education.[1] Part of the problem likely stems from the quip (attributed to Gerald Shove) that Keynes never put in the half hour necessary to learn microeconomics. This has left Post Keynesian micro underdeveloped relative to the macro side. Another part of the problem is that Post Keynesian microeconomists tend to focus on methodological and theoretical debates and to provide empirical evidence for the Post Keynesian theory of pricing, ignoring the policy side of microeconomics.

The goal of this paper is to help remedy this gap in Post Keynesian thought and get Post Keynesians to focus on microeconomic public policy issues. Toward this end, it outlines the fundamental principles

*Department of Economics & Finance, Monmouth University, West Long Branch, NJ 07764, pressman@monmouth.edu

American Journal of Economics and Sociology, Vol. 70, No. 2 (April, 2011).

of the Post Keynesian approach, explains how they can be applied to micro policy issues, and draws out some key policy conclusions that differ markedly from those of neoclassical theory on two issues— health care and productivity growth.

The Post Keynesian Approach

Five key notions distinguish Post Keynesian economics from neoclassical economics: (1) a recognition that the future is uncertain, rather than known with some probability distribution; (2) a view that individual decision making depends on social factors, such as habits and emulation, rather than on individual rational choice; (3) a belief that economic analysis should examine economies that move through historical time rather than economies that effortlessly reach some equilibrium; (4) a recognition that real world markets are not perfectly competitive; and (5) a focus on income effects rather than on substitution effects.

Uncertainty Versus Risk

One distinguishing characteristic of the Post Keynesian approach is its focus on uncertainty. Knight ([1921] 1971) argued that risk involved measurable probabilities while uncertainty involved unmeasurable and unknowable probabilities. We can know the chance that a 40-year-old man will die in the next year, and we can know the probability that a hurricane will hit land in Florida, because we have a good set of past observations about these events. For this reason private firms can insure against these catastrophes. However, past evidence is no guide when events happen infrequently or when dealing with situations that extend far into the future.

Keynes ([1936] 1964: ch. 12) applied this distinction to investment decisions, claiming they do *not* depend on an objective assessment of probable outcomes and the expected profitability of each possible outcome. Rather, firms operate under uncertainty, and investment decisions must be based on "animal spirits" or the state of confidence of business executives.

Rosser (2001) points out that Post Keynesians have two main arguments that many real world decisions require overcoming uncertainty. First, Loasby (1976) and Shackle (1955, 1972, 1974) claim that the world itself is unpredictable and constantly changing. So, we never know when things will change or how they will change. Important decisions are thus "experiments," to use Shackle's (1955: 63) evocative term. Davidson (1991, 1994, 1996) provides a more scientific defense of this view. Systems are ergodic if their structure remains stable over time. In this case, we can extrapolate from the past to the future. Non-ergodic systems experience structural change over time. It means that people cannot figure out what the future will be like.

Second, Arestis (1996) and Carabelli (1988) see uncertainty arising because we do not know what others will do. When economic outcomes depend on the behavior of others, and when such behavior is unpredictable, we face uncertainty. An investment decision may make sense only if the economy performs well over the next several years. But this depends on the investment decisions of other firms. If many firms invest, there will be sufficient investment and growth; if not, the investment will lose money. Thus, firms face uncertainty about what other firms will do.

At the macroeconomic level, such uncertainty leads to underinvestment and unemployment, and requires government intervention to remedy this situation. Similarly, uncertainty at the microeconomic level means that we need government policies to improve economic outcomes. If individuals are uncertain how long they will live, they may save too little for retirement. Adolescents may be uncertain about the consequences of working hard in school and getting a college education; so they will underinvest in their own education. Firms may be uncertain about the future and so spend too little for research and development. In each of these cases, overcoming uncertainty requires government intervention to improve economic outcomes—a public pension system, public investment in education, and government R&D spending.

Social Versus Economic Rationality

One consequence of uncertainty is that people tend to follow procedural rules, habits, and social conventions. They are not rational in the traditional economic sense of the term. Keynes's ([1936] 1964: 97) simple theory of consumption is about individual habits to consume a constant proportion of growing income, giving economies a relatively constant propensity to consume. Social interaction models go one step further; they recognize that individual behavior depends not just on gains, costs, and risk assessment, but also on the behavior of others. Such a view of human behavior underlies Post Keynesian economics. One famous example of this is Keynes's ([1936] 1964: 156) analysis of investment as a beauty contest, where the winner is not the one who picks the most beautiful contestant but the one whom others think is most beautiful.

For microeconomics, the important issue is identifying the habits and rules that drive individual behavior. Earl (1983) and Lavoie (1992: ch. 2) argue that individual choice depends on lexicographic orderings. People rank goods in a hierarchy based upon how they meet human needs. As our incomes rise, we move to consume goods that are higher and higher in the hierarchy. First, people choose to consume necessities (such as food, clothing, and shelter) that are required to survive. Once these needs have been met, they seek goods that make day-to-day living easier, that provide entertainment or diversions from the rat race, and so forth. Next, there are goods like books and education that lead to human betterment. Under lexicographic preferences, income effects are greater than substitution effects since income moves people up the hierarchy of goods.

The notion of social rationality takes things one step further. Individual decisions are interdependent, a function of what others do. Game-theoretic models let us analyze human behavior when it depends on the behavior of others. Individual decisions regarding whether to work or engage in crime may depend on social factors such as one's friends and the mores in one's neighborhood. And school choice or voucher systems may not lead parents to select the "best school" for their children for social reasons. Rather, parents tend to select the school other parents are selecting or the school that is closest to home (Bridge and Blackman 1978). In these cases, public policy needs to focus on improving undesired outcomes. For example, national education standards that most citizens accept and seek to meet will be necessary for better education outcomes.

Historical Time Versus Equilibrium

Joan Robinson (1974, 1976) and Nicholas Kaldor (1985) argued that economies could not be described in terms of some equilibrium toward which the economy is headed and that will be stable once achieved. Things change all the time—goods, production technologies and existing inputs. So even if the economy were to achieve equilibrium at one moment in time, that moment will be gone soon since the world is always in a state of flux or change. In addition, individual preferences, habits, and choices are always changing; again, due to these changes, a momentary equilibrium gets upset just as soon as it is reached.

For this reason, Post Keynesians contend that economists should focus on how economies evolve over time. Historical time differs from the logical time of neoclassical economics because it acknowledges that time is irreversible and recognizes that the path we take helps determine economic outcomes.

Post Keynesians recognize that choices are path dependent and that our current choices depend on what choices we made in the past (Georgescu-Roegen 1966). For example, buying a car requires purchasing gasoline, car insurance, parking spaces, and highway tolls in the future, while the decision to forgo buying a car requires the purchase of mass transit and car rental services in the future. At times, the short-run rational decision leads to long-run outcomes that are not utility maximizing. While buying a car may have been the best (that is, utility-maximizing) decision when it was made at one point in time, this does not mean it is the best decision in the long run, after gasoline prices soar unexpectedly or after we learn the environmental consequences of these decisions.

Another way history matters is that our tastes are a function of how we evolved as a human race, and so may not be optimal at present. In contrast to the neoclassical view, where tastes are regarded as given and not subject to dispute (Stigler and Becker 1977), a historical approach seeks the determinants of our preferences. Evolutionary psychology (see Pinker 1997, 2002; Barkow et al. 1992) traces the origin of our preferences to what enabled our ancient ancestors to survive and reproduce on the African savannah, and argues that these propensities are now part of the psychological makeup of humans.

To take just one example, hundreds of thousands of years ago survival required eating voraciously whenever food was present, since one could never know where the next meal would come from. Our ancestors who gorged themselves on food when it was available were more likely to survive. As such, these dispositions became part of the human genetic makeup. Today, with large agribusinesses and food distributors such as McDonald's, we have eliminated the uncertainty about whether food will be available next week and next month, but not our dispositions concerning food. Food producers have played upon our natural inclinations by increasing the fat and sugar content in foods because these are the sorts of foods we crave and tend to gorge ourselves on. The result is an epidemic of obesity, as individuals find themselves unable to control their urge to eat as much as possible when food is present (Crister 2003).

A Post Keynesian policy solution to this problem would recognize such mismatches between our world and the ancient world where human urges developed, and would seek to keep firms from exploiting them. We have banned Joe Camel to reduce smoking; to deal with the problem of obesity we may also need to consign Ronald McDonald to oblivion. Fat and sweet foods can likewise be banned from schools.

Oligopolistic Market Structures

History is also important because institutional structures develop over time and, once in place, are hard to reverse. Market structures are especially hard to change. This leads to the fourth main tenet of Post Keynesian economics—the proliferation of oligopolies.

Oligopolistic firms are not price takers; rather, they are price makers. Prices are administered; they are set by the firm after some good gets produced and is about to be offered for sale. In determining this price, firms rely on rules and customs and habits; they use some form of markup or cost-plus pricing, where some percentage gets added to the costs of production. This mark-up (and thus price) depend on the degree of monopoly in the industry (Kalecki 1971), the firm's desired rate of return to maintain growth and market share (Shapiro 1981), and the needs of the firm to engage in R&D and investment to promote firm growth in the future so it can maintain its oligopolistic status or stay ahead of the other oligopolies in its industry (Downward 1999; Eichner 1976; Lee 1998).

Neoclassical economics extols the virtues of perfect competition over imperfect competition. Post Keynesians have set forth several critiques of this view. First, Sraffa (1926) pointed out logical problems with the neoclassical supply curve for the firm and thus the neoclassical theory of perfect competition. Second, while competition may reduce prices for consumers, it also generates problems. Flexible prices can be volatile prices. When prices fall and are flexible downward, firms go bankrupt, sometimes bringing down other firms. The end result is that, retrospectively, capital has been misallocated.

Finally, oligopolies make a good deal of profit and use some of this money to invest in new technology (Eichner 1976; Galbraith 1967). In contrast, small firms in competitive markets earn meager profits, have little access to capital, and cannot invest in new technology and innovation. Given the large costs and the high degree of uncertainty in the process of developing new products, it is natural that firms will seek to develop market power and try to influence consumers.

For this reason the economic world comprises large oligopolistic firms that control the market and are not subject to the dictates of consumer demand. Rather, these firms mold consumer preferences and choices. To survive, firms need to try to reduce the uncertainty that exists in the marketplace by managing demand and by supporting Keynesian macroeconomic policies that promote full employment. Advertising by the firm is necessary because investment is expensive and its results are uncertain. A large part of the reason firms can do this is that for various reasons (such as the existence of uncertainty, or the fact that utility is derived *after* consumption but choices must be made *before* consumption), consumers do not know what they want to consume; they look at social behavior for clues. Advertising can thus affect tastes and preferences, and provides signals to consumers about what other people like and are consuming.

The microeconomic applications are clearest and most direct here. From a Post Keynesian perspective, we need to accept the existence of oligopolistic firms, but need to regulate them in the public interest. We must limit their influence on individual decisions, especially through advertising. We will need to limit the negative influence of oligopolies on the environment by putting in place strict environmental standards with stiff penalties for violators. And we will need to control the prices and wages set by large oligopolies (Galbraith 1952).

Income and Substitution Effects

Finally, there is the issue of income and substitution effects. Neoclassical economists see substitution effects as of paramount importance, sometimes to such a degree that they exclude all income effects. Economies are seen as supply constrained, and incentives become important to assure that scarce resources get used efficiently.

In contrast, Post Keynesians see income effects as more important than substitution effects (Davidson 2005: 459). This is the essence of Keynes's ([1936] 1964) rejection of Say's Law in *The General Theory* and for his alternative approach—the theory of effective demand. This means that for Post Keynesians creating income and increasing spending matters most for generating full employment and a virtuous cycle of economic and income growth. It also means that investment determines savings rather than savings determining investment. Investment is not constrained due to insufficient savings; rather, investment is constrained by the social and psychological forces in the real world that keep firms from expanding.

At the microeconomic level, income effects are also important. Income is important for good microeconomic outcomes and is the solution to many microeconomic problems. In contrast to the neoclassical position, which stresses the importance of capture and punishment as a disincentive to crime, a Post Keynesian approach would focus on jobs and income supports as a means to reduce crime. And in contrast to neoclassical economics, which views such supports as work disincentives and factors contributing to poverty, a Post Keynesian approach would see such spending (as well as full employment) as necessary for reducing poverty (Pressman 2007). Firm decisions are also likely to depend on income as much as on incentives. Firms may want to invest but have no retained earnings and no ability to borrow money, even at low interest rates. They may not be willing or able to engage in risky and innovative R&D without some guarantees about employment levels in the future (Courvisanos 1996).

Policy Issues

We saw above how the main Post Keynesian principles differ from the main neoclassical principles. We also saw how these principles have microeconomic applications as well as the usual macroeconomic ones. This section applies the main Post Keynesian principles to two public policy issues—health care and productivity growth. The goal here is not to provide a definitive set of Post Keynesian policy solutions to these problems, but to show how Post Keynesian tenets can be applied to these particular problems and to show how the Post Keynesian approach leads to markedly different policy implications when compared to neoclassical theory.

Health Care

Health care has become a critical issue in all developed nations. It is one of the largest categories of government expenditure, and the health care industry is a major source of national employment. Health affects the ability of children to learn in school and become productive adults, and it affects the ability of adults to hold jobs and earn a decent living. For these reasons, health affects economic growth and national living standards. The burgeoning area of happiness studies has found that little is more important to human happiness than good health (Layard 2005).

Most people recognize that the US faces a health care crisis. It spends more money per capita on health care than any other nation in the world. In 2004 OECD countries spent, on average, 8.9 percent of their national income on health care. Spending on health care in the US was 15.3 percent of GDP, by far the highest of all OECD countries (Peterson and Burton 2007).

This might not be of great concern if the US got a good return for its money—healthier individuals who are more productive at work, greater life expectancy, improved quality of life, and high quality health care due to the miracle of modern medicine. Then, one could argue, the money was well spent.

However, by most measures, the US does poorly relative to other countries that spend less on health care. Life expectancy in the US is not much better than life expectancy in other countries. Table 1 provides data on life expectancy at birth and per capita GDP in around 30 countries. Given that the US is the most affluent nation and spends more on health care per person than any other country in the world, we would expect the US to have the highest, or close to the highest, life expectancy in the world. But it ranks near the bottom of the list—below other developed nations, below several middle-income countries such as Chile, Malta, Greece, and Costa Rica, and barely above Cuba.

Infant mortality, one of the best indicators of general health and the quality of national health care, measures the fraction of newborns that die before reaching the age of 1 year. On this measure, the US performs very badly. In 2005, infant mortality was lowest in Singapore (2.29) and Japan (2.77). Canada's infant mortality rate was 4.75, and the EU average was 5.10. The US ranked 41st in the world, with an infant mortality rate of 6.50, a bit worse than Cuba (6.33) and a bit better than Croatia (6.84) (CIA 2007).

US citizens also express a great degree of dissatisfaction with their health care system. A survey of five English-speaking countries found that the percentage of citizens who thought their national health care system was good and required only minor changes was lowest in the US (16 percent). At the other extreme, around one-third of Americans surveyed felt that the US health care system required a fundamental rebuilding—by far the largest percentage of all five nations (Schoen et al. 2004).

More seriously, despite spending so much on health, many US citizens do not have health insurance. In 2006, 45 million Americans or nearly 16 percent of the population had no health insurance (US Census Bureau 2007). Of these, 80 percent are in families where someone is employed but whose employer failed to provide health insurance, or who made it optional and available only at a very high cost (Cohen and Martinez 2005). Consequently, many families are forced to choose between health insurance or paying the rent and putting food on the table. The result is that families do without

Table 1

Life expectancy at birth and GDP in 2005 US dollars adjusted for purchasing power

Country	Life Expectancy at Birth	GDP per Person
Japan	82.3	31,267
Iceland	81.5	36,510
Switzerland	81.3	35,633
Australia	80.9	31,794
Sweden	80.5	32,525
Spain	80.5	27,169
Canada	80.3	33,375
Italy	80.3	28,529
Israel	80.3	25,864
France	80.2	30,386
Norway	79.8	41,420
New Zealand	79.8	24,996
Singapore	79.4	29,663
Netherlands	79.2	32,684
Germany	79.1	29,461
Malta	79.1	19,189
Cyprus	79.0	22,699
United Kingdom	79.0	33,238
Greece	78.9	23,381
Finland	78.9	32,153
Belgium	78.8	32,119
Costa Rica	78.5	10,180
Ireland	78.4	38,505
Chile	78.3	12,027
United States	77.9	41,890
Korea	77.9	22,029
Cuba	77.7	6,000
Portugal	77.7	20,410
Mexico	75.6	10,751
Poland	75.2	13,847

Source: United Nations *Human Development Report, 2007/2008* (New York: Oxford University Press, 2008).

regular checkups and without treatments that can improve their lives and prevent more serious problems in the future.

In the neoclassical approach, health differences are due mainly to individual choices. The decision to not smoke, to exercise regularly, and to eat well comes from comparing the disutility I get today from doing these things and the utility I get in the future as a result of better health. If the utility of unhealthy behavior today exceeds the discounted value of future utility, I will act in ways that lead to future health problems. My choice to purchase health insurance, exercise, eat well, see doctors regularly, and receive treatment also results from calculating probabilities of future outcomes from prices and information about goods, applying my discount rate, and then deciding how to best spend my money. People will select the most desirable amount of health insurance and health care; government intervention in health care markets only distorts incentives and reduces utility.

In contrast, a Post Keynesian approach to health care policy would rely on many of the principles identified above—uncertainty, the pervasiveness of income effects, historical time, and imperfect competition (see Dunn 2006). This leads to a different approach to health care and a different set of policy prescriptions from those of neoclassical theory.

Even neoclassical economists recognize the importance of uncertainty in health care. In a famous paper, Arrow (1963) noted that health care markets were plagued by uncertainty, contributing to a less than perfect outcome, and he identified two main types of uncertainty in health care—uncertainty in demand (firms do not know how much health care will be needed at any give time) and uncertainty regarding effective treatments (we still do not know the best way to treat diseases). To this we can add a few other ways that uncertainty arises in the area of health. Few individuals are medical experts, and they do not have the knowledge to challenge the advice of health care professionals or judge the quality of doctors. People also do not know whether their doctor has financial ties to drug companies, research centers, or hospitals, or whether tests and treatments are recommended because they are in the financial interest of the doctor rather than the best interests of the patient. Facing such uncertainty, people follow rules, watch what other people are doing, and rely on past habits.

In Post Keynesian macroeconomics, one role for the government is to reduce uncertainty and improve economic performance. Similar things hold in the microeconomic case of health care policy. This is why governments need to establish "best practice" standards for doctors and hospitals (see Gawande 2009), why they need to license doctors, why they need to prohibit conflicts of interest, and why they need to assure that adequate health care is available to all citizens.

Regarding the importance of income, a good deal of empirical evidence supports the view that income inequality generates health problems. Rodgers (1979) was the first to show that life expectancy was related to both average income and income distribution using international data. Wilkinson (1992) showed that in the developed world income inequality was a more important factor than average income. Kaplan et al. (1996) and Kennedy et al. (1996) found that income inequality closely tracked death rates in US states and cities. Marmot (2004: 43–45) demonstrated this by looking at civil service positions in the UK and mortality rates, while Acheson (1998) documented a close association between income inequality and health in the UK overall. This relationship has been found in many other studies, employing different data sets and time periods, and using numerous control variables (Flegg 1982; Wilkinson 1992, 1994, 1996; Le Grand 1987; Waldmann 1992; Wennemo 1993). This helps explain why the US has relatively low life expectancy and relatively high infant mortality, yet spends the largest fraction of its GDP on health care—inequality in the US is the highest in the developed world.

Marmot (2004) provides a theoretical explanation for this in evolutionary terms. Inequality reduces the control that people have over their lives, and low-status individuals are subject to the arbitrary demands of others and are frequently discriminated against. This all leads to sustained and chronic stress. Stress, in turn, leads to problems with one's immune system, cardiovascular system, and glucose metabolism, and it can destroy brain cells involved in memory. Stress triggers "fight or flight" responses—chemical reactions in the body that were designed for emergency situations where an individual had to fight or flee. These responses helped save the lives of our ancestors (as well as other animals) during times of immediate threat. But with repeated stress, these chemicals remain in the bloodstream, disrupt normal body functions, and increase the probability of health problems.

This view receives further support in studies carried out with monkeys. Sapolsky and Mott (1987) found that when the social status of apes declines they are at greater risk for heart disease. In other experiments, monkeys were fed diets high in fat and cholesterol. High-ranking monkeys were less likely to develop atherosclerosis than were low-ranking monkeys. To control for genetic factors that might dispose monkeys to be high ranking and not develop atherosclerosis, the top monkeys and the bottom monkeys from different groups were put together and allowed to form a new hierarchy. Again, high-ranking monkeys were less likely to have heart problems as a result of eating a fatty diet (Shively 2000).[2]

This analysis points to one important cause of high US health care spending—great income inequality. The neoclassical theory of distribution holds that the existing distribution is the result of individual worker productivity, and that attempts to change this distribution are wrong ethically and economically. But Sraffa (1960) and the resulting capital controversy showed the logical inconsistency of this theory. It thus opened the door for social theories of distribution, theories that depend on the level of demand and worker bargaining power, and for economic policies that counter market inequalities. Thus, in contrast to neoclassical policy solutions, a Post Keynesian approach to health care would focus more on government programs to promote a healthy population (such as WIC, Food Stamps, and Medicaid) and redistributive government policies, especially focusing on households with children since childhood poverty is known to lead to long-run health problems (Children's Defense Fund 1994; Duncan and Brooks-Gunn 1997).

The good news is that such policies are likely to pay for themselves in the long-run. In a recent attempt to quantify some of these gains, Holzer et al. (2007) cull the results from numerous previous studies and find that the cost of childhood poverty in the US comes to around $500 billion per year, or 4 percent of US GDP. The costs involve reduced productivity, more unemployment, greater incarceration, and greater government benefits. One implication of this study is that a relatively large redistribution to low-income households in order to keep children out of poverty would effectively pay for itself on an annual basis. This is the obverse of Okun's (1975) leaky bucket. Rather than income redistribution reducing the amount of water we have, redistribution can give us more water.

Perhaps the major issue facing all developed countries is the sharp rise in health care expenditures. Following Arrow (1970), neoclassical economists have focused on making consumers pay more for their health care as a solution to this problem. Arrow argued that increasing co-pays and deductibles would create incentives for people to use health care efficiently and effectively. Cogan et al. (2005) and others advocate removing tax advantages for health insurance so that generous plans would not encourage the excessive consumption of health care. To help people afford the additional out-of-pocket expenses from such changes, many economists have proposed health care savings accounts. These accounts allow households to save money before taxes to pay for health care. With consumers paying for a large fraction of their health care, neoclassical economists assume they will be more cost conscious, which will help to bring down rising health care costs and expenditures.

Given large firms with substantial market power, a Post Keynesian approach would focus on a regulatory response to controlling health care spending and costs. It is important that regulatory agencies be independent of the companies they regulate. Government bodies that make important decisions about public health and safety should not be supported by pharmaceutical companies, and individuals who make key decisions should not benefit from them financially. In the US, this is presently not true of the Food and Drug Administration, which must approve all new drugs. We prohibit conflicts of interest for politicians and central bankers; regulatory officials should be held to the same standards.

Another part of the regulatory response needs to be controls on advertising by drug companies. Neoclassical economists generally regard advertising as benign. It just provides information to the consumer. It cannot manipulate consumer tastes and preferences since these are known and given to the individual. Following this line of reasoning, pharmaceutical company advertising informs and empowers patients. Yet, Moynihan and Cassels (2005) show that pharmaceutical companies typically hide the dangers of drugs from consumers and the FDA, extol the virtues of drugs with few or no benefits, and then use advertising to create fears so that consumers will see their doctor to get prescriptions for expensive medications. Faced with uncertainty, consumers tend to believe the "experts" pushing these drugs in advertisements.

From a Post Keynesian perspective, however, marketing does not provide information to consumers. As Galbraith (1967) notes, it is designed to aid the planning of the firm and manipulate the consumer. So, a Post Keynesian health care policy would support a ban on drug advertising in the US similar to the ban that exists in virtually every other developed country in the world. In addition, drug companies must be prohibited from influencing the decisions of doctors through direct payments to them and other perks. Doctors, like government regulatory agencies, should not face conflicts of interest when prescribing medication, running diagnostic tests, or providing treatment.

And Post Keynesians should oppose health savings accounts (and their cousin, flexible spending accounts) for several reasons. One problem is that low-income households cannot put much money into health savings accounts since they have accumulated little wealth and they need most of their annual income for day-to-day survival. Moreover, the main benefits of health care savings accounts go primarily to wealthy households in high tax brackets. Putting $5,000 into a health savings account costs only $2,500 for someone in a 50 percent tax bracket, but $4,000 for someone in a 20 percent tax bracket and $5,000 for someone in the 10 percent bracket. Looking at this another way, the government pays for a larger portion (50 percent) of health savings account contributions by wealthy households than other households. This just reinforces the trend towards greater income inequality that contributes to current health problems and the high health care expenditures in the US. Another problem with this approach is that in the face of uncertainty, consumers may not make good decisions about their own care. The famous RAND health insurance experiment found that when people are forced to pay more for their medical expenses they cut back on many valuable procedures. Its main conclusion is that for those who are sick or poor, the reduced health care was harmful to their overall health (Newhouse 2004).

Finally, innovation is particularly important in health care because it leads to life-saving discoveries that improve quality of life and life expectancy. Neoclassical economics looks to market incentives to assure appropriate health care innovation and new drugs. But such incentives already exist in the form of patents to pharmaceutical companies. Moreover, patents may stifle innovation, as firms seek to maximize profits from their current patent before introducing something better. Because R&D is so expensive and the end result so uncertain, even large oligopolies are reluctant to engage in R&D. Government investment is thus necessary for innovations in health care. In fact, governments already do most of the R&D in health care, so citizens rather than drug companies should receive most of the benefits of these efforts.

Productivity

Productivity is a measure of how efficiently an economy produces goods and services. Labor productivity equals national output divided by the number of (full-time equivalent) workers needed to produce this output. Productivity growth, the percentage change in productivity from one year to another, measures the *additional* output per worker that we get this year compared to last year. A broader notion, total factor productivity, seeks to combine labor and capital inputs in the denominator of the productivity measure. Because of the conceptual and practical difficulties of adding together such diverse things as labor and various kinds of capital, most economists focus on just labor productivity.

More than anything else, national well-being mainly depends on productivity. The more each worker produces, the more a nation has to consume; and the faster productivity grows, the faster average living standards rise. To take one simple example, productivity grew in the US by around 3 percent per year between 1947 and 1973. Since then it has grown only 2 percent per year. Had productivity growth not fallen, the average standard of living in the US would have been nearly 50 percent greater in 2010.

Productivity is also important because of its effect on inflation. As average productivity rises, fewer workers are needed to produce each good, reducing unit labor costs and prices. This relationship is expressed in the famous wage cost–markup equation, $P = kw/A$, where P is the average price level, k is the markup on costs, w is the average wage rate, and A is the average product per employee or average labor productivity (see Weintraub 1961: ch. 3). According to this equation, per unit (labor) cost is w/A, and prices are determined by a markup (k), which in turn is determined by the degree of monopoly (see Kalecki 1971). Given existing competitive conditions, and given current wage rates, higher levels of productivity will reduce unit costs and will exert downward pressure on prices.

The neoclassical approach to productivity growth focuses on market signals. It stresses the importance of competition among firms and on creating incentives to spur people to work hard so that they can become fabulously wealthy. If firms and workers get to keep the gains from productivity growth, they will have greater incentives to produce more efficiently. So, individual income taxes and taxes on corporate profits should be kept low, and we must not let the government interfere in the marketplace (imposing rules and regulations on firms regarding hiring labor, environmental standards, and so forth), thereby distorting prices. We also need to discourage employees from being lazy. If lack of effort leads to low income, and maybe even poverty, there is an incentive to work hard. Government programs, such as unemployment insurance and Food Stamps, which help people survive with little or no earnings, provide disincentives to work hard and be productive. In addition, these government programs must be financed; this will require higher taxes, further hurting productivity.

In contrast to this, a Post Keynesian approach to productivity growth would stress the importance of income effects rather than substitution effects for productivity growth, as well as the social notion of rationality. These social factors are important in a world where people work together in oligopolistic firms that control wages, prices, and income distribution. But first and foremost, for two reasons, a Post Keynesian analysis of productivity would stress the importance of full employment and economic growth.

Adam Smith ([1776] 1937) was the first to note that productivity improves when firms can divide tasks, when individuals can specialize in narrow duties, and when machinery can then be employed to assist workers in their jobs. This is possible, however, only when firms sell a sufficient quantity of goods to justify both the capital investment and the restructuring of production. For Smith, the greater the extent of the market, the more the firm would sell and the greater the productivity of workers.

More recently, Allyn Young (1928) argued that many firms operate under increasing returns to scale. As more and more gets produced, costs fall because fewer resources are used to produce each good. Increasing returns means that productivity grows as output expands, and during times of slow economic growth, productivity growth will slow. In addition, during recessions firms focus on maintaining sales and surviving the difficult economic times. They focus on cutting costs rather than on long-run growth and profitability. In contrast, during booming times, firms do not need to concern themselves with keeping afloat. With increasing sales and labor shortages, firms think about using workers more efficiently (Sylos-Labini 1983–1984).

Even more recently, Salter (1969) pointed out that productivity differences exist among industries and, over time, there are changes in the most efficient sector of the economy. Expanding on this, Harcourt ([1997] 2001: 268) argued that the way to achieve high productivity growth is to make sure that declining industries disappear quickly and production moves toward those industries where productivity is growing rapidly. But the flexible wages policies advocated by neo-classical economists hinder this outcome. With flexible wages, declining industries can survive as a result of falling labor costs. A better policy is to increase demand, which raises wages and promotes the transition to more productive economic sectors.

The second reason that productivity growth is demand driven stems from the nature of productivity in a service economy. For most service firms, demand must be the main determinant of worker productivity. Consider a symphony orchestra. The productivity of the orchestra does *not* depend on how fast the musicians play a piece or a few pieces of music. Rather, the productivity of the orchestra is measured by the amount of money received via ticket sales. When the economy is doing poorly, and people are reluctant to spend money, they do not go to the symphony. The productivity of the symphony orchestra thus languishes. In contrast, during booming economic times, the concert hall is full and the productivity of the orchestra (the value of its output divided by the number of players) increases as spending on concert tickets increases.

What is true of the symphony orchestra is likewise true of most service occupations. Teachers are more productive the more students they have in their classes. Greater demand for higher education thus improves the productivity of college teachers. The productivity of the sales force in a store, the productivity of real estate agents, the productivity of newspaper reporters, and the productivity of management consultants (who try to help firms become more productive) all depend on the value of sales.

A second ingredient of a Post Keynesian approach to productivity growth arises from the social nature of rationality. In a modern capitalist economy, productivity is discretionary because people work together in teams and across functions.

Simon (1957) was one of the first to argue that the relative distribution of pay within a firm was a critical determinant of employee behavior. Leibenstein (1966) then developed this idea, arguing that worker productivity is a variable at the control of the individual worker. He coined the term "x-efficiency" to indicate that a large part of worker effort is discretionary. When workers feel that their wages are unfair, and too much income is going to the owners and the heads of the firm, they do not quit; instead, they tend to work more slowly or less efficiently (producing more defective goods that cannot be sold and that do not count as output or in productivity data). Martin (1981, 1982, 1986) has shown that people lower in organizations do compare their rewards to those at the top and that large differences lead to feelings of injustice. These sentiments likely also affect worker productivity. This problem is encapsulated in the ultimatum game, which raises issues of productivity, inequality, and feelings about fairness. It also touches on another key Post Keynesian tenet, uncertainty, since in social settings there will always be uncertainty about how others will behave.

The ultimatum game is structured as follows. Two people are given a sum of money to divide. The first subject can propose any division of the money that they like; the second subject can only accept or reject this division. If the division is accepted, each person receives the amount of money proposed by the first subject; if the division is rejected, each person receives nothing. Kahneman et al. (1986) ran a number of experiments where individuals played this game for real stakes. He found that people do *not* behave as predicted by the rationality assumption of economists. Dividers tend to make substantial offers to the other subject, when they could have offered close to zero, reasoning that the second subject would not reject getting a very small amount of money. Furthermore, most people reject unfair or unequal offers, despite the fact that it is personally costly and economically irrational. These results have been replicated time and time again, including cases in which people rejected offers as large as one month's pay because they felt that the split was unfair (Cameron 1999; Henrich et al. 2001; Klasen 2008: 260f).

Neurological studies have shown that people are more likely to reject offers when there was strong activity in the anterior insula area of their brain, which is associated with negative emotional responses. It thus appears that rejecting unfair offers is not the result of rational, deliberative action in our brains; rather, it is an emotional response (Cohen 2005: 14). Humans seem to have some internal sense of fairness. When this is violated, we want to punish the violator, even at personal cost. Field (2002) argues that this arose because it contributed to human survival.

Consider now a modified version of the ultimatum game, something applicable to the issue of productivity growth. In this game, the original proposer still gets to divide a sum of money and the second subject still gets to accept it or reject it. However, the result of rejecting the pie is *not* that both subjects get nothing. Rather, the result is that both subjects get less—although distribution of the pie remains pretty much the same.

This revised ultimatum game approximates what goes on in real world economies. Large firms propose a division of the economic pie, or the revenues they receive. Some of this money goes to workers; the rest goes to senior executives and shareholders. Workers can ill-afford to reject this offer outright, since most workers need a job and an income to survive. But workers can *quasi-reject* any proposal they regard as unfair in other ways—by working less hard, by sabotaging production and firm efficiency, by causing firm resources to be used in setting rules, monitoring workers, and dealing with lawssuits. The net result is a loss of efficiency, or a smaller pie.

This analysis leads to a very different set of public policies than we get from the neoclassical approach. It means that to improve productivity growth we need to *reduce* income inequality. It means that high taxes are *not* a problem and are *not* a cause of slow productivity growth. Rather, high taxes are a solution to the problem and low taxes on the very wealthy may lower productivity growth.

This view even has some empirical support. If you look at when the US economy performed best, in terms of rising productivity growth, high and rising living standards, and low rates of unemployment, the past 25 years or so have not been very good (except, of course, for the very wealthy). Since the 1970s productivity growth has stagnated, unemployment has been relatively high, and average household incomes have barely increased (despite a large rise in the number of household members who are part of the labor force). All the policies enacted since the early 1980s to reduce government regulation of business firms, cut the top marginal tax rates, and reduce redistributive government spending have resulted in rather poor productivity performance for more than a quarter of a century. In contrast, the glory days for the US economy were the 1950s, the 1960s and the early 1970s. These were times of very high marginal tax rates. They were times of significant and growing income redistribution, of greater support for education, and of substantial regulation of markets.

Further support for this view comes from microeconomic studies. Economists typically focus on the benefits of inequality for individual performance. Some evidence for this comes from sports like golf and auto racing, where the greater the inequality of the prize money, the better the individual performances tend to be. While true for individual sports, it is not true for team sports. Bloom (1999) has analyzed baseball salaries and found that the wider the pay differences, the worse the team performance and the worse the individual performances on the team. There is further empirical support for this in studies of manufacturing firms. Cowherd and Levine (1992) found that firms with wider pay differentials have lower product quality. So while inequality is likely to enhance per-formance in individual competitions, in real world situations, where productivity and performance depend on social factors, inequality appears to harm performance.

Finally, a Post Keynesian approach to productivity would recognize the importance of government investment or what Keynes ([1936] 1964: 378) called "the socialization of investment" at the end of *The General Theory*. The problem Keynes identified and sought to address was insufficient investment at the macro level. But there is also insufficient investment at the micro level. The reasons for this are uncertainty (especially in the face of high up-front costs) and the fact that with large oligopolies we tend to be locked-in to existing practices and procedures that had developed over time. For example, why would Exxon/Mobile or BP invest in wind power when it makes so much more profit from oil? Moreover, new technology and new firms are at the mercy of energy firms, which can out-invest them and cut prices to drive potential competitors out of business before they threaten existing monopoly profits. This opens the door to government investment or government R&D as part of its stabilization functions.

In sum, the keys aspects of the Post Keynesian approach to improv-ing productivity are the same as those for health care policy. The hallmarks of a Post Keynesian micro policy will be full employment, greater income equality, and government investment. First, the gov-ernment needs to ensure full employment. As we have seen, full employment spurs productivity growth in a number of ways. It also reduces stress and so leads to a healthier nation. Second, the govern-ment needs to promote greater income equality. Our deep-seated feelings about justice can lead to cooperation rather than sabotage and enhance productivity growth. And, as we saw above, the literature is vast on the negative impact of inequality on health. Finally, govern-ment R&D and government investment are needed to promote both healthier and more productive societies.

Summary and Conclusion

This paper has argued that, although it is primarily a school of macroeconomics, key Post Keynesian principles can be applied to microeconomic policy issues. It has done so for two particular cases—health care and productivity. By doing so, it has shown how a Post Keynesian approach yields an analysis of contemporary problems and a set of policy prescriptions that differ markedly from neoclassical economics. As would be expected, Post Keynesian microeconomic policy will focus first and foremost on getting the macroeconomics right. Microeconomic policy must take care to ensure full employment, a more equal distribution of income, and government investment in the absence of private investment. There is still a great deal of work to be done in the area of public policy. It is now time for Post Keynesians to begin this important work.[3]

Notes

1. There are a few noteworthy exceptions—Courvisanos (1996) on innovation policy, Dunn (2006) on health care, Pressman (2007) on poverty and, of course, the work of Galbraith.

2. Another possible explanation, also consistent with Post Keynesian thought, is that inequality leads to lower civic participation. If low-income individuals are less likely to vote, then the government will be less responsive to the needs of the poor and near poor. There is also some empirical evidence for this view. US states with the greatest income inequality are less likely to invest in human capital and less likely to provide a generous social safety net (Kawachi et al. 1997). This analysis, of course, deserves much greater attention than is possible here.

3. The author thanks Fred Lee and two anonymous referees for their comments and suggestions on an earlier version of this paper. Any remaining errors are the responsibility of the author.

References

Acheson, D. (1998). *Independent Inquiry into Inequality in Health*. London: Stationery Office.

Arestis, P. (1996). "Post-Keynesian Economics: Towards Coherence." *Cambridge Journal of Economics* 20: 111–135.

Arrow, K. (1963). "Uncertainty and the Welfare Economics of Medical Care." *American Economic Review* 53: 941–973.

——. (1970). *Essays in the Theory of Risk-Bearing*. Amsterdam and London: North Holland.

Barkow, J., L. Cosmides, and J. Tooby (eds.) (1992). *The Adapted Mind: Evolutionary Psychology and the Generation of Culture*. New York: Oxford University Press.

Bloom, M. (1999). "The Performance Effects of Pay Dispersion on Individuals and Organizations." *Academy of Management Journal* 42: 25–40.

Bridge, R., and J. Blackman (1978). *A Study of Alternatives in American Education, Vol. 4: Family Choice in Schooling.* Santa Monica, CA: RAND.

Cameron, L. (1999). "Raising the Stakes in the Ultimatum Game: Experimental Evidence from Indonesia." *Economic Inquiry* 37: 47–59.

Carabelli, A. (1988). *On Keynes's Method.* London: Palgrave/Macmillan.

Children's Defense Fund (1994). *Wasting America's Future.* Boston: Beacon Press.

CIA (2007). *The 2007 World Factbook.* Washington, DC: Central Intelligence Agency.

Cogan, J., R. G. Hubbard, and D. Kessler (2005). *Healthy, Wealthy and Wise.* Washington, DC: American Enterprise Institute Press.

Cohen, J. (2005). "The Vulcanization of the Human Brain: A Neural Perspective on Interactions Between Cognition and Emotion." *Journal of Economic Perspectives* 19: 3–24.

Cohen, R., and M. Martinez (2005). *Health Care Coverage: Estimates from the National Health Interview Survey, January–March 2005.* Http:// www.cdc.gov/nchs/nhis.htm.

Courvisanos, J. (1996). *Investment Cycles in Capitalist Economies: A Kaleckian Behavioural Contribution.* Cheltenham, UK: Edward Elgar.

Cowherd, D., and D. Levine (1992). "Product Quality and Pay Equity Between Lower-Level Employees and Top Management: An Investigation of Distributive Justice Theory." *Administrative Science Quarterly* 37: 302–320.

Crister, G. (2003). *Fatland.* Boston: Houghton Mifflin.

Davidson, P. (1991). "Is Probability Theory Relevant for Uncertainty?" *Journal of Economic Perspectives* 5: 129–143.

———. (1994). *Post Keynesian Macroeconomic Theory.* Edward Elgar.

———. (1996). "Reality and Economic Theory." *Journal of Post Keynesian Economics* 18: 479–508.

———. (2005). "The Post Keynesian School." In *Modern Macroeconomics: Its Origins, Development and Current State.* Eds. B. Snowdon and H. Vane, pp. 451–473. Cheltenham, UK: Edward Elgar.

Downward, P. (1999). *Pricing in Post Keynesian Economics.* Northampton, MA: Edward Elgar.

Duncan, G., and J. Brooks-Gunn (eds.) (1997). *Consequences of Growing Up Poor.* New York: Russell Sage.

Dunn, S. (2006). "Prolegomena to a Post Keynesian Health Economics." *Review of Social Economy* 64: 273–299.

Earl, P. (1983). *The Economic Imagination.* Armonk, NY: M.E. Sharpe.

Eichner, A. (1976). *The Megacorp and Oligopoly.* New York: Cambridge University Press.

Field, A. (2002). *Altruistically Inclined? The Behavioral Sciences, Evolutionary Theory and the Origins of Reciprocity.* Ann Arbor, MI: University of Michigan Press.

Flegg, A. (1982). "Inequality of Income, Illiteracy, and Medical Care as Determinants of Infant Mortality in Developing Countries." *Population Studies* 36: 441–458.

Galbraith, J. K. (1952). *A Theory of Price Control.* Cambridge, MA: Harvard University Press.

———. (1967). *The New Industrial State.* Boston: Houghton Mifflin.

Gawande, A. (2009). *The Checklist Manifesto: How to Get Things Right.* New York: Metropolitan Books.

Georgescu-Roegen, N. (1966). *Analytical Economics.* Boston: Harvard University Press.

Harcourt, G. (1997). "Pay Policy, Accumulation and Productivity." *Economic and Labour Relations Review* 8: 78–89. Reprinted in *Selected Essays on Economic Policy,* 2001, pp. 263–275. Hampshire, UK and New York: Palgrave Macmillan.

Henrich, J. et al. (2001). "Cooperation, Reciprocity and Punishment in Fifteen Small-Scale Societies." *American Economic Review* 91: 73–78.

Holt, R., and S. Pressman (2001). *A New Guide to Post Keynesian Economics.* London and New York: Routledge.

Holzer, H. et al. (2007). "The Economic Costs of Poverty in the United States: Subsequent Effects of Children Growing Up Poor." Institute for Research on Poverty Discussion Paper #1327-07.

Kahneman, D. et al. (1986). "Fairness and the Assumptions of Economics." *Journal of Business* 59: S285–S300.

Kaldor, N. (1985). *Economics Without Equilibrium.* Armonk, NY: M.E. Sharpe.

Kalecki, M. (1971). *Selected Essays on the Dynamics of the Capitalist Economy.* Cambridge: Cambridge University Press.

Kaplan, G., E. Pamuk, J. Lynch, R. Cohen, and J. Balfour (1996). "Income Inequality and Mortality in the United States." *British Medical Journal* 312: 999–1003.

Kawachi, I., B. Kennedy, K. Lochner, and D. Prothrow-Stith (1997). "Social Capital, Income Inequality, and Mortality." *American Journal of Public Health* 87: 1491–1498.

Kennedy, B. et al. (1996). "Income Distribution and Mortality: Cross Sectional Ecological Study of the Robin Hood Index in the United States." *British Medical Journal* 312: 1004–1007.

Keynes, J. M. ([1936] 1964). *The General Theory of Employment, Interest and Money.* New York: Harcourt Brace and World.

Klasen, S. (2008). "The Efficiency of Equity." *Review of Political Economy* 20: 257–274.

Knight, F. ([1921] 1971). *Risk, Uncertainty, and Profit.* Chicago: University of Chicago Press.

Lavoie, M. (1992). *Foundations of Post-Keynesian Analysis.* Aldershot: Edward Elgar.

———. (2006). *Introduction to Post-Keynesian Economics.* New York: Palgrave Macmillan.

Layard, R. (2005). *Happiness: Lessons from a New Science.* New York: Penguin Press.

Le Grand, J. (1987). "Inequalities in Health: Some International Comparisons." *European Economic Review* 31: 182–191.

Lee, F. (1998). *Post Keynesian Pricing Theory.* Cambridge: Cambridge University Press.

Leibenstein, H. (1966). "Allocative Efficiency vs. X-Efficiency." *American Economic Review* 56: 392–415.

Loasby, B. (1976). *Choice, Complexity and Ignorance.* Cambridge: Cambridge University Press.

Marmot, M. (2004). *The Status Syndrome: How Social Standing Affects Our Health and Longevity.* New York: Times Books.

Martin, J. (1981). "Relative Deprivation: A Theory of Distributive Injustice for an Era of Shrinking Resources." In *Research in Organizational Behavior, Vol. 3,* Eds. L. Cummings and B. Staw, pp. 53–107. Greenwich, CT: JAI Press.

———. (1982). "The Fairness of Earnings Differentials: An Experimental Study of the Perceptions of Blue-Collar Workers." *Journal of Human Resources* 17: 110–122.

———. (1986). "When Expectations and Justice Do Not Coincide." In *Justice in Social Relations.* Eds. H. Biefhoff, R. Cohen, and J. Greenberg, pp. 317–335. New York: Plenum Press.

Moynihan, R., and A. Cassels (2005). *Selling Sickness: How the World's Biggest Pharmaceutical Companies Are Turning Us All into Patients.* New York: Nation Books.

Newhouse, J. P. (2004). "Consumer-Directed Health Plans and the RAND Health Insurance Experiment." *Health Affairs* 23: 107–113.

Okun, A. (1975). *Equality and Efficiency: The Big Tradeoff.* Washington, DC: Brookings Institution.

Peterson, C., and R. Burton (2007). *U.S. Health Care Spending: Comparison with Other OECD Countries.* Washington, DC: Congressional Research Service.

Pinker, S. (1997). *How the Mind Works.* New York: Norton.

———. (2002). *The Blank Slate.* New York: Viking.

Pressman, S. (2007). "What Can Post Keynesian Economics Teach Us About Poverty?" In *Empirical Post Keynesian Economics.* Eds. R. Holt and S. Pressman, pp. 21–43. Armonk, NY: M.E. Sharpe.

Robinson, J. (1974). "History Versus Equilibrium." In *Collected Economic Papers*, 5 Vols. Cambridge: MIT Press, 1980.

——. (1976). "The Age of Growth." In *Collected Economic Papers of Joan Robinson*, Vol. 4, pp. 122–127. Oxford: Basil Blackwell.

Rodgers, G. (1979). "Income and Inequality as Determinants of Mortality: An International Cross-Section Analysis." *Population Studies* 33: 343–351.

Rosser, J. B. (2001). "Uncertainty and Expectations." In *A New Guide to Post Keynesian Economics*. Eds. R. Holt and S. Pressman, pp. 52–64. London and New York: Routledge.

Salter, W. (1969). *Productivity and Technical Change*. London and New York: Cambridge University Press.

Sapolsky, R., and G. Mott (1987). "Social Subordinance in Wild Baboons Is Associated with Suppressed High Density Lipoprotein Cholesterol Concentrations: The Possible Role of Chronic Social Stress." *Endocrinology* 121: 1605–1610.

Schoen, C. et al. (2004). "Primary Care and Health System Performance: Adults' Experiences in Five Countries." *Health Affairs*. Web exclusive, W4-487-W4-503. http://content.healthaffairs.org/cgi/content/full/hlthaff.w4.487/DC1.

Shackle, G. (1955). *Uncertainty in Economics and Other Reflections*. Cambridge: Cambridge University Press.

——. (1972). *Epistemics and Economics*. Cambridge: Cambridge University Press.

——. (1974). *Keynesian Kaleidics*. Edinburgh: Edinburgh University Press.

Shapiro, N. (1981). "Pricing and the Growth of the Firm." *Journal of Post Keynesian Economics* 4: 85–100.

Shively, C. (2000). "Social Status, Stress and Health in Female Monkeys." In *The Society and Population Health Reader—A State and Community Perspective*. Eds. A. Tarvol and R. F. St. Peter, pp. 278–289. New York: New Press.

Simon, H. (1957). "The Compensation of Executives" *Sociometry* 20: 32–35.

Smith, A. ([1776] 1937). *The Wealth of Nations*. New York: Modern Library.

Sraffa, P. (1926). "The Laws of Return Under Competitive Conditions." *Economic Journal* 36: 535–550.

——. (1960). *Production of Commodities by Means of Commodities*. New York: Cambridge University Press.

Stigler, G., and G. Becker (1977). "*De Gustibus Non Est Disputum.*" *American Economic Review* 67: 76–90.

Sylos-Labini, P. (1983–1984). "Factors Affecting Changes in Productivity." *Journal of Post Keynesian Economics* 6: 161–179.

US Census Bureau (2007). *Income, Poverty and Health Insurance Coverage in the United States: 2006*. Washington, DC: Government Printing Office.

Waldmann, R. J. (1992). "Income Distribution and Infant Mortality." *Quarterly Journal of Economics* 107: 1283–1302.

Weintraub, S. (1961). *Classical Keynesianism, Monetary Theory and the Price Level.* Philadelphia: Chilton.

Wennemo, I. (1993). "Infant Mortality, Public Policy and Inequality—A Comparison of 18 Industrialised Countries 1950–85." *Sociology of Health and Illness* 15: 429–446.

Wilkinson, R. (1992). "Income Distribution and Life Expectancy." *British Medical Journal* 304: 165–168.

——. (1994). "Health, Redistribution and Growth." In *Paying for Inequality: The Economic Cost of Social Injustice.* Eds. A. Glyn and D. Miliband, pp. 409–460. London: Rivers Oram Press.

——. (1996). *Unhealthy Societies: The Afflictions of Inequality.* London and New York: Routledge.

Young, A. (1928). "Increasing Returns and Economic Policy." *Economic Journal* 35: 527–542.

Morgenstern's Forgotten Contribution: A Stab to the Heart of Modern Economics

By Philipp Bagus*†

Abstract. In contrast to physics, there is no estimate of statistical error within economics in spite of Oskar Morgenstern's book *On the Accuracy of Economic Observation*. The problem of error in economic observations is still a widely neglected problem. The various sources of error that come into play in the social sciences suggest that the error in economic observations is substantial. As the error might be substantial, this paper argues that the usefulness of econometrics becomes questionable.

In his classic book *On the Accuracy of Economic Observation*, Oskar Morgenstern deals with a common, yet widely neglected problem with which economic historians are faced, namely the quality of economic data. Morgenstern's "study aims at examining the conditions governing the accuracy of planned quantitative economic observations and, more widely, of economic statistics" (1963: 3). Thus, his work does not deal with economic information that stems from qualitative research approaches such as participant observations, interviews and questionnaires. The problem of the quality of (quantitative) economic data or economic statistics has not been addressed or solved until today, despite a striking call to attention by the co-founder of game theory.

The accuracy of economic data is a problem for all fields of economics. For an economic historian, the quality of economic data is

*The author is assistant professor at the Universidad Rey Juan Carlos (Madrid). He is author of the book *The Tragedy of the Euro*. His interests are monetary and business cycle theories. He would like to thank Nicolas Cachanovski, Jonathan Catalán, John Cochran, David Howden, Guido Hülsmann, Frederic Lee, Mateusz Machaj, Brian Ó Caithnia, Vincent Wolters and two anonymous referees for comments on earlier drafts.

†Departamento Economía Aplicada, Universidad Rey Juan Carlos, Campus de Vicalvaro, Facultad de Ciencias Jurídicas y Sociales, Pso. Artilleros s/n, 28032 Madrid, Email: philipp.bagus@urjc.es

American Journal of Economics and Sociology, Vol. 70, No. 2 (April, 2011).

of utmost importance, since false data or belief in inaccurate data can lead the economic historian to faulty interpretations of the past. For a policy maker the accuracy of data is vital, as policy makers base their decisions on economic data with far-reaching consequences for the whole economy.

Likewise, Morgenstern's insights are relevant for orthodox economics since the economics profession has been dominated by mathematical formalism since the 1950s. While there has been an increase in the variety of economic theories, the development on the methodological front has been leaning towards homogeneity (Dow 2007). The methodological monism in orthodox economics is manifested by a mathematical formalism. The mathematical approach to economics is affected by Morgenstern's arguments as it makes sense to perform computations and solve a system of mathematical equations only if one has reliable data. Morgenstern illustrates this in the following example:

> The equations
> $x - y = 1$
> $x - 1.00001y = 0$
> have the solution $x = 100001$, $y = 100000$, while the almost identical equations
> $x - y = 1$
> $x - 0.999999y = 0$ [sic]
> have the solution $x = -99999$, $y = -100000$. The coefficients in the two sets of equations differ by at most two units in the *fifth* decimal place, yet the solutions differ by 200,000 (1963: 109).[1]

Morgenstern's sample equations show the significance of a small error in the observation. Yet, in more complex equations with extensive mathematical operations, the extent of error due to unreliable data may increase (or, depending on the equation, the errors may cancel out).

The quality of economic data is at least as important for econometrics as it is for mathematics. Defined as "a combination of economics, mathematics, and statistics,"[2] econometrics is a mainstream approach to economic science and the interpretation of economic data is central to its methodology: one formulates a model, gathers data, and then estimates the model with this data, comparing the theoretical solutions with the observed data via hypothesis testing. Finally, one interprets the results.[3] Clearly, the economic data plays a crucial role in this procedure since it serves the econometrician in arriving at theoretical solutions by confirming or falsifying the models. If the accuracy of the economic data is not known, then the suitability of the data for this kind of procedure is also not known. In such a case, the econometrician may likely find a spurious relationship.

A Morgensternian critique of econometrics is different from other critiques that focus on econometrics as practiced by prominent economists. Edward Leamer (1983), in an influential article, stated that econometric analysis is not taken seriously due to the amount of "data mining" and "number crunching." Econometricians make implicit assumptions about the distribution of errors, the functional form, and the variables in the model. According to Leamer statistical interference is based on opinions and whims. In a similar way, Deirdre McCloskey and Steven Ziliak (2008) criticize the procedure of econometricians and the abuse of significance testing. Too often statistical significance is confused with real world significance. Morgenstern's critique is, however, on a different level. The critique of econometric practices and techniques does not deal with the accuracy of the underlying data but takes it as given. Morgenstern more fundamentally questions the accuracy of economic data and, consequently, the very basis for econometrics.

It is indeed surprising to note how much the problem of accuracy in economic data has been neglected. This is not the case in the physical sciences (Preston and Dietz 1991).[4] Within the physical sciences the error of observation is always explicitly mentioned, yet in economics there is simply no error estimate.[5] This means that economists do not know the accuracy of the economic data presented to them. This is even more troubling when one considers that in social or economic data there are more possible sources of error than in the physical sciences. Economists, therefore, face the question of why the problem of accuracy of economic data is rarely mentioned or passed over in silence in economics, while in the physical sciences this problem is widely acknowledged.

Sources of Error in Economic Statistics

Oskar Morgenstern names several sources of error that influence the accuracy of economic observation. One is a lack of designed experiments.[6] The observations are not produced by the user of an experiment, as in the natural sciences, but rather, statistics are simply a byproduct of business and government activities. There is a complete lack of incentive to provide accurate information for government statistics and economic researchers on the part of companies, because to do so would require a costly and burdensome process. Companies simply lack incentives to spend much time to accurately fill out the demanded forms.

In addition to the lack of an accurately designed collection of data, there is a related problem also absent in the physical sciences— namely, the possibility of the hiding of information or outright lying. Companies have strong incentives to hide information or lie in order to mislead their competitors about their competitive strategy or strength. Sometimes companies manipulate profits in order to pay out fewer dividends. Individuals and companies also have an incentive to mislead tax authorities and the government in general in order to seek subsidies or avoid taxation. By amplifying their problems they might receive more subsidies. By tax evasion or tax avoidance, companies increase returns for owners. Even though the incentive to mislead tax authorities is reduced by penalties for tax evasion, it is difficult to know the extent of misleading information and the real data. Income tax returns for countries such as Spain, Italy or Greece do not closely resemble the underlying income patterns of these countries. Nevertheless, as Machlup points out, "it is on the basis of tax returns that important and elusive problems, such as the validity of the 'Pareto distribution' . . . explaining the inequality of personal incomes, are minutely studied" (1963: 19). Apparently, the real income patterns may indicate a different conclusion than the official statistics. Thus, relying on inaccurate data may lead to erroneous conclusions and flawed theories.

Likewise, governments themselves have an incentive to falsify statistics, thereby improving their economic record. Doing so improves the ruling party's chances of staying in power. The falsification of economic statistics can also improve the likelihood of receiving some kind of foreign aid or foreign recognition. A recent example involves the Greek government, whose officials falsified the report on the Greek budget deficit in order to gain entrance into the European monetary union.[7]

Another potential source of error consists in the inadequate training of those who observe economic data. Whereas in the physical sciences the observers are the scientists conducting the experiment, the observers of economic data are often not trained at all. The lack of training can lead to error in data collection. For instance, errors may stem from questionnaires. The conductor of the research does not normally conduct all the interviews. Instead, the interviews are likely to be conducted by different persons. As a result, the delivering of the questions, the setting up, the interpretation and the recording of the answers are additional sources of error. Friedrich August von Hayek (1948) sees an additional problem with economic data collection. The nature of facts in the social sciences is subjective. The "social facts" are interpreted by the human mind. Therefore, different individuals might give different answers when asked about the same historical event. It must be pointed out that the errors in mass observation do not necessarily cancel each other out. Frequently, such errors are cumulative.

An additional potential source for errors is the lack of clear definitions or classifications. These problems apply, for instance, in the classification of goods, types of employment, or classification of companies within industries.[8] Companies like General Electric operate in various industries, making it difficult to assign its revenues or profits to distinct industries.

More fundamentally, unlike observations within natural sciences, economic observations are unique and not reproducible. While a stone always reacts in the same way to certain stimuli, human beings act differently in certain situations and have the ability to learn. Any human action is unique in its context of time and space. As there are no universally prevailing regularities in the social realm, scientific prediction of future actions based on past data is impossible (Mises 1957). In a similar way, Lawson (1997) and Bigo (2006) argue that society is an open and complex system. In an open system controlled experimentation is unfeasible. In the open social realm there is a lack of event regularities, which makes events in the social realm unpredictable. If prediction is not possible, then the econometrics projects are irrelevant in the first place, no matter how accurate the data is. Morgenstern's insights, however, address econometricians on another level. Even if prediction were possible in the social realm, the data used by econometricians may not be accurate enough, and the lack of accuracy has been thus far neglected.

The uniqueness of economic events also has implications for the accuracy of the observed data. With economic observations, one deals with processes, which means that the very same event can be observed by several independent observers at different places or points of time, leading to discrepancies in their observations. The time element is another potential source of error because it takes time to conduct certain types of statistical research, and within that time frame, the observed phenomenon might change. An example is the counting of inventories for a certain period or a large population for a certain day. As people immigrate, migrate, emigrate, travel, die, and are born, it is difficult to get an exact number.

The only points where, according to Morgenstern, the natural sciences are worse off in relation to the social sciences are errors resulting from the use of instruments.[9] This is so, because economic statisticians often do not use machines. For example, they do not have to measure a price by a machine, but can just observe a certain price paid on the market and already have a number at hand. However, in using machines to measure, natural scientists at least get their data immediately and probably more reliably as Wassily Leontief points out. Leontief also emphasizes some of the aforementioned advantages that the physicist holds versus the economist regarding the observation of data:

> The scientists have their machines while the economists are still waiting for their data. In our case not only must society be willing to provide millions of dollars required for maintenance of a vast statistical machine year after year, but a large number of citizens must be prepared to play, at least, a passive and occasionally even an active part in actual fact-finding operations. It is as if the electrons and protons had to be persuaded to cooperate with the physicist. (1971: 6)

While considering these problems with data collection, for example, a lack of trained observers and a lack of clear definitions, it is important to note that advances in data collection have also occurred since the appearance of Morgenstern's book. By virtue of increased funding for research, data has become more accurate in past years. However, there are some problems inherent in social science data collection that cannot be eliminated by pouring more money into statistical research.[10] One important point is that in most cases, the economist using the data is neither the originator nor the collector of the data. This is a possible source of error that cannot be eliminated. In addition, the incentive to lie remains, even in a surveillance state that threatens such misinformation with harsh penalties. Thoughts remain free. Morgenstern (1963: 21) reports that statistical authorities in the Soviet Union had developed "lie-coefficients" in the 1930s to correct statistical reports of different regions. A third point that must be raised is that statistical research itself might influence the observed data.[11] Pouring more money into the economic research of some particular data will change the same data under research. In other words, the introduction of a new variable, such as increased funding or time spent on empirical research, might change other variables, for example, those variables that are to be examined. For instance, when more economic resources are shifted from other areas of the economy towards the investigation of changes in the price level, this will change relative prices and most likely the prices that enter the price index as well.

The Illusion of Price Statistics

One of Morgenstern's examples of the questionable accuracy in which economic observations are presented is that of price statistics. Almost all possible sources of error mentioned above apply to price statistics: the desire to hide or lie about the true price, problems of classification or definition, and quality changes.

The history of the collection of price data is dominated by both advances and calls for more accurate data (Mills 1936). The collection of price data has become ever more sophisticated by expanding the observations and disaggregating the data. This has sometimes caused a revision of conclusions derived from price statistics. An interesting example is provided by Frederic S. Lee and Paul Downward (1999), who reassess Gardiner Means' doctrine of administered prices. Lee and Downward show that the data supports Means' claim that in the 1930s in the U.S. market prices declined relative to administered prices when demand declined, and vice versa. However, expansion and disaggregation of price and production data shows weak to non-existent support for Means' thesis that in an economic downturn the production of administered-price products would decrease greater than the production of market-price products. We are, therefore, faced with one instance where the aggregation of data had lead to a thesis that later proved to be problematic. Inaccurate data may induce faulty conclusions.

In addition to the problems of aggregation, classification and grouping of goods, price statistics face additional difficulties. In reality, a certain good has multiple prices. The price changes when the goods are sold in different units, at different times, and in varying quality. From this infinite number of possible prices only some are available. Sources of price quotations range from companies, boards of trade, trade associations, trade journals, labor unions and government institutions. Consequently, one product may have several price quotations available. Which price should be chosen and what about the infinite number of prices that are not available? There are also non-monetary components to prices, for instance, the quality of service before, during, and after the sale, which may vary. These, however, are not taken into account by merely measuring the monetary price. These non-monetary components of prices are, of course, relevant for an econometrician who wants to test the hypothesis that changes in the money supply have an influence on prices. Moreover, there are not only different qualities; there are also significant quality changes even on a yearly basis. For example, the prices and quality of PCs change very quickly. The provision for these quality changes in the changes of price statistics necessarily remains somewhat arbitrary.

When observed prices enter the calculation of index numbers, further problems are created. For one thing, the method of calculation itself is arbitrary, since many methods of calculating averages or price indexes exist, they all lead to different results. Furthermore, the components and their (changing) weight in the index are arbitrary.

One might grant the difficulties to calculate accurate price indexes but reply that this would pose no problem for the econometrician. For example, one could argue that an econometrician only wishes to test a hypothesis about the changes in the money supply and the behavior of a price index X calculated by the institution Y in the years W–Z. Yet, an economist is normally not interested in a price index X, but he really wants to know, for instance, if prices are influenced by changes in the money supply. He "has in mind some 'true' variables that he would like to measure" (Haavelmo 1944: 7). For an econometrician who is interested in the relation of "true" variables, error estimates are vital.

Keeping all of these problems in mind, it is surprising that no error estimate of price level statistics is provided. Even more surprising is that economists and politicians take changes in price indexes up to 1/10 of 1 percent at face value, without questioning their validity.

The Pretension of National Income Statistics

Another of Morgenstern's examples is that of national income statistics. National income statistics are widely considered to be relevant for economic analysis. They supposedly reflect the success of the government and are used in econometric models. These statistics are also of international importance. Morgenstern notes that, shortly after World War II, Japan and the United States "negotiated" the national income of Japan, because the national income influenced the size of economic help from the United States.

Morgenstern mentions several conceptual problems with national income statistics. The first involves the difficulty of the imputation of value. The problem lies in assigning a monetary value to goods and services produced. As Morgenstern states:

> A classical illustration is that of persons living in houses they own them-
> selves. If these same houses were owned by others, rent would have to be
> paid (in money, goods, or services), thereby swelling the national product.
> To avoid this, a value has to be imputed to owner-occupancy. This is,
> obviously, a tricky affair, with less certain results than finding out about

rent payments made in money. These estimates are uncertain and many arbitrary decisions have to be made. (1963: 246)

A similar problem arises when domestic help, which involves money payments, is substituted by housewives' labor, which does not involve money payments. Changes in the amount and quality of leisure, as well as in amount and quality of voluntary labor (other than housewives') imply problems of the same sort.[12] A professional football player contributes to national income, while playing for leisure does not. Furthermore, money payments can be substituted as the bartering in an economy or the black market increases.[13]

A second problem in calculating national income statistics arises from the treatment of government services. They are not sold on the market. How should we account for them in the national income? The common practice is to account for them with factor costs. However, this seems arbitrary. The monetary cost of a service is not important as a measure of wealth production. What is important, however, is what people are willing to pay for a service on the free market. One could even make the case that government expenditures should instead be subtracted from national income, because the government withdraws resources from the productive private sector and uses them for its purposes.[14] As an example of the absurdity of adding government services positively into national income statistics, consider the case of a government that builds a bomber and a bomb and destroys a newly built house in its own country. In today's national income statistics, the costs of building the bomber and the bomb are added into the national income, as is the house.

Another inconsistency is mentioned by Rittershausen (1962). Increases in real estate or stock market prices are not included in national income statistics because they do not imply a change in production. Profits of companies, however, are included in national income statistics, even though they may be, to a large extent, caused by fluctuations in asset price markets.

Besides these conceptual problems, there are, as Morgenstern notes, three principal types of errors in constructing the statistics of national income. First, there are errors in the basic data that occur because they are a mere byproduct of other activities, because of classification difficulties, lying, hiding of information, transmitting errors, and so on. A second type of error results from the adjustment of the basic data to a conceptual framework, as the collected data is not directly suitable for use in national income statistics. A third type of error arises when gaps must be filled where basic data is not available, for example, for a range of years or for industries where estimates are not known. Moreover, national income is not calculated by adding up physical goods like cows, cars, or petroleum, but by adding up monetary sums. Consequently, we are dealing with prices, their collection, and the problems mentioned in regard to price statistics.

With all these difficulties in mind, is it not very important to provide an error estimate for national income statistics? However, nothing is said about the degree of accuracy in the publications of the national income statistics. Economists have to rely on their own estimates about the accuracy of statistics, or they must rely on the expertise of those who make these judgments.

Simon Kuznets, a pioneer in national income accounting, argues that *10 percent* is a reasonable average margin of error for national income estimates (Morgenstern 1963: 255). We cannot take this margin of error at face value but must take it as a subjective estimation. At least, however, Kuznets provides an error estimate. His estimate is the confession of a leading expert on national income statistics of his time that there is a wide margin of error in national income statistics. Considering this, it makes no sense to state the U.S. GDP of about $14,000 billion with an accuracy of $0.1 billion! That is like having a yardstick and stating that a certain distance would be 4.333127 yards. It aspires to have an accuracy that is impossible. However, many economists take national income statistics at face value and use them, for instance, to confirm or falsify econometric models of the business cycle. In the light of Morgenstern's analysis this procedure is highly questionable.

International comparisons of national income statistics are even more difficult to conduct due to different classifications, definitions, different hidden non-monetary incomes, interventions of the government into their respective price systems, and different measurements of inflation and deflation in the respective countries. From the difficulties of national income statistics, it also follows that growth rates, too, should not be taken at face value. Clearly, they are subject to the same errors as national income statistics, since they are based on them. And again, these errors do not necessarily cancel each other out. Furthermore, the choice of the base year introduces ambiguity and the base year estimate will contain error. The margin of error in the base year (again Kuznets suggests an average error of 10 percent) has a significant influence on the growth rate.

It might be claimed that growth rates would somehow be better than absolute national income statistics because there would always be the same bias in national income data. However, this is a daring and unproven assumption. Why would the possible sources of inaccuracy, for example, the lying, hiding of information, and the transmission error always produce the same bias? Why would the error always be in the same direction and to the same extent? Is it not possible that classification problems, changes in government activity, changes in the amount of non-monetary transactions, the adjustment of data, and the filling of gaps lead to very different errors in different periods?

As national growth rates are already problematic, these problems only increase more so for international comparisons. Morgenstern concludes that one can only make qualitative judgments about growth over longer periods of time.

The consequences of inaccurate national income statistics have been important both for economists and policy makers. The falsification of national income statistics allowed Greece to enter the European Monetary Union in 2001 with far-reaching consequences. Based on the inaccurate statistics, policy makers believed that Greece would maintain a sound fiscal policy. The recent sovereign debt crisis in Europe was triggered when Greece announced high deficits and acknowledged additional falsifications. The Euro zone was at the verge of collapse. Inaccurate Greek statistics played a part in the upheaval.

Another instance of inaccurate statistics misleading economists is the alleged war time prosperity of the U.S. economy in the 1940s. Robert Higgs argues that inappropriate and inaccurate statistics misled historians and economists in their assessment of the war years; "it is difficult to understand how working harder, longer, more inconveniently and dangerously in return for a diminished flow of consumer goods comports with the description that 'economically speaking, Americans had never had it so good' " (1992: 53).

Similarly, Richard K. Vedder and Lowell Gallaway (1991) maintain that inaccurate statistics may induce misinterpretations concerning the post war years in the United States. In 1946 real GNP declined by 19 percent, the largest single decrease of the century according to official statistics. Government data indicates a Great Depression in 1946 while conventional wisdom regards the transition from war to peace as relatively smooth or even prosperous. It is interesting to note that revisions of the data actually increased the size of the decline in real GNP. Revisions of data do not necessarily imply improvements.

A famous example of an economist who was misled in his analysis by government statistics is mathematical economist Paul Samuelson. As late as the 1989 edition of his text book Samuelson maintained that "The Soviet economy is proof that . . . a socialist command economy can function and even thrive" (Samuelson and Nordhaus 1989: 837). Samuelson predicted that the Soviet Union would finally catch up with the United States in per capita income. He based his prediction in part on a comparison of national income statistics of the Soviet Union and the United States. Even if we assume, for the sake of the argument, that scientific predictions in the social realm are possible, we see that deriving predictions from inaccurate data or basing a theory on such data is a method bound to fail.

Implications for History and Econometrics

The absence of error estimates and the potential of relatively high errors in data of the social sciences imply for historians that they should not take the data at face value. Historians must be very careful in interpreting the data, keeping in mind the potential error. Sentences such as "in the following decade, consumer prices rose 11.7 percent" or "in the first war year, economic growth fell back to 0.3 percent" do not make much sense as they portray an accuracy that the data does not contain. Writing "in the following decade, the consumer price index X as calculated by institution Y rose 11.7 percent" and "in the first war year, GDP as calculated by institution Z increase 0.3 percent" would be a better formulation. However, this still might pretend an accuracy that is not available. Hence, data must be interpreted carefully, in a largely qualitative manner, as it should not be taken at face value.

Furthermore, Morgenstern's concerns imply another, unique critique of econometrics. This critique of econometrics is often neglected. Indeed, discussing this implicit critique would violate one of the good rules of econometrics, "namely that econometrics is something that should be done, rather than talked about" (Haavelmo 1958: 351). Morgenstern's implicit critique of econometrics sets in before the econometrician really gets started. It consists in the accuracy of economic observations. As the quality of economic data is doubtful, this raises the question of what is precisely the point in investing human energy and resources for developing ever more sophisticated statistical methods of testing hypotheses and estimation.[15] Expressing this concern, Christopher Worswick feels that econometricians are more interested in developing additional statistical tools than troubling with the quality of economic data; "they [some econometricians] are not, it seems to me, engaged in forging tools to arrange and measure actual facts so much as making a marvelous array of pretend-tools which would perform wonders if ever a set of facts should turn up in the right form" (Worswick 1971: 79).

Indeed, if we have to guess the error in economic data, it raises doubts about the suitability of the data for econometric testing. What is the point of constructing macroeconomic business cycle models including growth rates, price indexes, capital accumulation, population figures, and running them for different countries? Is this not futile considering that error estimates are not published and an expert like Simon Kuznets regards 10 percent error in GDP as realistic? One is reminded of Keynes' sarcastic statement in his famous review of Jan Tinbergen's book, *Statistical Testing of Business-Cycles Theories*, emphasizing the futility of econometric research:

> No one could be more frank, more painstaking, more free from subjective bias or *parti pris* than Professor Tinbergen. There is no one, therefore, so far as human qualities go, whom it would be safer to trust with black magic. That there is anyone I would trust with it at the present stage, or that this brand of statistical alchemy is ripe to become a branch of science, I am

not yet persuaded. But Newton, Boyle, and Locke all played with Alchemy. So let him continue. (Keynes 1940: 156)

Keynes also speaks about "the frightful inadequacy of most of the statistics employed" (1939: 567).[16] Yet, Keynes' main critique of Tinbergen's method does not aim at the quality of statistics or data. His main critique of econometrics is more devastating. Keynes points out that one cannot assume economic variables to be constant and homogeneous through time. He, therefore, rejects the possibility of prediction through econometrics.[17] If Keynes was right, we do not even have to worry about the quality of economic data that is used in econometrics.

Morgenstern's contribution, however, is slightly different from Keynes' or other critics of econometrics. Although he does not claim that econometrics is alchemy,[18] Morgenstern agrees on the inadequacy of economic statistics and attacks mainstream economic tools on a different level than Keynes. He asserts that the nature of economic observation makes it categorically different from physical observations and more error-bearing. It follows as an important implication for modern economics that the data in social science might not be good enough for the type of research that econometrics engages in. Even if prediction in the social sciences based on econometrics would be possible, the quality of the available data may well be insufficient. Moreover, Morgenstern's insights have important implications for economic historians, policy makers, and journalists to not take economic data at face value.

Why Does the Pretense of Accuracy Continue?

Considering the sources of error in economic data it would be more scientifically honest to provide error estimates, for example, limits of accuracy, in economic statistics as it is done in physics. Another author beside Morgenstern that argues for such an error estimate is Heinrich von Rittershausen (1962: 545). Ritterhausen criticizes the pretense of accuracy when data on income statistics or the price level is provided with decimal points. One might wonder why these voices calling for error estimates have been neglected.

One reason why Morgenstern's contribution might have been widely neglected is the unfavorable reviews of his book in prestigious journals. Simpson (1951) in *The American Economic Review* and Carter (1951) in *The Economic Journal* are the only generally favorable reviews. These reviews are of the first 1950 edition of Morgenstern's book, published at a time when the econometric approach was on the rise. For negative reviews, see Barna (1951, 1965) in *Economica*, Clark (1952) in *Econometrica*, Ruggles (1964) in *The American Economic Review*, and Telser (1965) in *Econometrica*. Mainly published in journals championing the econometric approach, these reviews often criticize only minor and rhetorical points without grasping Morgenstern's central point and its implications for econometrics.

A more fundamental reason for the neglect of the error problem may be that the existence of important errors in economic data is an inconvenient truth for the modern economic profession. Modern economics builds heavily on econometrics and, therefore, relies on the accuracy of economic data. There are several explanations for the extensions of mathematical and statistical research in economics, such as econometrics. James Surowiecki (2004) argues that the increased use of mathematics results from the "wisdom of crowds." Referees, journal editors, and members of hiring committees believe in the efficacy of econometrics. Clive Beed and Owen Kane (1991) indicate where this "belief" might stem from. Mathematical rigor can insulate against critiques from people without mathematical knowledge. Sophistication also diverts attention from more theoretical deficiencies and from the accuracy of economic data. Moreover, mathematics may be used to attain scientific respectability (Katzner 2003). Attracted by the success of the natural sciences, economists may have adopted econometrical research to gain respectability. Daniel Sutter (2009) offers a reinforcing explanation for an excessive mathematization of economics. Academic research lacks a suitable medium of exchange because most of the academic publications do not yield direct monetary revenues. Economists, in general, have nothing attractive to offer their colleagues from mathematical departments in exchange for mathematical input. Therefore, mathematical and statistical research cannot be outsourced from economics departments. Economics departments must directly hire mathematicians, leading to a high level of sophistication in faculty and economics curriculum. Consequently, Surowiecki's crowd increasingly becomes experts in mathematics and statistics.

For a profession heavily engaged in econometrical research, the problem of the quality of economic data is an inconvenient issue. The publication of possibly high error estimates could reveal the illusion of the accuracy of economic data. Econometric research relying on exact data would be severely challenged. This may explain why Morgenstern's arguments have been ignored.

It is true that the publication of error estimates would just add another layer of subjective data. Therefore, it is essential to call the error estimate for what it is: an estimate and not an accurate measure. Another reason why error estimates are never given may be that there is no precise way of calculating them. Yet, if the error estimate is provided with sufficient honesty and caution, it would help to increase the quality of historic research based on economic data. The advantage of such an error estimate is that economic historians could continue with their research without creating an air of false accuracy. The error estimate would put their findings into perspective and reduce the chance of hasty and daring interpretations induced by an assumed accuracy of the data. An error estimate would also demand more cautious decisions of policy makers based upon the available data.

Conclusion

In contrast to physics, there is still no estimate of statistical error within economics. Albeit subjective, error estimates would at least acknowledge the problem of faulty data and provide a caveat against too hasty conclusions. The various sources of error that come into play in the social sciences suggest that the error in economic observations is substantial. Classification problems, inadequate training of observers, filling of gaps, transmission errors, lying or the concealment of information add up to a substantial source for errors. Price and national income statistics are especially prone to substantial errors.

The accuracy of economic data is a widely neglected problem and should be taken into account by the economic profession. Economic statistics cannot be accepted at face value. This skepticism of the accuracy of economic data does not imply that one should ignore available statistics altogether. There is much to learn from analyzing available statistics. History teaches and illustrates, yet statistics have to be analyzed with the appropriate caution and with an awareness of potential errors. For instance, long term growth rates may give us certain insights about the evolution of a certain economy. They have to be interpreted with caution. Substantial errors become likely particularly when comparing data internationally.

Pretending an accuracy that is unrealistic may lead us to erroneous conclusions. The consequences of Morgenstern's insights are far-reaching. Based on faulty data, economic historians may misinterpret the past. Policy makers may make fateful decisions, and econometricians develop flawed theories applying an inadequate methodology. In fact, Morgenstern's *On the Accuracy of Economic Observation* has an important implication for modern econometrics. It shows that the solution of a system of economic mathematical equations or econometric models is, due to the quality of the data, problematic. In ignorance of the error in economic observation, econometric research seems to be vain. Thereby, Morgenstern's critique of econometrics is different from other approaches that aim at arbitrary assumptions made by econometricians or the abuse of significance testing. Some economists regard econometrics as irrelevant, considering that no scientific prediction in the field of human action and the social realm is possible. Morgenstern's critique is complementary to the other approaches. Even if we assume, for the sake of the argument, that scientific prediction would be possible in the social realm, economic observations may not be accurate enough to provide econometricians with meaningful results.

The challenge for econometrics and modern economics posed by Morgenstern's arguments may explain why these arguments have been neglected. Instead of investing resources in new econometric techniques and trying to squeeze more out of the existing data, the economics profession should invest these resources to improve the accuracy of data or to investigate the potential for error.

Notes

1. Morgenstern took this example from W. E. Milne (1949: 30–31). For mathematical correctness the second set of equations must be:

$$x - y = 1$$

$$x - 0.99999y = 0,$$

leading to the solution x = −99999 and y = −100000.

2. See, for this definition and alternative definitions, Tintner (1953: 31–32).

3. The econometrical concept of the standard error refers to a problem different from the accuracy of economic data. The standard error measures the standard deviation of the sampling distribution associated with the estimation method. The data of the sampling distribution is assumed to be the true data.

4. Preston and Dietz (1991) in their book *The Art of Experimental Physics* dedicate one chapter to "Error Analysis." On page seven we find the statement that: "A measurement alone, without a quantitative statement as to the uncertainty involved, is of limited usefulness. It is therefore essential that any course in basic laboratory technique include [sic] a discussion of the nature of the uncertainty in individual measurements and the manner in which uncertainties in two or more measurements are propagated to determine the uncertainty in the quantity or law being investigated. Such uncertainties are called experimental errors and their analysis is called error analysis."

In econometrics textbooks, we usually search in vain for a discussion of error analysis of the data. See, for example, Ramanathan (1998), Amemiya (1994) or Kelejian/Oates (1981). An exception is Gujarati (1995: 26–27), where less than two pages out of 838 pages are dedicated to the problem of accuracy of economic data. Gujarati makes no case for a quantitative statement of the error.

5. For example, the U.S. GDP for the second quarter of 2006, seasonally adjusted, is stated as $13,209.7 billion, implying a tremendous accuracy of 0.1 billion, with no error estimate being provided (Federal Reserve Bank of St. Louis 2006a).

Similarly, the not seasonally adjusted consumer prices with index 1982–84 = 100 is reported to be 203.5 on July, 1st 2006 (Federal Reserve Bank of St. Louis 2006b). We find the statement that the "cumulative nonsampling error can be much greater than the sampling error" (Bureau of Labor Statistics 1997). Again, we are not provided with an error estimate.

Likewise, Lawrence Summers (1981: 609) states that the sum of uncertainty in measuring unemployment is never reported by the Bureau of Labor Statistics.

6. Regarding this, also see Darnell and Evans (1990: 13).

7. See BBC News (2009).

8. On this point, see also Leontief (1971: 6).

9. This minor advantage was emphasized by Joseph Schumpeter to justify the econometric method in the first volume of *Econometrica* (1933: 5–6) and is also quoted in one of the rare modern econometric text books that raises the issue of the nature of economic data. See Mittelhammer, Judge, and Miller (2000: 4–5).

10. Indeed, economists have frequently suggested or asked governments to increase spending in these areas. See Hendry (1980: 398) or Frisch (1946: 4). Also Haavelmo (1944: 5) claims that economic observations "could possibly be measured rather accurately" if there were only more time and more money.

11. See, for example, Popper (1961), Lucas (1983) or Hoppe (1983). Individuals have the ability to learn and will, therefore, adjust to experiments, as well as statistical and econometric research—hence, Lucas' critique of econometric policy evaluation.

12. For the problem of the value of voluntary work and national income, see Fogel (1999: 7).

13. Anderson (1917: ch. 11) argues that the amount of barter in the economy is highly underestimated.

14. Rothbard (2000: 253–256), develops the concept of Gross Private Product, which subtracts government receipts or expenditures (whichever is higher) from the GNP.

15. The poor quality of the data might be one explanation for Lawrence Summers' famous critique of econometrics, which questions the little impact econometric research has had, in relation to the resources spent on it; "given the tremendous professional investment in econometric work, it is natural to ask why it has so little impact in either the short or long run" (1991: 133).

16. For Tinbergen's reply, see Tinbergen (1940).

17. For a discussion of Keynes' view on prediction and econometrics, see Lawson (1985).

18. On the question if econometrics is alchemy or science, see Hendry (1980). For other critiques of econometrics, see Phelps Brown, who states that "running regressions between time series is only likely to deceive" (1972: 6). Worswick argues that "[t]oo much of what goes on in economic and econometric theory is of little or no relevance to serious economic science" (1971: 83).

References

Amemiya, T. (1994). *Introduction to Statistics and Econometrics.* Cambridge, MA: Harvard University Press.

Anderson, B. (1917). *The Value of Money.* New York: MacMillan Company.

Barna, T. (1951). "On the Accuracy of Economic Observations." *Economica* 18(72): 440–443.

———. (1965). "On the Accuracy of Economic Observations." *Economica* 32(126): 237–238.

BBC News. (2009). *Timeline: Greece.* http://news.bbc.co.uk/2/hi/europe/country_profiles/1014812.stm.

Beed, C., and O. Kane. (1991). "What is the Critique of the Mathematization of Economics?" *Kyklos* 44(4): 581–612.

Bigo, V. (2006). "Open and Closed Systems and the Cambridge School." *Review of Social Economy* 64(4): 493–514.

Bureau of Labor Statistics. (1997). *Handbook of Methods. Ch. 17: The Consumer Price Index.* http://stats.bls.gov/opub/hom/pdf/homch17.pdf.

Carter, C. F. (1951). "On the Accuracy of Economic Observations." *Economic Journal* 61(244): 856–857.

Clark, C. (1952). "On the Accuracy of Economic Observation." *Econometrica* 20(1): 105–106.

Darnell, A., and L. Evans. (1990). *The Limits of Econometrics.* Worcester: Billing & Sons.

Dow, S. (2007). "Variety of Methodological Approach in Economics." *Journal of Economic Surveys* 21(3): 447–465.

Federal Reserve Bank of St. Louis. (2006a). *Gross Domestic Product,* 1 Decimal. http://research.stlouisfed.org/fred2/data/GDP.txt.

———. (2006b). *Consumer Price Index for All Urban Consumers: All Items.* http://research.stlouisfed.org/fred2/data/CPIAUCNS.txt.

Fogel, R. (1999). "Catching Up with the Economy." *American Economic Review* 89(1): 1–21.

Frisch, R. (1946). "The Responsibility of the Econometricians." *Econometrica* 14(1): 1–4.

Gujarati, D. (1995). *Basic Econometrics.* 3rd ed. New York: McGraw-Hill.

Haavelmo, T. (1944). "The Probability Approach in Econometrics." *Econometrica* 12 Supplement: iii–vi, 1–115.

———. (1958). "The Role of the Econometrician in the Advancement of Economic Theory." *Econometrica* 26(3): 351–357.

Hayek, F. A. (1948). "The Facts of the Social Sciences" In *Individualism and Economic Order.* Chicago: Henry Regnery: 57–76.

Hendry, D. (1980). "Econometrics-Alchemy or Science?" *Economica* 47(188): 387–406.

Higgs, R. (1992). "Wartime Prosperity? A Reassessment of the U.S. Economy in the 1940s." *Journal of Economic History* 52(1): 41–60.

Hoppe, H.-H. (1983). *Kritik der kausalwissenschaftlichen Sozialforschung. Untersuchungen zur Grundlegung von Soziologie und Ökonomie.* Opladen: Westdeutscher Verlag.

Katzner, D. W. (2003). "Why Mathematics in Economics?" *Journal of Post Keynesian Economics* 25(4): 561–574.

Kelejian, H., and W. Oates. (1981). *Introduction to Econometrics*. New York: Harper & Row.

Keynes, J. M. (1939). "Professor Tinbergen's method." *Economic Journal* 49(195): 558–557.

———. (1940). "On a Method of Statistical Business-Cycle Research. A Comment." *Economic Journal* 50(197): 154–156.

Lawson, T. (1985). "Keynes, Prediction and Econometrics." In *Keynes' Economics: Methodological Issues*. Eds. T. Lawson and H. Pesaran, pp. 116–133. London: Croom Helm.

———. (1997). *Economics and Reality*. London and New York: Routledge.

Leamer, E. (1983). "Let's Take the Con Out of Econometrics." *American Economic Review* 73(1): 31–43.

Lee, F. S., and P. Downward. (1999). "Retesting Gardiner Means's Evidence on Administered Prices." *Journal of Economic Issues* 33(4): 861–886.

Leontief, W. (1971). "Theoretical Assumptions and Nonobserved Facts." *American Economic Review* 61(1): 1–7.

Lucas, R. E. Jr. (1983). "Econometric Policy Evaluation: A Critique." In *Studies in Business-Cycle Theory*. Cambridge, MA: MIT Press: 104–130.

McCloskey, D. N., and St. T. Ziliak. (2008). *The Cult of Statistical Significance: How the Standard Error Costs Us Jobs, Justice, and Lives*. Ann Arbor, MI: University of Michigan Press.

Mills, F. C. (1936). "Price Data and Problems of Price Research." *Econometrica* 4(4): 289–309.

Milne, W. E. (1949). *Numerical Calculus*. Princeton: Princeton University Press.

Mises, L. v. (1957). *Theory and History. An Interpretation of Social and Economic Evolution*. New Haven, CT: Yale University Press.

Mittelhammer, R., G. Judge, and D. Miller. (2000). *Econometric Foundations*. Cambridge: Cambridge University Press.

Morgenstern, O. (1950). *On the Accuracy of Economic Observations*. Princeton, NJ: Princeton University Press.

———. (1963). *On the Accuracy of Economic Observations*. 2nd ed. Princeton, NJ: Princeton University Press.

Phelps Brown, E. H. (1972). "The Underdevelopment of Economics." *Economic Journal* 82(325): 1–10.

Popper, K. (1961). *The Poverty of Historicism*. 3rd ed. New York: Harper and Row.

Preston, D., and E. Dietz. (1991). *The Art of Experimental Physics*. New York: Wiley.

Ramanathan, R. (1998). *Introductory Econometrics with Applications*. 4th ed. Fort Worth: Dryden Press.

Rittershausen, H. v. (1962). *Die Zentralnotenbank. Ein Handbuch ihrer Instrumente, ihrer Politik und ihrer Theorie*. Frankfurt am Main: Fritz Knapp.

Rothbard, M. N. (2000). *America's Great Depression.* 5ᵗʰ ed. Auburn, AL: Ludwig von Mises Institute.

Ruggles, N. (1964). "On the Accuracy of Economic Observations." *American Economic Review* 54(4) Part 1: 445–447.

Samuelson, P., and W. Nordhaus. (1989). *Economics.* 13ᵗʰ ed. New York: McGrawHill.

Schumpeter, J. (1933). "The Common Sense of Econometrics." *Econometrica* 1(1): 5–12.

Simpson, P. (1951). "On the Accuracy of Economic Observations." *American Economic Review* 41(4): 695–696.

Summers, L. H. (1981). "Measuring Unemployment." *Brookings Papers on Economic Activity* 81(2): 609–620.

———. (1991). "The Scientific Illusion in Empirical Macroeconomics." *Scandinavian Journal of Economics* 93(2), Proceedings of a Conference on New Approaches to Empirical Macroeonomics: 129–149.

Surowiecki, J. (2004). *The Wisdom of Crowds.* New York: Doubldeday.

Sutter, D. (2009). "The Market, the Firm and the Economics Profession." *American Journal of Economics and Sociology,* 68(5): 1041–1061.

Telser, L. (1965). "On the Accuracy of Economic Observations." *Econometrica* 33(4): 886–887.

Tinbergen, J. (1940). "On a Method of Statistical Business-Cycle Research. A Reply." *Economic Journal* 50(197): 141–154.

Tintner, G. (1953). "The Definition of Econometrics." *Econometrica* 21(1): 31–40.

Vedder, R. K., and L. Gallaway. (1991). "The Great Depression of 1946." *Review of Austrian Economics* 5(2): 3–32.

Worswick, G. D. N. (1971). "Is Progress in Economic Science Possible?" *Economic Journal* 82(325): 73–86.

Index

for